NEW VISIONS FOR THE AMERICAS

Religious Engagement and Social Transformation

David Batstone,
Editor

FORTRESS PRESS
Minneapolis

NEW VISIONS FOR THE AMERICAS
Religious Engagement and Social Transformation

Cover graphic: Claudia Racha
Cover design: Pollack Design Team

Library of Congress Cataloging-in-Publication data

New visions for the Americas : religious engagement and social
    transformation / edited by David Batstone.
        p.   cm.
    Includes bibliographical references.
    ISBN 0-8006-2690-7 (alk. paper) :
        1. Christianity and justice—America.   2. Liberation theology.
    3. Church and social problems—America.   4. Sociology, Christian—
    America.   I. Batstone, David B., 1958-.
    BR115.J8N48   1993
    230'.046—dc20   93-28257
                                                             CIP

The paper used in this publication meets the minimum requirements of American National Standard for Information Services—Permanence of Paper for Printed Library Materials, ANSI Z329.48-1984.

Manufactured in the U.S.A.   AF 1-2690

97   96   95   94   93   1   2   3   4   5   6   7   8   9   10

For Athol Gill (1937–1992)
Who opened my eyes to a world of injustice
and taught me to care
and
Jade and Zachary
Who daily remind me that
the struggle is worth it

CONTENTS

CONTRIBUTORS

William Baldridge. Associate Professor of Native American Ministries at Central Baptist Theological Seminary in Kansas City, Kansas, Baldridge is a member of the Cherokee nation of Oklahoma.

David Batstone. The founder and president of Central American Mission Partners (CAMP), Batstone is author of *From Conquest to Struggle: Jesus of Nazareth in Latin America*.

Robert McAfee Brown. Professor Emeritus of the Pacific School of Religion (Berkeley) and internationally renowned spokesperson for peace and justice, Brown's numerous works include *Unexpected News: Reading the Bible with Third World Eyes; Theology in a New Key; Religion and Violence; Gustavo Gutiérrez: An Introduction to Liberation Theology;* and *A Spirituality of Liberation*.

George C. L. Cummings. Associate Professor of Theology at the American Baptist Seminary of the West (Berkeley), Cummings is co-author of *Cut Loose Your Stammering Tongues: Black Theology in the Slave Narratives*.

Miguel D'Escoto. The former Foreign Minister of Nicaragua, D'Escoto is a Maryknoll priest and a visionary leader of the movement of ecclesial base communities throughout Central America.

Ignacio Ellacuría. Theologian, author, and former rector of the University of Central America, Ellacuría was assassinated along with five of his Jesuit brothers and two Salvadoran women in October 1989. He authored numerous works, including *Freedom Made Flesh: The Mission of Christ and His Church*. His essay in this collection was contributed by Jon Sobrino and was written shortly before Ellacuría's murder.

Jon Sobrino. A Jesuit priest, Sobrino teaches theology at the University of Central America in San Salvador and is an internationally recognized author on liberation theology; among his major works are *Christology at the Crossroads; Jesus in Latin America; The True Church and the Poor;* and *Spirituality of Liberation.*

Bill Smith. Executive Director of the Northern California Conference of the United Church of Christ AIDS Ministry, Smith has dedicated himself to the promotion of social justice via education and theater in grassroots communities. Smith also served as the Director for African-American Student Services at the University of New Mexico for six years.

Elsa Tamez. Professor of Biblical Studies at Seminario Bíblico Latinamericano in Costa Rica, Tamez is a prolific writer on liberation theology and feminism; among her major works are *Through Her Eyes: Women's Theology in Latin America; Bible of the Oppressed; The Scandalous Message of James;* and *Against Machismo.*

Mark Lewis Taylor. Associate Professor of Theology and Culture, Princeton Theological Seminary, Taylor is author of *Remembering Esperanza: A Cultural-Political Theology for North American Praxis; Beyond Explanations: Religious Dimensions in Cultural Anthropology;* and *Paul Tillich: Theologian at the Boundaries.*

Emilie M. Townes. Assistant Professor of Christian Social Ethics at Saint Paul School of Theology, Kansas City, Missouri, Townes is a respected spokesperson in the womanist theological movement arising out of African-American culture and author of *Womanist Justice, Womanist Hope.*

Jim Wallis. Founder of the Sojourners Community in inner city Washington, D.C., Wallis is an author, political activist, and editor of *Sojourners* magazine. His works include *The Call to Conversion* and *Agenda for Biblical People.*

Sharon D. Welch. Welch is Associate Professor and Director of the Women's Studies Program at the University of Missouri and author of *A Feminist Ethic of Risk* and *Communities of Resistance and Solidarity.*

Ellen K. Wondra. Wondra is Assistant Professor of Theology at Colgate Rochester Divinity School/Bexley Hall/Crozer Theological Seminary.

INTRODUCTION
David Batstone

*L*iberation theologies have undeniably and irrevocably altered the
self-understanding and practice of the global Christian faith community in the last three decades. Simultaneously arising within such diverse contexts as the black community in the United States, feminist
circles in North Atlantic countries, and the grassroots base communities of the Two-Thirds World, theologies of liberation have evolved as a
resource and inspiration for those seeking historical and political freedom. Each community has sought in its own way to fashion a "theology which does not stop with reflecting on the world, but rather tries
to be a part of the process through which the world is transformed."[1]

Nonetheless, that movement now ever more keenly appreciates that
refashioning hermeneutical and ethical frameworks for liberation
requires—however much the proposition that they are a "second act"
proceeding from praxis may be authentically claimed—an ever deeper
immersion "on the ground." Though uncomfortable to admit, an uncritical discourse of inclusion, tolerance, plurality, diversity, and rights
has all too often blinded us to more concrete, specific realities. What we
have voiced in the name of principled freedom and justice has masked,
or at least ignored, potent social dynamics that actually produce and reinforce existing relationships of unequal power.

Yet how does one critically, passionately, honestly, justly, and effectively address those dynamics, especially the relationships and concerns
of class, gender, and race?

Exposing these covert social forces demands a frank, open, and active
dialogue between embodied identity groups about the meaning of particular historical events for their community. That very practice, however, is regularly avoided in contemporary culture because it is feared
that such discussions are likely to become mired in conflictive and mutually exclusive interpretations and commitments. Given the propensity
within a decidedly postmodern age to avoid, at all costs, making state-

1

ments of value—or perhaps more accurately, to own up to the value judgments that have already indeed been made—the potential conflict becomes too much to bear, is often submerged, and thereby bolsters existing power relationships. In the age of tolerance it is fine to say anything one likes, as long as one does not let on that he or she believes it is actually true.[2]

To work together for real transformation, therefore, it will be necessary to come forth honestly with our own concrete identities and commitments, social locations and engagements. There is no room for dispassionate, disinterested discourse for, as Henri Nouwen suggests, neutrality as a starting point for conversation with another will always generate a false consciousness within the relationship:

> No real dialogue is possible between somebody and a nobody. We can enter into communication with the other only when our own life choices, attitudes and viewpoints offer the boundaries that challenge strangers to become critically aware of their own position [and we ours!] and to explore it critically.[3]

It is also necessary to recognize, however, that structural conditions will largely determine whether social conversation may take place on the basis of mutual vulnerability and relatively equal power. When those conditions do not exist, it is not really conversation that is taking place but rather a subtle, or not so subtle, form of dictation. In the Americas during the last quarter of this century, the possibilities for fruitful dialogue have grown frightfully slim. It is the market which has become the primary dispenser of the "common good." It functions to set communities against each other and effectively to break down the potential for even provisional truces. The strong have been elevated over the weak, and the shrinking middle classes have been convinced that they have more to gain by siding with the powerful against those who occupy the bottom rungs of society.[4] In a world dominated by the market, the "laws" of social Darwinism become self-confirming prescriptions.

Given this environment within the United States, the individual's experience of community is typically quite limited and, at best, intermittent. A compelling metaphor for community at the present moment of our history was manifest at a rock concert I attended recently at the renowned Warfield Theater in San Francisco. The expansive space between the stage and the back of the hall at the Warfield was jammed mostly with younger people in their early twenties who "slam danced" along to the slashing rhythm of the guitar. Both men and women frantically jumped up and down in chaotic movements, intentionally bouncing into each other in such a way that would send them flying off toward their next collision. It was indeed a community. Yet it was experienced as a shared space of isolated individuals who entered into relationship with one another through a series of random encounters. The intimacy of human contact, though also celebrated, was transacted on an anonymous level that precluded the interrelatedness and bonding implicit in personal human relationship. By the end of the night, the individual was free to walk away from the concert "community" unfettered by mutual responsibilities and accountabilities, "free" to act according to the dictates of competition in the market.

In view of all the above, now more than ever we of the Americas sense urgency in the task to define clearly the meaning of liberation for the complex social and cultural realities of race, class, and gender. It is time to move through and beyond a rhetoric of liberation to explore specific strategies for transformation, to uncover particular obstacles to human freedom, to engage in the formation of holy alliances and the destruction of "unholy" alliances, to nurture the intersubjectivity of particular identities, to link and contrast the results of exhaustive analyses, and to celebrate the new creation of sacred spaces of freedom, justice, and peace.

It might very well be asked whether theologians and ethicists, who reside most comfortably in the discourse of meaning and value, possess the competency to address these demands. After all, would not this work more appropriately fall on the broad shoulders of sociologists, psychologists, political scientists, anthropologists, economists, and other social scientists?

In times past, such a division between value and analysis, as well as that separating meaning and objective reality, would have lent credence to such a distribution of knowledge and vocation on the basis of specialty. However, it has become increasingly apparent that social systems can no longer simply be understood as essentialist elements of organic existence that merely want objective description. Rather, social systems are now commonly seen as humanly constructed realities that rely on a foundation of values for their production and a universe of meaning for their sustenance. For that reason, the issues at hand are too important to be left to technocrats who hide behind the positivistic garb of the "expert." We now live in a world of "blurred genres" that demands an interdisciplinary conversation between the humanities and the social sciences.[5] Every analysis of social reality must be critiqued on the basis of its presumed value and meaning while, in turn, every statement of value and meaning must be linked to its concrete social location.

With that in mind, each of the authors in this volume was asked to approach issues of race, class, and gender in the Americas through a specific entry point of their own choosing. The results were unpredictable, as were the methods employed. In that regard, it is significant to point out that the sections that have been imposed to organize the material for the reader's clarity did not organically determine the content or shape of the chapters. For example, only one person of color is found in the section on race; the other authors of color do indeed address issues of race, but they do so in relation to particular class and gender concerns. For that matter, the reader will discover that nearly every chapter moves from its point of entry to encompass the wider connections linking the dynamics of race, class, and gender in American societies.

The first section points toward a new framework for constructing theology and ethics in a pluralistic, multicultural, interreligious, global community. In doing so, the first three chapters attempt to deconstruct those frameworks that have provided spiritual guidance and resource for imperialism in the Americas during the last five centuries. Robert McAfee Brown removes some scales from the way we understand recent history and the connections essential to a "realistic idealism." He reflects on his own participation in the peace-and-justice movement over three decades and addresses the significance of rewriting our histories with a clear sense of our own social locations. William Baldridge, a member of the Cherokee nation, encourages the Native Indian people to explore the richness of their way while walking the path set before them by both the Corn Mother and Jesus of Nazareth. He then encourages his people to share freely that truth in grace with their conquerors who are choking on their own self-absorption. Elsa Tamez further enriches that discussion of a post-colonial worldview with her presentation of the many gods of the native people of Mexico and the many gods of the European people who came to take their land, their inheritance, and their very lives. The true God, Tamez argues, is revealed through the divine givers of life who are revered in both the Mayan and the Christian religious traditions.

Part Two critically considers economic class structures in the Americas and their determination of human relationships within interdependent societies. Three significant Latin American figures, Miguel D'Escoto, Ignacio Ellacuría, and Jon Sobrino, raise the specter of economic domination and injustice toward the poor countries of the world. The foreign minister of the Nicaraguan government for most of the 1980s, D'Escoto compares the relationship of the United States toward small countries like Nicaragua to that existing between a *patron* (plantation owner) and his day-worker. Ellacuría was one of the six Jesuit brothers brutally assassinated in their home by the Salvadoran military because of their strong voice in favor of peace and justice in El Salvador. This chapter, which challenges modern capitalist societies to create economies based on the possibility of work rather than ones designed primarily for the production of capital, was written shortly before his murder and serves as a personal harbinger of what would be his tragic fate. In the following chapter, Jon Sobrino develops a spirituality of compassion, which will be necessary to make Ellacuría's suggestions real. Liberally borrowing language from the Ignatian *Spiritual Exercises*, Sobrino's "principle of compassion" stands in sharp opposition to "principles" that, whether consciously intended or not, directly lead to the division of society into communities of poverty and wealth. In the final chapter of the section, Mark Lewis Taylor exposes the tentacles of economic power emanating from the transnational corporations of First World countries, and provides the religious community in the United States with specific strategies to resist and restrict their exploitative practices.

The third section explores personal identity and the politics of sex and gender. First, three North American women raise particular obstacles that impede woman's liberation in a social world imbued with resilient and pervasive sexism, while at the same time indicating how their strategies must extend to resist racism and classism as well. Emilie Townes, a womanist ethicist, shares an "unctuous" rhetoric of justice that teaches the reader how to listen to the stories and the traditions of one's people before offering prescriptive agendas, thereby building communities to which women may come home. Ellen Wondra, noting the dual location of privilege and oppression experienced by white feminists, demonstrates how the resistance of the subjugated is both a historical phenomenon and a transcendent reality which may be elaborated within the construction of a Christology. The more specifically political implications of these affirmations are demonstrated in the subsequent chapter written by Sharon Welch, who directs a women's studies program on a midwestern state university campus. Welch evaluates strategies for the liberation of women based on both workshops she has facilitated and those led by other feminist activists. Bill Smith concludes the section with a consideration of creating sacred spaces of justice and freedom for gay men of color, and explores its implications for a local theology. Linking the experience of his community to blues music, the chapter is written with a cadence and style that invites the reader to enter into the transforming power of the blues for oneself.

Part Four takes racism as its point of entry to the larger discussion, holding it up as an ugly social force deeply interwoven into the fabric of U.S. society. Jim Wallis, editor of *Sojourners* magazine, contends that racism is the "original sin" of the Americas and ties its redemption to far-reaching enactments of repentance and restitution. Theologian and social activist George Cummings then evaluates the mutually beneficial dialogue that has developed between the black liberation movement in the United States, with its unrelenting experience of racial oppression, and the Latin American liberation community, which has focused its attention primarily on economic exploitation and class analysis. Cummings concludes his chapter with an exploration of how black culture and black religion have served as dynamic expressions of resistance against the hegemonic culture of white racists. My own chapter closes the section with a critical debunking of oft-touted claims of "racial progress" and "integration" within the United States. Drawing on the specifics of an autobiographical event, I construct a method for understanding racism on both personal and social levels, and then promote an ethic of intervention.

Although heightened understanding of the import of our diverse social locations will require fundamental changes in liberation theologies, they might thereby nurture a vision and praxis that more fully embodies the character of our hope. Indeed, at the dawn of the twenty-first century we in the Americas desperately need new visions and strategies which may make our dreams effective and real. The human family, the earth, and all of creation cry out for their recreation.

Part One
Christianity after Colonialism

1

RETHINKING
OUR HISTORIES

Robert McAfee Brown

*I*n the summer of 1979, when it already began to look as though Ronald Reagan would be elected president, I attended meetings of the Christian Peace Conference in Matanzas, Cuba. I was asked to reflect on the American political scene. The respondent to my paper, a Catholic from Peru, commented that the paper seemed to him a description of a "never, never land." I was describing "political choices," the importance of "working through the electoral process," "the possibility of change" in the United States, the "importance of the leaven of the churches," and so on. But to my respondent, none of these was even remotely possible south of the Rio Grande, where there were few *real* "political choices," where the "electoral process" involved a recognition that rallies, demonstrations, political parties, ballots and "free elections" were not even on the horizon. As for the possible "leavening of the church," that, too, seemed remote, although the documents of the Latin American Episcopal Council (CELAM), promulgated only a few months earlier at Puebla, Mexico, had kept open some doors that many had thought would be closed. (A Latin American theologian, present at Puebla and Matanzas, told us with a measure of excitement in his voice that "there are fifty phrases in the Puebla documents we can use," but it was clear that even in the most avant-garde circles of Latin American Christianity it would be uphill all the way.)

And now, years later, even though some of the most blatant military dictatorships in Latin America have been toppled, the picture is no more encouraging than it was then. How can we in the United States, in the light of Watergate, Irangate, military aid to the Salvadoran and Guatemalan governments, ongoing attempts to unseat Castro in Cuba, the extravagant support of the contras in Nicaragua, the invasion of Grenada, the invasion of Panama, and intervention in Iraq, anticipate the possibility of change in the Americas, rather than simply more of the same?

MOMENTS OF UNDERSTANDING ON THE JOURNEY

At the risk of sounding as naive to present-day Latin Americans as I must have sounded to my critic years ago at Matanzas, I want to try to sketch something of the personal journey of people like myself reaching toward a realistic and hard-nosed idealism about methods and possibilities for change. I cite my own reactions and experience, not because they are unusual, but because they are typical of the movement of many of us in responding to the events we did not anticipate or know how to cope with when they first confronted us. If there are lessons to be learned for the future, they come in part at least out of these experiences (and mistakes) in the past.

Here, then, are seven moments of new understanding:

1. Mine is the generation of World War II. It was the occasion of death for many of my contemporaries, and I resist the current retrospective attempt to call it a "good" war. But there were some clear moral issues at stake. My initial response to World War II was as a pacifist, who applied for conscientious objector status and was granted a deferment to go to seminary. I accepted the latter classification (something I would not have done in relation to Vietnam or any subsequent American military endeavor). I was going to prepare for reconstruction work overseas once the war was over, thus doing good in a time when others were doing evil. What I discovered, of course, was that none of us was going to be able to "reconstruct" Europe unless the Allies defeated Hitler. And to me it became morally intolerable to let others do the dirty work of defeating Hitler so that people like myself could do good works in the aftermath of the war. So my personal odyssey from pacifism to a U.S. naval uniform, and duty on a troop transport in the Pacific theater, was informed by a reluctant but increasingly clear recognition that *there are no pure choices*. We are not offered clear-cut instances of good or evil; the notion of living in a land of unambiguous moral purity was an illusion.

2. As our nation moved into the fifties and then the sixties, one particularly domestic cancer became so inflamed that there was no way to avoid dealing with it. This was the civil rights struggle, particularly as waged by blacks. I think middle-class Christians learned at least three things during this period: (*a*) We learned that there was no way to remain on the sidelines. As William James once put it, "not to decide is

to decide"—it is to decide, in this case, to give power by default to the structures of evil, which could (and did) mount powerful pressures to "keep the nigra in his place." (*b*) We also learned that for most of us nonviolence was not a principle carved in stone to be adhered to whatever the outer context; *nonviolence was, in certain situations, a useful, creative, and moral way of challenging social evil*. That Martin Luther King, Jr., accomplished so much is in no small part due to the tone of moral authority that nonviolent protests and sit-ins could command. And (*c*) we learned, more reluctantly, that *civil disobedience* could be both a moral obligation and a "realistic" option. This was a hard lesson for middle-class folk to learn. Taking a few risks now and then, yes; but "breaking the law"? It had always been ingrained in us since infancy that respect for law, which meant obeying the law, went with the territory of being a Christian, especially a middle-class Christian: if you did not like the law, you worked to change it at the ballot box. It had not occurred to us that one way to change the law might be to break it, be arrested, and take the case to court. Many evil laws fell as local and state ordinances crumbled when confronted with the Constitution in a federal court.

3. As the sixties wore on, and some gains were registered in the civil rights struggle through the courts, a complication arose that was initially very troubling: the escalating war in Vietnam, and the immorality of sending hundreds of thousands of U.S. troops into the midst of a Vietnamese civil war. The initial impulse in the civil rights movement was: don't fudge the issues, keep the focus on domestic civil rights rather than on a war six thousand miles away. And the moment of clarity that finally emerged (symbolized by King's famous speech at Riverside Church pledging the resources and commitments of the civil rights struggle to oppose the war in Vietnam) was that *they were not, in fact, two struggles; both were part of the same struggle*. In both situations, racism was dominant—racism in terms of the denial of civil rights to African-Americans throughout U.S. history, racism in the reality that blacks were drafted twice as often as whites to kill and be killed in Vietnam, and racism in the fact that in both cases light-skinned people were pitted against dark-skinned people. Why should blacks be drafted for such a war? A sign displayed at many anti-Vietnam rallies by black participants read, "No Vietcong ever called me 'nigger.' " Additionally, the economic forces that thrive in a wartime economy overseas thrived in a "peacetime" economy at home in which blacks and other minority groups could be exploited without recourse to collective bargaining or unions. The two struggles could not be disentangled.

It is part of the picture of this period that the churches got into the struggle over Vietnam very late in the day, if at all. Despite some strong initial involvements in the civil rights struggle (sparked, of course, by the black churches, who were able to bring increasing numbers of whites on board), the churches did not take gladly to the extension of the "same struggle" to Southeast Asia. This reluctance made clear that individuals are often at places on a moral spectrum that their churches have not yet reached. To me, the most important discovery here was the need for additional, almost ad hoc groups to provide solidarity and witness on specific issues–not as "substitutes" for the church, but as extensions to it. People did not "leave the church" to join Clergy and Laity Concerned about Vietnam, but joined as a way of expressing concerns that could not yet find expression in the mainline churches within which the members of CALC still continued to work. There are clearly some analogies here with the base communities of Latin America that we in the North need to adapt to our own situations.

4. As the U.S. military presence in Vietnam grew, and the moral ambiguities became more intolerable, another insight began to permeate middle-class Christians, almost as unnerving as the earlier option for civil disobedience. This was the realization that *we could not trust our leaders*, or, put more bluntly, our recognition that our leaders were lying to us. This was a devastating discovery for middle-class folk, whose assumptions about civil life had always been predicated on the norm of honesty and trustworthiness. Take away that norm and it is hard, initially, to know where to turn. This led to a new dimension of realism, sometimes bordering on the cynical, but other times being a catalyst for attempting not only to discover the presence of lies, but with equal determination to ferret out the truth, even if it meant turning to the "underground press," or the magazine articles and books that began to "tell it like it is." Church periodicals, likewise, began to make such information available.

Events emanating from the Watergate break-in italicized the untrustworthiness of our public officials. We had to struggle with the erosion of most of what our high school civics courses had taught us, and put our trust in the very few officials we felt were *still* dealing honestly with us. (Even this was difficult. One of the huge ironies of this period was that one of the few elected officials we could all trust, Fr. Robert Drinan, S.J., of the House of Representatives, was forced by the Catholic Church to give up his seat after serving five terms, because of a vote on abortion legislation that did not satisfy the hierarchy.)

5. The history of U.S. involvement in the internal affairs of Nicaragua was an extremely important watershed in the life of U.S. churches. Through the impact of groups like Witness for Peace, thousands of U.S. citizens went to Nicaragua and saw firsthand how U.S. money and munitions were being used to fund the contras in all of their terrorist activities. Once again we were reminded not to trust our leaders, particularly Messrs. Reagan and Bush, who used palpably false information to rev up ongoing support for the contras.

But there was a plus this time. As a result of people going to Nicaragua and returning, U.S. public opinion, both in the churches and outside, became increasingly antagonistic to the official White House line, and led slowly—all too slowly—to the diminution and finally discontinuance of U.S. aid. One can never say for sure what would have happened in history had alternative courses been taken, but I feel confident that one reason the Reagan administration never directly invaded Nicaragua was because of the pressures on members of Congress from their constituencies. (One very conservative member of the House of Representatives reported, "Every time I go back to my district and have an open meeting on funding for the contras, there is somebody in the audience who just got back from Nicaragua last week and knows more about the situation there than my legislative assistant for Central American affairs.")

The hopeful lesson: *Sometimes keeping the pressure on produces results.* To be sure, the results came late—thousands of deaths too late—but the situation for Nicaraguans would have been arguably worse without that pressure. If one cannot produce massive good through the political process, one can sometimes forestall a modicum of evil, and if that does not sound like a ringing endorsement of the political process, we should remember that it is impressive testimony for those who live rather than die as a result of the pressure.

6. Many of the same things can be said about U.S. involvement in El Salvador: the same lies, the same phony claims, the much more massive number of deaths, the clear complicity of the United States in financing "death squads" who could engage in random killings (to the figure of 70,000 in ten years) with such active Salvadoran government support that not a single member of a death squad was ever brought to justice. What is so shocking was our government's unwillingness truly to put pressure on a succession of Salvadoran governments, and its shallow attempts to claim that "democracy" was ensured whenever there was an election, no matter how badly it was rigged. To the degree that there *are* some beginnings of a democratic process in El Salvador, they must

be credited to the ongoing pressures of the guerrilla forces rather than to the massive U.S. support for regime after regime exercising power corruptly.

Perhaps the most important impact of the Salvadoran war on our U.S. churches was the presence of the sanctuary movement. A few churches, aware of the true state of terrorism in El Salvador created by the death squads and governmental fanatics, declared themselves willing (in apparent disregard of the U.S. law) to receive and house refugees fleeing from the death squads, providing them sanctuary from U.S. law enforcement agencies until their cases could be adjudicated in the courts and their right to remain in the United States could be guaranteed. The presence of such refugees personalized the Salvadoran war for many North Americans who were now confronted not with the abstract concept of "refugees," but with Carlos, Elvira, Pablo, María, José, who shared their stories of being full-time targets for extermination. That the Department of Immigration and Naturalization kept trying to discover where such people were hiding and send them back to the likelihood of torture and death is one of the low points of recent U.S. social policy.

7. If one detects in the above material an increasing sense of disillusion with the nature of our political life, such disillusion is well founded. It has been brought about not only in terms of our indirect subsidies of death dealing—aid to Pinochet, Marcos, Somoza, the contras, the death squads, and a legion of other "foreign policy decisions"—but in terms of our active military invasions as well, of which three—Grenada, Panama, and Iraq—stand as the most overt symbols.

No justification for invading Grenada can any longer hold currency, save that President Reagan needed an event to divert attention from the catastrophe of the 241 Marine deaths in Lebanon, and that a war with Grenada was "a war we could win," and thus serve notice to Nicaragua that it might be next on the list if it failed to "say uncle," as Mr. Reagan demanded. The situation in Panama, meanwhile, is demonstrably worse today than it was before our military invasion in December 1989, which decimated the population around Panama City, destroyed cavernous areas of the capital, and installed a puppet government under which the drug traffic has become worse than it was before the United States intervened.

The issue of Iraq is too massive for more than cursory treatment here, but a few facts cry out for attention: our casualties were about

200, Iraq's casualties perhaps as high as 150,000, which suggests not a war but a massacre; the baleful state of affairs in the postwar Middle East where a moderately powerful Saddam Hussein is now almost a political necessity; the callous neglect of the postwar refugees by the Bush administration; the inordinately high civilian deaths in what the media (at the behest of the Pentagon) presented as a "clean" military operation; Mr. Bush's peremptory decision to invade militarily despite advice to the contrary from former secretaries of state and defense and highly placed military officials within Mr. Bush's own White House coterie; and the fact that the decision-making process was not in the hands of elected officials, but a tiny handful of Bush-appointed advisors who (in a manner similar to Panama and Vietnam) were not truly answerable to the electorate.

Unlike the Vietnam years, when the churches became involved only late in the day, the war in the Middle East engaged almost all of the major church groups long before it actually began. Church groups affirmed, with a surprising unanimity of opinion, that if one employed the criteria for a "just war," no war in the Middle East would be able to meet the test. The widespread reactivation of the ancient categories of a "just war" was surprising to many; the theme was so persistent that the president had to reply with *his* own version of how the administration's stand met all seven criteria of a "just war"—a piece of theological apologetic that was scarcely Mr. Bush's finest hour. Whatever theologian in Pharaoh's court wrote the speech for Mr. Bush served the commander in chief of the U.S. armed forces very badly.

However, the downside of the fact that the churches condemned the war is that despite declaration after declaration, *nobody listened*. It should be a sobering reminder of the churches' lack of real impact on public policy that they could be so united in their condemnation yet so totally disregarded by the policymakers.

U.S. military actions in the Middle East suggest that when our leaders do not know what to do internationally they start a war, and this can only spawn disillusionment with the way our nation plays its role in the world. As Tom Fox, editor of the *National Catholic Reporter*, reminds us, although the war in Iraq was clearly a military victory of stunning proportions, it was a moral defeat of just as stunning proportions, even though not many U.S. citizens recognize it as such. The rest of the Third World surely recognizes the contradiction: what Third World country that causes difficulties for the United States' imperial designs can help wondering, "Are we next?"

WRITING (AND REWRITING)
OUR NATIONAL HISTORY

This little slice of personal history raises some larger questions about the writing (and rewriting) of our national history. Three comments:

1. *We need to recognize how our own national history has been written, and by whom.* Like other national histories, it has been written by "the winners," those who represent, broadly speaking, North American upper-middle-class white males. In an image Leonardo Boff has popularized, "History is written by those with white hands." The term "white hands" is meant both literally and metaphorically. Literally, it is members of the white race who are almost always the "winners" (at least until the present), while those of another skin color (red, yellow, black, brown — take your pick) are the "losers." Metaphorically, those with white hands are those who sit at desks, drive cars past construction sites, and live in suburban subdivisions where such amenities as running hot water are taken for granted. They are distinguished from "the others," those who engage in manual labor on the construction sites, work on the production lines in factories, dig ditches, live in "low-cost housing," and are often denied such amenities as running hot water. On a wider scale, the divisions run: First World "winners" vs. Third World "losers;" men in charge vs. women in subservient roles; financial wheeler-dealers vs. bankrupt small-business owners; those whose faith is in armaments or the almighty dollar vs. those who get no health benefits because of the defense budget. Our history has not been written (until very recently) by Native Americans, African-Americans, women, or a whole host of other "hyphenated-Americans": Irish-Americans, Hispanic-Americans, Filipino-Americans, gay-and-lesbian Americans.

So our knowledge of our history, a knowledge that molds our attitudes for the future, has been very much a "class" production. If we ever balked in a high school civics course at such a reading of our situation, we were probably subjected to intense efforts to get us back in line or face a failing grade.

However, as the parenthetical qualifiers in the above scenario suggest, it is not so easy to maintain these distinctions anymore. Those who have been excluded from the process are now demanding a hearing and are forcing the rest of us to take a fresh look at interpretations that up to now have been sacrosanct. A new process is underway.

2. *We must rewrite our own history.* The crucial terms in this second proposition are the apparently insignificant words "we" and "our." To whom do they refer? While some people among the "winners" are able

to transcend their class background and listen seriously to "the view from below"—Page Smith and Howard Zinn are two who come to mind—it is clear that the initial authors of a *new* U.S. history are going to have to come from among the "victims." The rest of us are going to have to listen to them, maybe for a long time, before earning the right to propose our own rewriting. While we all aspire to transcend class differences that are only abrasive, when those differences blind or destroy us, the only way we can deal with them creatively rather than destructively will be for all of us to be as upfront as possible about where we are really coming from, and count on the others to tell us in what ways we are still bound by biases apparent not to us, but ever so apparent to others.

I recall one such lesson I had to learn during the Vietnam years. Like many "liberals" of that generation I had a few experiences of being inside jails. Many of us advocated breaking what we felt were unjust laws, being arrested, taking our cases to court, and finally winning vindication as the unjust laws were declared unconstitutional by higher courts. But as an upper-middle-class white, I had a lot of built-in protection and privileges that were denied to others. When I anticipated being indicted for "aiding, counselling, and abetting" draft-age youth to resist induction, a panel of faculty from the Stanford Law School (the university at which I was then teaching) came to my defense, and had an indictment actually been served, I would have had the best legal help the profession could provide. Anticipated result: "the system works."

But I was brought up short by the realization that blacks without much education, without access to the Stanford Law School faculty, without the promise of contributions from friends to defray legal fees, would have had little or no chance of making it through the system, and would be likely to end up spending years in jail, without even a principled if pyrrhic victory to show for it. The justice system in the land of the free and the home of the brave, I discovered, was a two-track system. Folks like myself could use it, maybe even creatively, whereas other folks would be ground down and destroyed by it. So there is a shadow across the ringing praises of the judicial system so often sung by white middle-class people: we benefit from a system that threatens to destroy those who occupy a lower rung on the civic pecking order. If we are truly to know the history of how justice works in our country, we will learn about it only as we are able to listen to the victims.

Where do the class biases come from that make it so difficult for those with white hands to write authentically?

Part of the problem is naïveté—a belief that somehow our own perspective is pretty universal and that we see things the way they truly are. Fortunately, that claim is harder and harder to maintain, and those who nevertheless try to do so simply demonstrate their location in a "never, never land," comfortably insulated from what is really going on.

But I think the real difficulty in transcending our biases is much deeper, and is based on an inherent fear of change, since we have it so well "made" the way things are. As a result, we may be willing to entertain the notion of personal inner change, since all of us could become at least a little "better" without threatening our outer security, but we resist like the plague the notion of corporate or structural change. The latter is what is really scary, for it would threaten the place we have carved out for ourselves within a set of structures always tilted in our favor.

This means, as the bottom line, that economics is a long-neglected clue in understanding how and why we operate as we do. We do not want to scrutinize the sources and resources of our economic privilege, nor especially do we want (God forbid) to have things change as a result of such scrutiny. If there is to be a rewriting of our history that takes account of the fact that so many are disadvantaged for the sake of so few, we will have to take economic factors more seriously into account than we have before. Consider a few examples:

Since the arrival of Christopher Columbus and the conquistadors, the history of our hemisphere has been a story of rape, pillage, exploitation, and slavery, for the purpose of obtaining gold, or property translatable into gold. Gustavo Gutiérrez rightly entitles the first volume of his series on Bartolomé de las Casas, *Dios o el oro*—God or gold,[1] establishing in his text that for the settlers in Latin America, God and gold were finally indistinguishable. In a *New Yorker* cartoon, one of the Pilgrims on the *Mayflower* is saying to another, "Oh, I'm going for religious liberty, too, but my long-range plans are real estate." The greatest blots on our national moral escutcheon—slavery and the ongoing subjugation of minorities—are both examples of the way one class exploits another class for the sake of greater economic profit. In the settling of the West, and in the Industrial Revolution's expression on our eastern shores, the name of the game has always remained "profit." The free enterprise system that "made our nation great" is a system affirming competition and greed as high virtues, traits rendered honorable and desirable to those who want the rewards of "the American way of life." Our recent forays into the Third World, described in the earlier pages of this essay, depict our nation as a whole still motivated primarily by the promise of high economic return; behind all the moralistic rhetoric, for example, of our chief executive in justifying the war with Iraq, the bottom line, and everyone knew it, was "o-i-l."

We will be able to see the truth of this side of history only as we open our ears to the victims and hear their side of the story. This claim has been clearly, if diabolically, clarified by the recent discussion about free trade with Mexico. Those who listen to the view from below will not be taken in by presidential rhetoric about the benefits of free trade for Americans. Our ear must be attuned to what Mexican workers are saying about its baleful effects on *their* livelihood: still more sweatshops with no minimum wage, no health and safety standards, no means for disposing of toxic chemicals, no matter what may be written in the formal agreements. A "free trade package" might be great for a certain sector of the U.S. economy, thereby enabled to hire workers at less than minimum wage, and for a few already wealthy Mexican entrepreneurs as well. But for the workers, whether U.S. or Mexican, the reality will be a nightmare.

(An example of the cynical way such proposals are foisted on the electorate was offered by former President Bush's early pressure for immediate legislative approval for his "free trade" proposals so that workers could be helped, coupled with the fact that when such legislation began to look like a liability in his 1992 bid for reelection, Mr. Bush put the whole proposal on hold for the indefinite future.)

A helpful tool in learning how others see us and insist that we rewrite our history has been furnished by the documents *Kairos: Central America* and *The Road to Damascus*, written by Third World Christians living in poverty in Central America, Asia, and South Africa.[2] Both documents identify the United States as part of the problem rather than part of the solution. They are unsparing in their critique, but it is finally a critique informed by love rather than spite, holding open the possibility that even at this late date we North American Christians could undergo a "Damascus road experience" and begin to orient our national priorities in new directions. If the churches as a whole do not hear that message, those who do must create within the church what might be called "kairos communities," ad hoc groups modeled on what happened in the Vietnam years, and on the current Latin American experience of the base communities, not only to keep new hope alive but to transform it into reality.

I am not particularly sanguine that we as a nation can even contemplate, let alone adopt, such a perspective. But I am sure that if we do not we will increasingly find more and more of the world ranged against us, and what we might once have voluntarily shared we will increasingly be forced to surrender, whether we wish to do so or not. Here is one place where altruism and hard-nosed realism might join hands.

3. *We must recover a sense of the importance of history.* In many circles — both those who fear social change and those who advocate it — there is a disdain of history in any form. It is either "romantic" to look to a past we cannot retrieve today, or it is "diversionary" to reflect on the past when it is toward the future that we must direct our gaze. While few would agree with Henry Ford's blunt assessment that "history is bunk," many would just as soon bypass preoccupation with it.

To all such it must be responded (in the well-known and overquoted dictum of George Santayana) that "those who forget history are condemned to repeat it." We never start de novo, particularly as institutions or societies or cultures. We inherit an incredible amount of ideological baggage from the past. We can ignore that baggage at our peril (as Santayana reminds us) or we can use it, either to our peril or to our emancipation, for we are creatures of memory whether we will it or not, and memory is a two-edged sword. The crucial fact is not *that* we remember but *what* we remember.

Germans can remember the golden days of Schiller and Goethe, or they can remember the dark days of Hitler and Auschwitz, and their choice between such memories will dictate the direction and quality of their future. Catholics can look back to the days of the imperial medieval papacy, or they can remember the servant papacy of John XXIII, and the choice they make will determine the quality of the church of the future. Similarly, who and what we remember out of our own national history will determine the quality of our national future. Will we remember Martin Luther King, Jr., or George Wallace? Susan B. Anthony or David Duke? Ronald Reagan or Jimmy Carter? The Emancipation Proclamation or the *Dred Scott* decision? Sojourner Truth or partisans of white supremacy?

Memory sifts between past events in ways that focus toward a dream nourished with hope, or a nightmare invested with power.

The Christian faith, in whatever manifestation, is a faith squarely immersed in history, and Christians, too, invoke memory. We look back not to a golden age, but to what Gutiérrez has bluntly called "an irruption smelling of the stable"[3] — earthly events, earthy events, firmly fixed as to time and place, that tell us that the truth about God and about ourselves will be found in a stable rather than a palace.

TOWARD A CREATIVE FUTURE

To conclude, what do we learn from a (rewritten) past that can empower us to work toward a creative future?

• We do not get pure choices, and must not render ourselves irrelevant by demanding them.

• We do not have the privilege of neutrality, since inaction strengthens the hand of whatever despotic power is trying to consolidate its gains.

• In a time when violence seems only to breed more violence, we must explore nonviolent methods of social change more assiduously than we have previously done.

• We need to remember that humanity is so interwoven that there is one overall struggle to which we must all be committed: a struggle for justice that must be waged simultaneously against all the institutions of injustice.

• When our institutional churches falter, we must create ad hoc groups within them to keep specific concerns alive.

• We must nourish a healthy suspicion and skepticism about whatever promises our political leaders make.

• Simultaneously, we must put unremitting pressure on those in public office, realizing that sometimes (as in the case of Nicaragua) paths of greater evil can be abandoned if the public will is firm enough.

• We must keep the dialectic of reflection and action alive and well (as the sanctuary movement illustrated).

• We must speak directly on the moral dimension of public social issues; and, when we discover that nobody is listening, we must respond by speaking more clearly and even, if necessary, more stridently.

• We must engage in a new (and more economically informed) re-reading of our past if we are to prepare ourselves for a different future. As Karl Barth wrote about the task of the churches, "Better something doubtful and overbold and therefore in need of forgiveness than nothing at all!"[4] It has been a long time since any U.S. church was accurately pilloried for being overbold—and that is surely the direction in which we must move.

For that, we need hope, something our Third World friends, in particular, have taught us. They, who have so little tangible reason for hope, have much more actual hope than we. Theirs is a hope founded not on human ingenuity, nor even on economically informed rereadings of history. It is founded on a belief that history (including our own

U.S. history) is somehow still in the hands of a living God who will not (for reasons we cannot fathom but for which we must always be grateful) give up on such recalcitrant human clay as we, but keeps presenting us with new opportunities to see the constant in-breaking of the reign of God, so that we, like those who first saw that in-breaking, can also repent and believe the good news. Since the human venture has already been graced by the divine presence of the Son, and continues to be the arena of the ongoing divine presence of the Spirit, we are not permitted the luxury of disengagement or despair.

Augustine has a final word for us. "Hope," he wrote, "has two beautiful daughters. Their names are anger and courage; anger that the world is the way it is, and courage to see that it does not remain that way."

2

RECLAIMING OUR HISTORIES

William Baldridge

*I*n the middle of one of Jesus' sermons in Capernaum, Mark's Gospel relates, four people battered a hole through the roof of Jesus' home and lowered a paralytic into the crowded room. I wonder if Jesus had to stop talking when the banging and busting started, or if he just talked louder while the dust and chunks of roof began to rain down on his head. I wonder what the disciples were doing while all this was happening. Ever vigilant to keep the children away from Jesus, what were they doing while strangers were dismantling his family's house? I would have thought that somebody around there, perhaps old Joseph, who presumably was going to have to do the reroofing, or impetuous Peter, or just anybody who wanted to hear Jesus, would have been up on that roof pronto.

Anyway, these men made a hole in the roof big enough to lower a man through. What they did so pleased Jesus that he began to bait the scribes, who with all the dust flying must have looked like coal miners at the end of a double shift. Without a word to the demolition crew, Jesus looked down and forgave the paralytic. Taking the bait, the scribes questioned the right of Jesus to forgive sins: "It is blasphemy. Who can forgive sins but God alone?"

Jesus boldly reinforced the terms of their challenge: "Which is easier, to say, 'Your sins are forgiven,' or to say, 'Get up and take care of yourself?' " In other words, the authority to forgive sin rests on the authority to define sin. Then, to demonstrate that he had the authority to do both, Jesus defined the man's sin by prescribing its cure, "Get up and take care of yourself." Called to live out his potential, the man got up and walked, presumably at a speed fast enough to keep ahead of the four men who had been carrying him.

From a Native American's perspective, one way to describe the spiritual significance of 1492 is to realize that for the last half-millennium Columbus and his spiritual children have usurped the role of God and imposed their definitions of reality onto this continent. People now go through life believing that trees went unidentified until Europeans came to name them, that places could not be distinguished and directions could not be given until Europeans arrived to designate one place New York and another Los Angeles. People in the United States accept as self-evident that this continent could not produce food until row cropping was introduced, that water was not pure before filtration plants were introduced, and that conservation is a concept introduced by the U.S. Forestry Service. It is believed without question that this land was godless until the arrival of Christianity.

For Native Americans, perhaps the most pervasive result of colonialism is that we cannot even begin a conversation without referencing our words to definitions imposed or rooted in 1492. The arrival of Columbus marks the beginning of colonial hubris in America, a pride so severe that it must answer the charge of blasphemy.

COLONIAL CHRISTIANITY

A central agent in the colonization of this hemisphere has been the Christian church. Whatever the church likes to believe its intentions were or are in making us the object of its missionary endeavors, history shows the missionary system to be colonialism in the name of Christ. The foundation of colonial Christianity rests on its power to monopolize definitions: who is godless, godly, and most godly, all stemming from Christianity's definition of the essential nature of God. When Christians confuse their confessions of faith with absolute knowledge of reality, they invite a challenge of hubris. When Christians confuse the limitations of their humanity with the nature of God, they invite a challenge of blasphemy. Who can claim absolute knowledge of reality but God alone?

Native Americans have not been passive toward Christian colonialism. Today's generation of Native Americans, like the generations that preceded us and those to follow, are bound by the spiritual power of freedom and dignity, gifts from our Creator. We are often dismissed as trying to change the past or trying to return to the past. Having our intelligence questioned is a familiar experience. But being underestimated is one of our most effective and constant weapons. We are not denying history or the weight of the forces pushing us down. We are also not willing to forsake our spiritual birthright as children of God. Colonial Christian definitions to the contrary, we will not label our ancestors nor teach our children that they are spiritually illegitimate. So, as well as resisting we are retrenching, reaching down, down to the bedrock of our continent, down where our spiritual vitality is grounded. Native people's thoughts need not be determined by the definitions of the colonizer if they know who they are and where they stand, if their identity is anchored in bedrock. We are the embodiment of this hemisphere. God made us and placed us here.

Identifying and attacking the enemy is a time-honored means to gain respect and admiration within one's community. As a Native American Christian I have done my warring with the missionaries. They are a target as easy to hit as dirt and just as difficult to eliminate. I am not making claims to be a seasoned, veteran missionary fighter, but I do know the taste of battle. In my first firefights I joined those presenting a more balanced picture of the Christian missionary work. Many of the missionaries were people of good faith who sacrificially brought us the gospel of Christ. I was raised on the praise and publicity generated by the churches concerning these people.

On the other hand, many missionaries served as federal agents and in that role negotiated treaties which left us no land. Most missionaries taught us to hate anything Native American and that of necessity included hating our friends, our families, and ourselves. Most refused to speak to us in any language but their own. The missionaries functioned and continue to function as "Christ-bearing colonizers." If it were otherwise the missionaries would have come, shared the gospel, and left. We know, of course, that they stayed, and they continue to stay, and they continue to insist that we submit to them and their definitions. The vast majority of Native people have experienced the missionary system as racist and colonial, and our most prevalent response has been passive resistance: A very small percentage of Native Americans are practicing Christians.

I realize that such language makes some people anxious and others quite indignant. If Native American Christians do not use colonial formulas for confessing Christ such people claim that we are not "real Christians," they believe that we are questioning the ability of these formulas to satisfy *their* spiritual needs, and they bristle at being defined as "Christ-bearing colonizers" when they "were only trying to help." Still, the list of injuries to hurl back at the missionaries is long, yet it remains essentially unknown outside of Indian communities. I continue to be impressed by the number of people, active in the life of their various denominations, who are shocked to hear about the realities of current mission programs to Native Americans and who assumed that "we stopped doing missions like that a hundred years ago."

One of the spin-offs of the quincentennial celebration of the European invasion of this hemisphere was a proliferation of information, produced by non-Indian historians, concerning the church's role in colonialism. When whites turn on themselves with their technological expertise—graduate degrees, computers, data banks, ethno-histories, and such—a defiant arrow from an Indian becomes a flame amidst laser beams. Furthermore, as the new official history continues to roll off the press, some of us warriors are realizing that the power of our arrows comes not so much from the historical evidence as it does from the anecdotal experience we own. We Indians lived the missionary history, we continue to live this history, and the power of our stories cannot be matched by "the cold hard facts." It is encouraging to watch the academic historians revisit history and bring a greater degree of balance to the subject. At the same time, it is discouraging to remember that such "objectivity" typically comes at a point in a political struggle when the issues have been decided and the victors, that is, the ones writing the history, can afford to admit that "nobody is perfect" without any real threat to their power base.

In the 500-year war against Christian colonialism we have had our successes. If on no more than a few occasions of hit-and-run skirmishes, we have had our moments. For me, the sense of comradery with brothers and sisters has become a lasting satisfaction. Yet the spoils of our small victories have faded into an ironic lesson: the very act of fighting the missionary system concedes too much to colonialism. It concedes too much because it accepts the premise that our dignity must be granted to us rather than be recognized in us. It accepts the premise that God loves one people more than God loves all people. It accepts the premise that a God of justice would condemn a people to hell because of where they were born and when they were born. Fighting missionaries has taught me that the end of the missionary system begins with a change of heart, my heart, not the heart of the missionary nor the heart of the institutions that commission missionaries. Fighting the oppression of the missionary system is a struggle for justice that unavoidably becomes a struggle for power. Power lies at the core of Christian colonialism. Refusing the terms of the struggle is an essential first step in regaining the spiritual perspective of Native America.

REAFFIRMING OUR SPIRITUAL HERITAGE

Before the Europeans came the Cherokee were taught the following story as spiritual truth. The Daughter of God loved her children.

Loving them, she provided food so that they never knew hunger. The day came when her children realized that their mother fed them without labor; it was miraculous. Human nature being what it is, the children developed an insistent need to know the source of the food that sustained them. When their mother retreated to the private place from which she brought them food, they followed her and from their hiding place they witnessed the miracle that gave them life. The food came from their mother's body. "She is a witch!" they whispered to each other. "She is evil! We must kill her! Kill her!" Their mother knew their thoughts and said to them, "When you kill me, take my body and place it in the ground. I will rise from the dead and you will be given life and never hunger." So the children killed their mother and placed her in the ground and in the fullness of time, corn, the source of bread for the Cherokee, rose from the grave.

When the Christians came we were taught a second story as spiritual truth. The Son of God loved his brothers and sisters. Loving them, he provided food for them so that they never knew hunger. On one occasion he fed a great multitude with five loaves and two fish; it was miraculous. Human nature being what it is, his brothers and sisters developed an insistent need to know the source of the food that sustained them. When they questioned him he responded, "I am the living bread that came down from heaven. Whoever eats of this bread will live forever; and the bread that I will give for the life of the world is my flesh" (John 6:51). One day his brothers and sisters brought to him a man who was blind and mute and he cured him. His brothers and sisters said, "It is only by Beelzebul, the ruler of the demons, that this fellow casts out the demons." The Son of God knew what they were thinking (Matt. 12:22-25). After that the Son of God began to show his brothers and sisters that he must be killed and on the third day be raised (Matt. 16:21). So, in time, his brothers and sisters killed him and placed him in the ground, and on the third day the bread of life rose from the grave.

Having reaffirmed our spiritual heritage, some of us who are both Native American and Christians have lost the ability to distinguish "us" from "them." When we hear again the words of the Daughter of God and the Son of God we look in vain for the children either one would not feed. We cannot identify the injured brother or sister either one would pass by on the other side of the road. When we recall how we have abused those whom the Creator has sent to us, we find ourselves looking with less hate and more compassion toward those who have abused us.

THE SACRIFICIAL NATURE OF THE SPIRITUAL LIFE

> How could we sing the Lord's song in a foreign land?
> If I forget you, O Jerusalem, let my right hand wither!
> Let my tongue cling to the roof of my mouth, if I do not remember you,
>   if I do not set Jerusalem above my highest joy. (Psalm 137)

As a Native American Christian, I find it helpful to remember the experience of the people of Jerusalem during their exile in Babylon. The people had so identified God with the place of their origin and with the shape of their temple they could not recognize that God was present in all times and in all places. None of us can know God directly. All of us experience God as through a darkened glass. The color, the shape, and the size of that glass is always a mirror of our particular culture and our particular time and place. Having never seen a ship, some of us Native people believed that the first ones we saw were floating islands. Having never seen a man riding a horse, some of us believed horse and rider were one entity. Having never experienced God except through their own cultures, those who came in ships believed that God had only been revealed to them and that God must be brought to this place. We who first mistook the Daughter of God for a witch must not be too eager to condemn European Christians who did the same. Somehow, Native Americans must find the means to forgive our white brothers and sisters and accept that they too did not know what they were doing.

Whether one eats only at the table of the Corn Mother or only at the table of the Son of Man, both are compelled to come to terms with the sacrificial nature of the spiritual life. Those who refuse to give up all that they have cannot move from death into life. Those who hoard their spiritual life lose it and are left with nothing but religion. Those who refuse to die become the agents of death.

After five hundred years of battle, Native American people are in danger of forsaking the lesson of the Corn Mother and of hoarding her seeds. The lesson—to plant in faith—is being lost in the shouts of our fears and anger. When the Europeans first came we met them and freely shared. We shared because we knew that what we had did not belong to us; it was a gift from our Mother. When the Europeans ignored the spiritual basis of life on this continent and made claims that as creatures they could own the creation, we refused to cooperate with their witchery. Now we are in danger of adopting the fear that produced their greed.

More and more, Native people protest that non-Indians are stealing the only thing we have left: our spiritual lessons. My Native brothers and sisters, spiritual lessons cannot be owned any more than the source of those lessons can be owned. All that we have has been given to us. If we have wisdom about the waters of this land it is because the waters have taught us. If we have wisdom about the rocks and trees it is because the rocks and trees have spoken to us. If we have wisdom about the rhythms of this land it is because the seasons have sung to us. We do not own the voice of the wind, we do not own the light at dawn, we do not own the colors of the grasses, we do not own a single thing. All that we have of value has been given to us by God.

For five hundred years the missionaries have been trying to save us. Look at the water, look at the sky, look at all the hungry children, look at all the machines of war. Brothers and sisters, it is now time for us to save the missionaries; it is time for us to return to sharing.

The way of sharing is sacrifice. The lesson of both the Daughter of God and the Son of God is sacrifice. Not only must the evil be sacrificed, but the good must also be sacrificed. Sacrificing the gains of evil is but the first step toward following the Corn Mother or the Christ. The temptations of evil came to Christ early in his life and were not difficult for him to reject. It was the temptation to hold on to the good that caused his sweat to become like great drops of blood. He had fed the hungry, healed the sick, raised the dead! So much good called to him to reject the final sacrifice. As the old ones have taught us, good, not evil, is the most powerful enemy of the beast. That is also the lesson of Jesus in Gethsemane.

It is good and just to struggle for the right to practice Christianity within the context of our Native cultures, and we will struggle on. Affirming sweat lodges as appropriate places for Christian prayers is good and just, and we will continue to make our claims. The use of Native symbolism in Christian churches is good and just, and we will continue to bring them into our sanctuaries. The insistence that Native Americans do not have to acculturate before they can become Christians is good and just, and we will not abandon our cultures.

As Native people, we have as much right to our heritage as any other people. As Native American Christians, we have a right, as well as an obligation, to express the coming of Christ in a manner that is meaningful within our cultures, and that is what we will do. A unique Native American expression of Christianity, a Native American theology, is a worthy, a good, and a just goal, and we will continue to develop it. Evangelical theology, liberal theology, black theology, feminist theology, liberation theology, why not Native American theology? Still, as desirable and just as all these agendas are, they fail to reach the ultimate goal of a gospel that proclaims neither Jew nor Greek, male nor female, European nor Native American.

Justice, when defined as "our getting ours as you have yours," does not rise above the level of "an eye for an eye." In light of our colonial history, claiming the moral high ground tempts us to the hubris of "owning" our own version of the gospel and of claiming that our definitions are the only ones that belong here. But there are greater spiritual needs than getting a higher place within the ecclesiastical hierarchy or getting a piece of the theological power pie. Life on this planet cannot survive if our, and your, and their, and everyone's spiritual agenda does not move beyond colonialism, nationalism, racism, tribalism, sectarianism, and denominationalism. The form of Christianity that has served the needs of separation and has promoted a disdain of the earth is now a deadly anachronism. In this light, for the follower of Christ justice as law or justice as "equal but separate" are continuations of colonial values, and both must be transcended by love.

Today, Christianity stands in need of the courage to fulfill the work of Christ. We stand in need of the courage to follow him into self-sacrifice. The fulfillment of Christianity will come, indeed it is coming, through the sacrifice of colonialism for hospitality, through the sacrifice of imperialism for invitation, the sacrifice of power for service, the sacrifice of fear for fellowship, the sacrifice of isolation from the world for the joy of living at peace with mother earth. Through self-sacrifice, Christianity can fulfill the promise of Christ's birth: glory to God, peace on earth, good will throughout creation.

TRANSFORMING IMAGES OF GOD

We know that Almighty God, the Ground of Being, is neither defined nor confined by the limits of our imagination. Still, all but the mystics are forced to pray to the Great Mystery through familiar associations. The Hebrew laws forbidding graven images address the tendency to confuse an image with the unimaginable and thus to slip into material idolatry. The laws forbidding even the writing or speaking a name for God address the tendency to slip into conceptional idolatry. "Father" has become a conceptional idol for colonial Christians. "Father" has, to this point, defined the limits of the Christian understanding of God.

But the term has never defined God. The colonial experience of this continent is a witness that "Father God" is not only inadequate but destructive. The god of military conformity, violence, and brutality thundering from the pulpit has suffered neither a witch to live nor a country the size of Grenada to threaten the national insecurity. God is not confined to "Father," but confining our concept of God to "Father" distorts, skews, and throws out of balance our relationship with God and the fullness of God's creation. For example, consider this early colonial representation of "Father God":

> The God that holds you over the Pit of Hell, much as one holds a Spider or some loathsome Insect over the Fire, abhors you, and is dreadfully provoked; his Wrath towards you burns like Fire; he looks upon you as Worthy of nothing else but to be cast into the Fire; he is of purer Eyes than to bear to have you in his Sight; you are Ten Thousand Times so abominable in his Eyes as the most hateful venomous Serpent is in ours. . . . "[1]

The time has come for the sacrifice of seeing God as only Father for a concept that allows the next generation of children to live. The time has come for the emerging Christian experience of God as Father and Mother. Transformation of our images from God the Father to God our Parent(s) will not destroy Christianity but fulfill it. Mother God is not an alternative to Father God; she is an expansion of our possibility to experience God. God as Father will not be lost by including the experience of God as Mother. Father images of God will still tend to discipline, order, history, progress, judgment, duty, transcendence, and all that the masculine has to offer. Mother images of God will make more available God's acceptance, creativity, eternity, grace, enduring nurture, immediacy, and all that the feminine has to offer.

We who are Native American can contribute to Christianity's transformation and fulfillment by sharing our experience of God as both Mother and Father. Even so, we Native Americans do not "own" the experience of God as Parent(s), for many other peoples join in the sharing. In fact, God as Mother as well as Father is not something that colonial Christians do not know; they just do not have images or the security that would allow them comfortable familiarity.

Within the Native American Christian community our history must be owned, our pain must be acknowledged, the present must be realized, and a future for our children must determine how we spend our energy. Our anger must be sacrificed to love as we reaffirm our spiritual heritage and offer it up for the benefit of all our relations. I do not suggest that this will be an easy task, but I am suggesting that our spiritual heritage, as well as our spiritual health, demand it.

The challenge for the larger Christian community is one that is impossible to meet without the grace of God. It is a call to sacrifice what has been good for what can be better. It is a call to sacrifice the good that has allowed us to come to this time and place along the paths of "us" and "them." It is a call to follow Christ to the cross, placing our faith in the power of God to raise us from the dead. The colonial history of the church contains much pain, suffering, and harm. As a community, the body of Christ has never attained the level of sacrifice expressed through the spirit of Christ. The saving news is that we do not have to make the way; we must, however, be willing to follow the way. The path has been well marked whereby we, too, can pass from death into life. The time and the place have come for us to follow the Christ, to share sacrificially, so that all our children might live.

Come spring rains. Come new life. Come Lord Jesus.

3

RELIVING OUR HISTORIES

Racial and Cultural Revelations of God

Elsa Tamez

*T*hese reflections are not directed to the indigenous people who maintain their native religions, but to white and *mestizo* Christians who live out their faith under rigidly set boundaries and who undervalue other living expressions of faith which are not their own. Perhaps for those indigenous people who are politically aware [*conscientes*] of their reality this contribution will say nothing new and will be of little consequence. In reality, that would be appropriate, since what this essay hopes to demonstrate on a theoretical level they are already experiencing daily within their own lives: the alliance, continuity, and struggle of Gods. In that regard, the Second Ecumenical Consultation on Indigenous Pastoral Service, held in Quito, Ecuador, proclaimed:

> We the indigenous people believe, and are convinced, that God, before Christianity, acted through men and women because they were moved by the experience of God. . . . God reveals Self and makes Self present through the myths of the indigenous people, myths which are mediated through nature. God is also present through our work and therein accompanies us.[1]

Indeed, this essay is not addressed to the indigenous people. It seeks to accompany them in their history, a challenge explicitly elaborated by those gathered in Quito at the Second Consultation who recognized that God has revealed God's Self in their cultures and that their religions have a salvation history which is their own.[2] To articulate that history will be our modest goal.

33

THE REVELATION OF THE GOD OF LIFE
BEFORE THE INVASION

The God of life, creator of the universe, lover of truth and justice, did not begin to reveal Self in these lands when the Spaniards and Portuguese, along with their religious representatives, arrived. It would be pure arrogance to declare that the true faith of the native people came into being with the arrival of Christianity, or to suggest that they had previously practiced a "primitive" faith. It would also be an expression of arrogance to suggest that previous generations of indigenous people perished because they did not know the God of the Christians. Such declarations reveal to us a very limited God, reduced to a small, western European circle.

The Presence of God

From the Christian perspective, is it possible to recognize the presence of God in Latin America before the imposition of Christianity? Leonardo Boff suggests an answer to that question from a theological point of view:

> Cultures, in that they produce feelings of life, in that they have an ethical dimension and, particularly, in that they give expression to religion, are the echo of the voice of God, who always addresses society and every subjective human being within it. Cultures are the conduit of God's revelation to humanity, in their different times, places, and cultural expressions.[3]

The Bible, with its poetic Hebrew thought, expresses the presence of God and the works of God in the form of a doxology so that everyone might know Yahweh: it is the heavens that tell of the glory of God and the firmament God's handiwork (cf. Ps. 19:1-4). In the Gospels, Jesus is astounded by the strength of faith demonstrated by several non-Jews (Luke 7:1-10; Mark 7:24-30). But it is Paul, in the New Testament, who gives us the key to reflect more fruitfully on the revelation of God before the arrival of the Spaniards.

In his Letter to the Romans, Paul repeats the extra-testamental idea of the revelation of God for all humanity based on his conviction that the practice of the Jewish religion during his time sought to reduce access to God to the fulfillment of the law and to circumcision. The artist Paul, who is a witness of the great multitudes that are excluded from the salvific message of the reign of God, manifests in his analysis of the society of his day (Rom. 1:1–3:20), that from the creation forward God has made Self known by means of divine works, power, and deity. Human beings have the capacity to perceive that God since they have been given the ability to "see" rationally (Rom. 1:20). The fact that they do not do it, according to Paul, is another matter.

God has given human beings *nous*, that is, reason, the ability to judge morals or principles based on intelligence, and humans are thereby able to describe the God of life. Furthermore, the human person has the capacity to desire to do good (Rom. 7:18). Whenever it is impossible for one to realize good it is because sin has dominated that very person, one's local conditions, and the society at large.[4]

It is of some note that in the same letter Paul gives us a means by which to argue for the existence of faith before the Conquest: the supremacy of faith over the law. As far as he is concerned, true knowledge of God is verified through the actions of human beings, not by virtue of fulfilling a law or circumcision. It was not important for the author of the Letter to the Romans whether someone was circumcised or uncircumcised, but that one has a "faith working through love" (Gal. 5:6).[5] On that basis, Paul exhorts the Christians in Rome not to be conformed to the style of life of their own time, but that their understanding (*nous*) be transformed and renewed so as to discern (*dokimazo*) what they ought to do in accordance with the will of God (Romans 12).

So as to free the Jewish religion from all exclusiveness which claims itself to be the sole heir of the promises of God, and so as to annul the requirement that one must fulfill the law in order to belong to the people of God, Paul returns to a time before Moses to prove that one is not justified by the law but by faith. The apostle points to Abraham, who before he was circumcised was received by God. By faith, Abraham was able to believe that he could have children despite his old age. Therefore, one may either be just before the law, by faith in the God of life, or by faith in the God who raises the dead and brings life out of nothingness (see Rom. 4:17).

This Pauline argument also basically serves to include within the liberating plan of God other people who do not know the Jewish law or circumcision, or, for that matter, the Christian religion. Access to God, or its flip side, God's solidarity with the human person, is made possible by the primacy of faith over the Jewish law or over Christian dogma. The openness of the Christian faith to other religions, therefore, is justified not by the law but by faith in the God of life. That affirmation leads to a consideration of some underlying christological problems that merit reappraisal in the light of other religions and in the light of the compassion of God for all people.

To preface that discussion by the terms "a reappraisal of Christology" does not mean that the centrality of Jesus Christ for all Christians is thereby being displaced. That central affirmation does not change, for our faith is rooted in the belief that we have been justified by faith in Jesus Christ [*pisteos Iesou Christou*] and by faith in the One who raises the dead. The obedience of Jesus Christ, the second Adam, has inaugurated the new humanity for everyone. Jesus Christ represents the human presence and solidarity of the triune God, an essential aspect of any religion which does not seek to escape the challenges of history. However, it ought to be remembered that the task of theology is not to "establish the God of Jesus Christ as superior or absolute and so convert the principles of other beliefs to the Christian religion, but rather its task is to testify to the victory of God over death through the weakness of the crucified one."[6]

Nor is our interest here apologetics, but to demonstrate that the revelation of God in history goes far beyond our Christian circle, for God's grace extends to the totality of creation, in its different times and different places.[7] The argument from the Scriptures utilized by Paul to introduce the arrival of God's justice, independently of the law, is the same that may be employed, contrary to certain forms of Christian sectarianism, to recognize other experiences of faith. Abraham was neither circumcised nor was he a Christian, but the strength of his faith in the God of life "was counted unto him for righteousness [justice]." It may also be remembered that the early Christian community grounded its faith in the Scriptures and believed themselves to be accepted by the same God of Abraham, who for them was also the God of Jesus Christ.[8]

We can also speak of the God of life in Latin America before the invasion, and there are elements of the Náhuatl culture that permit us to at least catch a glimpse of it.

The God of Life in the Náhuatl Culture

To speak of the God of life in the cultures of Mesoamerica, it is necessary to refer to the God or Gods who created the world and humanity, who are concerned for the life of human beings, and who do not demand human sacrifice. In the Náhuatl culture, for example, it is essential to go back to the God Quetzalcóatl, which, in the Náhuatl language, means "feathered serpent." The serpent is a symbol for the material realm and the feather is a symbol for the heavenly realm. Quetzalcóatl, then, is a synthesis of two combined forces that moves both to ascend (the reptile) and descend (the bird).

It is complicated to speak of Quetzalcóatl, since the tradition is a mix of myth and history that is, by nature, very ambiguous. Stories that narrate the life of a very concrete, historical personality are placed together with stories that refer to a God, and it is impossible to separate the two. To carry out a study of the Náhuatl religion adequately, then, it would be necessary to enter into its own theological elaboration and vision of the cosmos, something that will not be done in the present study. This essay simply seeks to present some aspects of the religion of the Náhuatl culture through which the revelation of the God of life may be seen.

The worship of Quetzalcóatl is present in almost every epoch of Mexican history, although it is always the Toltec culture which is characterized by its veneration of Quetzalcóatl as the only God: "The only God, Quetzalcóatl is that God's name. Quetzalcóatl demands nothing but butterflies that you must offer."[9] To praise Quetzalcóatl as the only God, all of the other divinities—like Tlaloc, God of the rain, or Huehuetéotl, God of fire—appear in the city where "the Gods are born" (Teotihuacán). These other Gods are, at root, more than "symbols of the forces of nature, water, wind, fire, and the earth, but by their actions make known the only supreme principle, which is invoked and remembered by the name Quetzalcóatl, Yohualli, Ehécatl—the One who is like the night and the wind."[10]

If there was great admiration and love for Quetzalcóatl, it was due to Quetzalcóatl's actions on behalf of humanity. There are many ancient testimonies which assign to Quetzalcóatl all those things which are good for human beings: Quetzalcóatl created the new human person through the Fifth Sun; life and movement were given to human beings through Quetzalcóatl's own blood, and Quetzalcóatl discovered corn for their sustenance; Quetzalcóatl gave humans the wisdom to build homes, and invented the calendar, art, and many other things.

There are three stelae in Xochicalco, Morelos (Mexico), that, through their images and hieroglyphics, narrate the actions of the God Quetzalcóatl—self-sacrifice, the creation of the Fifth Sun, discovery of corn, and so on—but it is in the Annals of Cuauhtitlán where the beautiful story of the fifth creation may be found.[11] The core of this story relates how the God Quetzalcóatl struggles against the lord of death and his reign so that a new humanity might rise into existence; the struggle is taken to such a degree that Quetzalcóatl injures Self in order to give humanity life. Quetzalcóatl's intention is to recreate humanity, to recover the material of other failed creations, and, after devising a way to escape the realm of the dead with human bones, use them to bring human beings, known as the *macehuales*, or "those worthy of penance," to birth.

However, the work of creation turns into a painful event for Quetzal-cóatl because the God must offer part of the God's life in the act, for only thus can the existence of humanity be made possible. Therein lies the success of this fifth creation: the blood of God is mixed with those human bones rescued from the world of death. Quetzalcóatl injures his penis so as to unite the material—the bones—and thereby infuse life into the new humanity. The God Cihuacóatl helps Quetzalcóatl in this act of creation:

> And suddenly Quilaztli,
> who is Cihuacóatl, arrived
> and crushed the bones
> and then put them into a precious bowl.
> Quetzalcóatl, who was over Cihuacóatl, then bled from his penis.
> And immediately the Gods made penitence,
> among whom were named:
> Apantecuhtli, Huictlolinqui, Tepanuizqui,
> Tlallamánac, Tzontémoc
> and the sixth of them, Quetzalcóatl.
> And they said: "The *macehuales*, oh Gods,
> have been born."[12]

Those who narrate this story are very aware that their existence is due to the self-sacrifice of Quetzalcóatl.

Another self-sacrifice of the Gods on behalf of human life is found in the story of the creation of the sun and the moon. The Gods Tecuciz-técatl and Nanahuatzin perform self-sacrifice by throwing themselves into the fire, and out of that act are born the sun and the moon, respectively. Quetzalcóatl, in the form of Nanahuatzin, sacrifices Self in order to create the sun, the name of which is Nahui Ollin (fourth movement), another name for Quetzalcóatl.[13]

Although the sun and the moon rise to the firmament, they have no movement. Movement is intrinsically related to life, it is the condition for life to exist. The Gods in Teotihuacán become concerned about that life which truly depends on movement:

> How will life come about?
> The sun does not move!
> How will we truly make people live?
> If through us the sun becomes strong
> we will sacrifice ourselves and we will all die![14]

Thus it is through the sacrifice of the Gods, who follow the example of Quetzalcóatl, that the dynamic of human life is initiated. Thanks to their death, everything begins to move: the sun, the moon, and every living thing on earth.

In yet another story we discover that the Gods are concerned about life, and once again Quetzalcóatl assumes the task of joining with them in their struggle. They are concerned about what human beings will eat. In the Annals of Cuauhtitlán it is recorded that the Gods decide to share their own food, corn:

> What shall we eat, oh Gods?
> May our sustenance, corn, descend.

Meanwhile, Quetzalcóatl sees a red ant carrying a grain of corn and asks it where the grain had been found. The ant answers, "in Tonacatépetl, the mountain of our sustenance." Quetzalcóatl then turns Self into a black ant, accompanies the red ant to the mountain, and carries corn away from it. Quetzalcóatl then carries the corn to Tamaonchán and there the Gods eat a great deal, and the narration announces: "Afterwards Quetzalcóatl put corn on our lips in order to make us strong."[15]

These are revelations of the God of life, the God who understands, a compassionate being who gives life to God's creatures. Hence, revelation is not known solely through the Hebrew or Judaic culture, but also through other cultures like those of our ancestors. The revelation of certain elements of the human God of life, who delivers Self so that humanity might live, cannot be denied.

The God Quetzalcóatl was always remembered with affection, and in the fifteenth and sixteenth centuries Quetzalcóatl was remembered with both love and nostalgia, especially by those people who were subdued by the Aztec warriors, whose God Huitzilopochtli could not be made congenial with Quetzalcóatl.[16]

THE PERVERSION OF RELIGION

In the measure that Gods are worshipped in history wherever human beings construct a social reality, it is inevitable that there will be differences in the perception of divinity. In that context, one may speak of the betrayal of both Quetzalcóatl and the God of the Bible.

The Betrayal of Quetzalcóatl

As society moved from theocracy to militarism and the Aztec empire became established, the perspective of Quetzalcóatl, the God of life, progressively declined. Meanwhile, the Sun God Huitzilopochtli, who has the vocation of a warrior and conquistador over other people, was progressively imposed. In the official religion Quetzalcóatl was relegated "to the thirteenth heaven, in the mythical Tamoanchán, the place of old Gods of generations past." Despite that fact, Quetzalcóatl as the God of the wind (Ehécatl) was still the most adored deity in the time of the Conquest.[17]

Nevertheless, during that period all of the principal morals and virtues that had been taught by Quetzalcóatl, such as interior perfection and the mystical union with divinity that the individual could reach after a period of penance, were attributed to Huitzilopochtli. The Aztecs claimed the tradition of Quetzalcóatl as their cultural inheritance, and they also took it on as a legitimization of their power. It is well known how prestigious it was to descend from the Toltec culture, which was appreciated for its art and wisdom. It was also prestigious because the image of Quetzalcóatl had been spread far and wide by its famous priest-king of the same name, who had been born as Ce Acatl Topilzin. The Aztecs, therefore, became recognized as the descendent heirs.

Already before the Aztec empire and after the decay of the theocratic cities, Mesoamerican societies were developing a warlike spirit, together with a religion more accommodated to that spirit—there are paintings, or stelae, which depict such an attitude. But it is with the Aztecs, led by their God Huitzilopochtli, that one may observe a transition toward a process of perversion of the religion itself. Beginning with the appearance of Huitzilopochtli one can see this God's mythical vocation—war:

> My principal coming and my work is war. . . . I have to gather and maintain the lot of every nation . . . but I do not do so graciously. . . . From the four corners of the earth you have to conquer, win over, and enslave others for yourselves . . . , you likewise have to pay with your sweat, work, and pure blood.[18]

Laurette Séjourné, an expert on the cultures of ancient Mexico, puts forward evidence for the religious ambiguity of the Aztec empire, noting that one may find a high level of spirituality on an equal par with the practice of human sacrifice. Their spirituality, she contends, has not been well understood, or has been left to one side, and understandably so, due to the barbarity of the culture's human sacrifice. The following fragments depicting a confessor's speech to his penitent is totally dissonant with everything else that is known of the highly stratified Aztec society and of the human sacrifices which were a daily part of its religion:[19]

> You were created and sent out, and your father and mother Quetzalcóatl formed you as a precious stone . . . but through your own volition and free-will you have defiled yourself . . . and now you have confessed . . . you have discovered and shown all of them (your sins) to our lord who is the defender and purifier of every sin.

Following the speech, and after granting him penance for adultery and the use of foul language, he continues:

> And for the inhumanity that you have shown to your neighbors, for not having offered to them from the goods that God has given you, for failing to impart to the poor those temporal goods that were imparted to you by our lord. You will have the charge of offering paper and copal, and also of giving alms to the hungry with needs, and to those who have nothing to eat, nothing to drink, nothing to wear, though you know to take away from your own food in order to give it to them, and to gather clothes for those who walk around naked and ragged; look how their flesh is like your flesh and that they are human beings like you.[20]

These texts are incomprehensible when examined next to other narratives which put forth evidence for unjust economic and social relationships throughout the empire. The following is a small example of the inhuman practice of human sacrifice on behalf of the extremely "human" God:

> They held a very solemn festival for the God called Xipe Tótec, and also to honor Huitzilopochtli. During the festival they killed all of the prisoners: men, women and children. . . . The owners of the prisoners delivered them to the priests at the foot of the Cu and each priest grabbed one by his or her hair and led them up the stairs; and if someone did not go willingly they were dragged to the chopping-block made of stone where they were killed. And taking from each one of them their hearts . . . they threw them down the stairs below where other priests were standing.[21]

In regard to the question how one might justify an apparently "noble" spirituality with homicidal activity, Séjourné contends that the elements of a compassionate spirituality were foreign to the warrior Aztecs; and, therefore, this is evidence that they took possession of the ancient spiritual inheritance of Quetzalcóatl and transformed it into an

arm of domination.[22] If that is so, then the process of perversion in the
Aztec religion is grounded in adopting the theology of Queztalcóatl (of
penitence, of the necessity of interior perfection, of striving for the goal
of the integration of opponents, of reaching the light of Venus or other
planets after death) while at the same time transforming it by wrapping
it up in a theology of human sacrifice. In Séjourné's words:

> The laws of interior perfection taught by Quetzalcóatl serve the Aztecs to
> support a reasoned state of bloodshed; the mystical union with the
> divine, which the individual may only reach through successive steps and
> only at the end of a life of contemplation and penance, is now determined
> by the manner in which one dies: the material transmission of human
> energy to the sun.[23]

Quetzalcóatl, the God of life, was betrayed. The tradition of Quetzalcóatl confessed that just as love may be found in the midst of life, even
more so is it to be found in the life beyond. Or, as our ancestors used to
say: "When we die, we do not truly die, we are resurrected, we continue
living, we are awoken. That makes us happy."[24]

The Aztecs grossly inverted that attitude into one that wished for
death as a pretext for acquiring life. In that manner, those Aztecs in
power felt themselves to be the elected people who would save humanity from the cataclysm under which the Fifth Sun was suffering. Since
the Sun protects the life of all people, it is necessary to save it in order
to save everyone. But the only way to save it was by killing human
beings—principally slaves, prisoners of war, and children and women
from the rest of the Mesoamerican cultures which were subjected to the
Aztec empire—thereby delivering them to the Sun. The God of life
came to be the God of death, the God who sacrificed Self in order to
give life to humanity came to be the God who demanded human sacrifice in order to live and move.

But the worse perversity was not the co-optation of Quetzalcóatl by
Huitzilopochtli, but that Huitzilopochtli was considered and adored as
Quetzalcóatl. Even the executioner priests called themselves Quetzalcóatl.
In reality, what made that possible was the effort to erase the God of life at
the very moment that other lords and principalities were implanted
through force. For some, at least the most lucid, Quetzalcóatl went away:

> Our prince Quetzalcóatl set off to sea in order to take a place in the land of
> the red color, in the place of cremation. Then we acquired through strong

force the lords, the princes, the kingdoms. And the princes, the lords and the chiefs governed, and they established cities.[25]

It should not be thought that this process was linear, that is, that the God of life came to be the God of death simultaneously or that this God came to prominence in all of the region. It is true that the Aztec warrior Gods were imposed, of which Huitzilopochtli and Tezcaltipoca were dominant. But that does not imply that they were received by all of the different nations, not even within the empire itself. As will be treated at more length below, what eventuated was a struggle between Gods.

The Betrayal of the God of the Bible

The fact that Christianity confesses its faith within the mark of monotheism and defends it as such does not change the reality that God can be interpreted in diverse ways; therefore, in effect, different Gods are being worshipped within Christianity.[26]

When the Spaniards arrived in Latin America with their God, the reversal of the God of life within Christianity had already taken place. The God of Abraham who would not sacrifice his son,[27] and the God of liberation who set the slaves free from Egypt, and the Son of God who came to give abundant life and is the source of life, this God was absent.

In the first place, God was perceived as the God who conquers or who directs the elect, the Spaniards, in all of their designs toward conquest. For instance, Hernán Cortés, with total sincerity, mentions the help of the Holy Spirit in the battle in Tenochtitlán against the native people of Mexico. In one of his memoirs, he writes:

> But our Lord wanted to show his great power and compassion to us, for despite all our weakness we broke their pride and arrogance and many of them died, among whom were included many key and celebrated persons. . . . [28]

The natives' battle against the Spaniards dissolved due to the large massacre by Pedro de Alvarado in the high temple, carried out with treachery during the feast of Tóxcatl.[29] Assuming the perspective of the Náhuas toward the massacres carried out by the Spaniards in Mexico, it is not hard to see why for them the God of the Spaniards was shown to be more impotent than even Huitzilopochtli in regard to the mass murder of humans. In less than two hours a European man sent six thousand people (unarmed), who were gathered at the temple, to be beheaded.

These people, too, were sacrificed, though the action was driven by the God of gold. In essence, there was no difference between the reigning God of the Aztec empire and the God of the Spanish empire; they both subdued and murdered, because they were both empires. The difference, in respect to human deaths, lies in the moment of the murder. The Aztecs did not kill those whom they had overwhelmed immediately after the battle because they preferred to offer the lives of prisoners of war to Huitzilopochtli, while the foreign invaders simply carried out massacres so as to possess the people's land and gold, and to subdue them beneath their power. In effect, that goal became their God.

Certainly, the missioners who defended the native inhabitants saw it that way. Fray Bartolomé de las Casas, addressing himself to the deaths caused by this greed for gold, asked: "Perhaps the eyes of divine mercy will be grateful for these our sacrifices?"[30]

Gustavo Gutiérrez analyzes the reversal of the true message of the Christian faith, whereby the God of life is substituted for gold. Possibly from the perspective of the indigenous people themselves that reversal was viewed without any sophistication; indeed, that seems to be the case in many instances. For example, Gutiérrez narrates the history of some indigenous people who believed that the God of the Spaniards was gold. A chief ordered the members of his community to gather together all of their gold, to dance around it, and then to throw it into the sea, hoping that if the God of the European foreigners would disappear then they would be assured to leave as well.[31]

Gold, the God of death, replaces the true God of life. It is a God that is imposed by force as the only God. It is a God of the law of orthodoxy, a God that does not know grace but offers salvation in exchange for gold, slavery, tribute, and submission.

Christ, the God-human, appears dead on the crucifix, but not like someone who has given his life for other creatures as was done by Quetzalcóatl, the God of life, or Jesus Christ, the Son of God of the Gospels. Possibly the Náhuas or Mayas could not understand a dead Savior who demands that others believe in his death unto salvation. And whoever did not believe and submit oneself to this God through baptism was put to death; and whoever submitted oneself but refused to render his or her gold and other belongings, or refused to pay tribute, or conspired against the Spaniards, was equally sacrificed. So Cuauhtémoc, the chief emperor of the Aztecs, was baptized and had his head chopped off because he conspired against those Spaniards led by Hernán Cortés:

. . . he seized Quatémuc and threw him into prison, and on the third day after he was put in prison they took him out and baptized him—it is not certain whether the certificate of baptism read Don Juan or Don Fernando—and then they chopped off his head and nailed it to a ceiba tree behind the house of the Gods in the village of Yaxam. . . . [32]

The betrayal of the God of the Bible is observed through the violent means by which the lordship of the new foreign God was imposed. For example, the *Códice Ramírez* narrates the reaction of Yacotzin, mother of Ixtlilxúchitl (who was brother of the lord of Texcoco) to the Christian God. Two religions, already inverted, are evident in the story: the Christian God imposes lordship over the defeated village and, Ixtlilxú-chitl, the ex worshipper of the Aztec God, acts as if he is still serving the ancient God Huitzilopochtli. The passage of dominance between two Gods who love power and the blood of victims is not problematic for leaders like Ixtlilxúchitl:

> And if it were possible, more than 20,000 people were baptized that day; but, regardless, many were baptized. Ixtlilxúchitl immediately went to his mother Yacotzin and told her what had happened and that they were coming to baptize her. She responded that he must have lost his mind, since only a few barbaric Christians were allowed to overcome them so quickly. Don Hernando then said that if she were not his mother, he would have her head cut off at the shoulders, but what she had to do, though she did not want to, was to hand over the life of her soul. She gently responded to him that he best leave, and that she would look at it another day in order to see what she ought to do. And he left the palace and ordered that they put on fire the rooms where she was to be found, although others say that he did so because he had found a temple of idols there. Finally, she came out, saying that she wanted to become a Christian. And, for that purpose, she, together with a large company, was brought to Cortés and was baptized. And Cortés became her godfather [*padrino*] and they called her Doña María, since she was the first Christian. And the same they did to her four young daughters and many other women. As it is written, three or four days later there were baptized a great number of people.

This sacrificed God-Christ, due to the law of the purity of faith—the inquisition—is guided by the additional law which demands the death of those who sacrificed him. The well-worn argument of European theologians and philosophers of the era was, in effect, that the indigenous deserved to be submitted to slavery, made to pay tribute, and lose all of their lands and possessions, because they sacrificed human lives, worshipped the devil, and were idolatrous.[33]

The God of the Castilians was the Antichrist for the victims, those who had also been victims of the Sacrificer God Huitzilopochtli. From their perspective, there was no difference between tribute and Christianity; the arrival of Christianity and suffering were synonymous. The Mayan prophet Chilam-Balam expressed this many times:

> Only due to crazy times, to crazy priests, was that sadness visited upon us with the arrival of Christianity. Because those who were very Christian arrived here with the true God, and that was the beginning of our misery and our charity, which caused many to leave the oppository occult, the beginning of battles with fire arms, the beginning of the abuse, the beginning of the plunder of everything, the beginning of slavery through debt, the beginning of debts tied to the sword. . . .

For that reason, the Christian God was called the Antichrist, for that God enslaved men, women, and children, sucking the blood of the indigenous people:

> They were just small children from the villages, and great sufferings were inflicted upon them! How unfortunate were those poor little ones! They did not protest against those who, for their own pleasure, enslaved them, those who are the Antichrist over the land, the tiger of the people, the mountain lion of the people, blood-sucker of the poor Indian.[34]

Given the reality of such misery which was attributed to the "true God"[35] brought by the Spaniards, and identified as the Antichrist by the Mayan prophet, all that was left was to wait for the arrival of the true God who would adhere to justice and put an end to the oppressors. It was that One whom Chilam-Balam awaited:

> But that day will arrive when the tears of our eyes will reach God, who will all at once put the world under justice. Truly, it is the will of God that Ah-Kantenal and Ix-Pucyolá return in order to gnaw away at the surface.[36]

The recognition of a God that will do justice and the understanding that thereby the truth of God will be shown signal to us that the victims see God beyond the manipulations which are done by those who worship God.

THE STRUGGLE OF THE GODS

The essential foundation of every revelation of the true God rests in the many dimensions of the concrete life. If Quetzalcóatl, or any other God, is eminently a God of life, then God must be revealed in life itself. Monotheism does not in itself guarantee the revelation of the God of life, for God is revealed in the very life of human beings who live with dignity, justice, and in communion with all people. For that reason, polytheism is not a stumbling block for the expression of a true divine revelation, as long as it is demonstrated in a life lived in favor of others.

However, this vital foundation for all true, divine revelation becomes quite complicated once it is brought to real history. Social systems of power come to pass not only within a culture but also between distinct cultures. In other words, life is lived in a human history, a reality that inevitably bears with it conflict. Thus, a diversity of life-styles is apparent in our history, some that function according to a logic of death, and others which function against this necrophilia and in favor of life. On that basis arise Gods, or interpretations of Gods, which are opposed to each other and are in a struggle.

It is for that reason that the struggle of the Gods should not be conceived, even principally, only as a conflict between Christianity and the indigenous religions, but more as a struggle within Christianity itself and within the different Toltec-Náhuatl religions. In regard to the latter, it has already been shown how Quetzalcóatl rejected human sacrifice in opposition to Huitzilopochtli, for whom such sacrifices were necessary for existence. And within the Christian religion this struggle between Gods can be detected in the various perceptions which exist of God that may only be verified through practice. The gospel therefore insists that "By their fruits you will know them," and affirms that "not everyone who says Lord, Lord, will be an heir of the reign of heaven."

The Struggle of Gods in Ancient Mexico

With respect to the struggle between Gods in the Aztec world there exists some very interesting data. It is important to delineate a difference between Gods because, at first appearance, there is a certain confusion between the God Huitzilopochtli and the God Quetzalcóatl in regard to human sacrifices. Of course, that confusion is understandable given the fact that the Aztec warrior God assumed the spiritual values of Quetzalcóatl. Nevertheless, the difference between the Gods is radical, and its significance must be underlined so that there can be no generalization made that the ancient Mexican culture, as a whole, practiced human sacrifice. The practice of human sacrifice has been a controversy from the Conquest to our present day, and has been used not only to justify the Spanish invasion, but also to silence or disorient those Mexicans, indigenous or *mestizo*, who seek to reappraise the culture of their ancestors.

It is relevant to ask the question why such practices existed in some cultures and not in others. It is suspected that empires with a strong military arm are obliged to carry out human sacrifices in order to remain in power.[37] However, there will always be a resistance to that practice which is compelled by a distinct religious vision of the cosmos.

In the ancient Mexican world there were many cultures which rejected human sacrifice. The Annals of Cuauchtitlán, for example, are clear that such practices were rejected by the priests of Quetzalcóatl, who also called themselves by the name Quetzalcóatl and lived their life as an example of their God. It clearly appears in the mystical attitude of the famous priest Ce Acatl Topilzin:

> When he was living he did not show himself publicly: he was inside a very dark and guarded habitation. . . . His habitation was remote . . . and he built four houses for his fasting. I refer to when Quetzalcóatl was living, repeatedly the demons wanted to trick our God, so that Quetzalcóatl would make human sacrifices, to kill human beings. But Quetzalcóatl never desired or condescended to it, because our God greatly loved God's subjects, who were the Toltecas. . . .[38]

Later, when the Tula society became oriented to militarism, the historical narrators clearly identify the shift in the cultic practices surrounding Quetzalcóatl. It appears that the change began with the priest-king Huémac:

> In this seventh-rabbit [7 *Tochtli*] there was much hunger. . . . And from that time began the great butchery of men and women through sacrifice. . . . It is related that first, during the time and when it was in power Quetzalcóatl, who was the one named by Ce Acatl, never wanted to sacrifice humans. In that year the Toltecas began to weaken, in the time that Huémac was ruling. . . . [39]

It is of vital importance to emphasize the fact that there are ancient testimonies that reveal many people—including those subjected to the empire, or who had been forced into alliances with it, or even Aztecs themselves—who rejected the God Huitzilopochtli. One of those testimonies is from King Nezahualcóyotl, who, in reaction to a large statue which he is obliged to build for the God Huitzilopochtli, builds an even more elevated and luxurious temple to the unknown God, who has not been seen until the present and for whom no other statue has been built.[40] The same occurs in the story of the murder of Tzompantecutly, chief of a people subjected to Aztec rule. He rejects, in the name of religious principles, an increase in tribute which has been demanded by the emperor Moctezuma, who, in turn, alleges that the increase was a divine necessity.[41] The rejection of the warlike conception of the Aztec myth is also found within the city of Tenochtitlan, the Aztec capital, where a song was found that speaks out ironically against Itzcóatl, the king who defeated the Tepanecas and imposed the vision of the God Huitzilopochtli.

In some cases, however, the attitude of the victims is one of resignation because they accepted the promises which would be fulfilled in agreement with the religious tradition. In other cases, the victims, generally prisoners of war, resisted being sacrificed.[42] For example, there is the story of a Mayan youth from Chichén Itzá who did not wish to cooperate with his sacrificers. According to some records, once they were taken to the temple many victims cooperated because of the guarantees of what they would receive in heaven, but this shrewd young man categorically assured his sacrificers that if they threw him into the sacred waters of the cave they could never "ask the Gods for a good harvest or anything akin to it"; they therefore had to search for another victim.[43]

The Struggle of Gods within the Christian God

Within Spanish Christianity, as well, a struggle between Gods was evident. The moment at which the difference between Gods in conflict can be noted with lucidity is when, a few years after the Spanish invasion, an intense struggle took place among Christians themselves over the exploitation, enslavement, and devaluation of the indigenous people. The God of the Dominicans, led by Fray Antonio de Montecinos, is quite opposite to that God presented by the majority of missioners who accompanied the Conquest. Montecinos, who claimed that he spoke with "the voice of Christ," stood up against those who, by their greedy and cruel practices, were reflecting a very different conception of God. In a well-known speech he delivered a day before the Christmas celebration, he dared to boldly address the issue:

> I have risen up here to be the voice of Christ in the desert, which is this island. . . . That voice says that you are in mortal sin, and therein will you

live and die, for the cruelty and tyranny that you have used against these
innocent people. Are they not human beings? Do they not have a rational
soul?[44]

That sermon was disapproved by the authorities and the colonists of
that locale, and indeed by King Ferdinand and the superior of the Do-
minican order. Montecinos was thereafter forced to return to the Ibe-
rian peninsula.

Hence, a campaign was initiated in favor of those enslaved by the
Conquest, and it utilized Christian criteria. For instance, the notion of
Christian liberty supported these scholastics in their argument against
the doctrine of natural servitude, a subject that was on the discussion
table in Spain.[45] Inspired by the liberal doctrine, biblical texts began to
be read in favor of the indigenous people. What was being invoked was
another God, different from the One put forward by the envoys and
missioners who legitimated theft and massacre.

The bishop of Chiapas, Fray Bartolomé de las Casas, was the best-
known defender of indigenous rights. His writings reflect his skill for
emphasizing a theology which accepts the indigenous people as the
children of God and which combats all injustice carried out in the name
of God. It was he who went to see the king of Spain in order to manifest that the behavior of the Spaniards was contrary to the gospel:

And the Indians do not take from anyone what is not theirs, nor do they
injure others, nor bother them, nor aggravate them, nor kill anyone; and
they see Christians committing every type of crime and evil; . . . finally,
they ridicule and mock what is taught them about God but that which
some of them do not believe, to the extent of mockery, is not what is
truly esteemed by God, for they see God as the most iniquitous and evil
of Gods, based on the example of those who worship that God. . . . [46]

This struggle between the legitimation of the Conquest and the defense of the indigenous is already well known, and there is an abundance of information available on it, especially in the writings of Fray
Bartolomé de las Casas. Hence, we will not dig very deeply into that
subject here. It would be sufficient for one to read Gustavo Gutiérrez's
book *Dios o oro* in order to understand the two Gods and their antagonistic theologies: the true God who rejects the massacres and the plunder, and the other God whom they call, or at least conceive of as, the
Christian God, but who at root is nothing more than a God of gold.
These are Gods in struggle, one for life and the other for death. And, it

must be said in passing, that fact must not leave us indifferent to the
Christian world today, not only due to the burden and debt which we
Christians bear for that sin, but because even today we perceive the
same phenomenon in our modern societies.

The Struggle between the Indigenous and Christian Gods

The struggle between two Gods belonging to two different worlds is
not quite as monolithic as it is commonly seen or as it might appear on
the surface. Viewed from an underlying perspective, one does not
simply find a confrontation between the Christian God and the indigenous Gods. It has already been shown that there are internally different
conceptions and practices toward God, within both the Christian and
indigenous worlds. What we have, then, is, simultaneously, a coincidence and an antagonism between Gods.

Traditionally, in order to extol the arrival of Christianity with the
Spaniards and to legitimate the imposition of Western civilization, the
Náhuatl people are portrayed as barbaric, idolatrous, demonic, and
fully supportive of human sacrifice. Given that vision, the conquistadors are handed free reign to impose the Judeo-Christian religion, evidently according to their own interpretation. And in defense of that
religion, they take on the right to destroy every sacred book and every
temple that is not Christian, even to kill those who refuse to align themselves to that religion (several examples of this already have been noted
above, such as the case of Yacotzin).

The Christian vision of the Spanish empire which was unveiled on
the Latin American continent could not tolerate the existence of other
living faiths, even when they might contain features similar to the
gospel. On the one hand, it is understandable why the warrior God
Huitzilopochtli would be rejected; on the other hand, one would have
to think very carefully about what vision of Christianity would not
know what to do with a God like Quetzalcóatl. Indeed, some theologians have been able to see in Quetzalcóatl the apostle St. Thomas
(Ramírez, Vetancurt, Boturini, Veytia, etc.) or the Lord Jesus Christ
resurrected, who appears a little later in Latin America (Hanson). From
the negative side, others have seen in Quetzalcóatl the demon who went
ahead of the Spaniards in order to take on the honor of being the God
of heaven who sent the message of their arrival (Padre de los Ríos).[47]

But in general terms, the Christian God, betrayed and imposed by the
Spaniards, was victorious because, if the correlation of forces is judged cor-
rectly, that God's supporters were stronger. That God fought against every

other manifestation of religion beyond the borders of the Christian faith and, in so doing, did not distinguish between the Gods of life and the Gods of death. In other words, what took place was the Christianization of the continent, at first by violent means and later by peaceful means. From the beginning the inhabitants of this continent were forced to recognize the superiority of the Christian God, not because the proclamation of that message was superior, but due to the superior military force which imposed it. Three ancient testimonies verify that fact.

First, the Mayan prophet Chilam-Balam made a call for his people to mourn due to the arrival of the Christian God, whom the Spaniards qualified as "true." The arrival of the Christian God was stained for these people because that God's entrance meant the institution of a tribute.

> Ay! Let us mourn for they have arrived! Ay for Itza, Sorcerer-of-the-Water [a priest], who will no longer be worth anything! This true God who comes from the heavens will speak only of sin, only sin will be his lesson. His soldiers will be inhuman, cruel his brave dogs. . . . They will bring an excess of misery through the tribute united with violence. . . . Let us prepare ourselves to take on the burden of misery that is coming to you people. . . . [48]

A second testimony, from the document called "dialogue of the twelve" (Tenochtitlán, 1524),[49] makes it clear that the missioners wanted the native people to leave behind their Gods:

> You are greatly lacking, you despise yourselves, you scorn each other, you do not wish that good might come to pass, you spit at those whom you consider Gods because they are not Gods.

But in the dialogue the indigenous priests put up resistance:

> You have spoken to us a new word, and we are disturbed by it. . . . Shall we destroy the ancient rule of life? Because in our heart we understand to whom we owe our lives, to whom we owe our birth, to whom we owe our growth, to whom we owe our development. For that reason the Gods are invoked. . . . Our lords, that which you have told us we do not take as the truth even though we confuse you. It is already enough that we have lost the war, that we have lost the power to rule. Do with us what you will. . . .

Although it has already been cited before, it is worth repeating here again, "That we may not die, that we may not perish, even though our Gods have died."[50]

The third ancient testimony comes from Chief Tecpanécatl. It is a document that, in the first place, accepts the God of the Spaniards for strategic reasons, that is, in order to survive, but also because he sees something in that new God which reminds him of his other Gods. After speaking of the past when they were owners of the land and reminding his people how much blood was shed at the time of the invasion, Tecpanécatl proposes,

> From there below where the earth is ours, they have moved us to leave behind our grandparents . . . and agree to form a new temple of adoration where we have to place the new God that the Castilians have brought to us. They want us to worship this God. What are we to do, my children? It is advantageous for us to be baptized, and to surrender to the men from Castile, for by doing so they will not kill us. . . . I now make known to you, so that they do not kill you, my will is that all of us become baptized and worship the same God, because I have discerned that their God is the same as ours. . . . [51]

The people accept the proposal of their ruler, but ask him only that when "Lord Marques" comes to take more land away from them, that he go out and meet him at their borders so as to dissuade him. Tecpanécatl promises to do it.

In light of these testimonies, it is clear that with the arrival of Christianity to Latin America there was no evangelization, at least in the biblical sense of the term, nor was there "good news." That message did come later when in the name of the gospel some missioners attacked the injustice being carried out against the natives. There was only Christianization, imposed by one religion over another; and what is worse, it was "bad news." In order to have integrity, every Christian must recognize that this happened.

THE GOD OF LIFE AND THE GIVER OF LIFE AS THE TRUE GOD

Any understanding of the Mesoamerican religion (Mayan or Náhuatl) which classifies it as barbaric, idolatrous, or diabolical is completely in error. Such judgments reveal little more than the ignorance of foreigners, for "everything that passed the comprehension of the Spaniards was considered by them as idolatrous and the work of the devil."[52] Serious investigations, all too often disgracefully relegated to anthropological knowledge, indicate that the indigenous vision of the cosmos, which bears with it a profound theology, merits thoughtful dialogue.[53]

The conquistadors never recognized the God of life in the native culture. Of course, that is a lot to ask of the missioners who at that time professed a religion that had set its borders in an extremely rigid orthodoxy. Not even the good missioners, who proclaimed and practiced the gospel as a word of justice and defense of the natives, had the capacity to accept that the God of life was already present and worshipped before the arrival of the Spaniards.

A contrary attitude is observed in various indigenous testimonies. In the "dialogue of the twelve," the Náhuas do not understand why their Gods are demonized, since they see in the biblical creator God, as that God is presented by the twelve missioners, many of the same attributes which their Gods possess. Tecpanécatl, likewise, affirms, "We will worship their God, because I have discerned that their God is the same as ours." And in that same document, when he arrives at the conclusion that the only way to survive is to surrender to the Spaniards, he says, "May the God who is the true God, who runs above the heavens, favor us in the hands of the Castilians."[54] In that statement, it is clear that he commends himself and his people to God because that God's truth is demonstrated through the manifestation of justice. Beyond that, the proper name one gives to God is of little importance.

When Bartolomé de las Casas, or other missioners, condemn in the name of God the practices of slavery and plunder, his God is the same God that the native victims accept, even though they do not accept his God as such. If we say that it is the same God it is because both the missioners, who are the defenders of the indigenous, and the native inhabitants themselves share a coincidence in their perceptions of reality. For example, Chief Tecpanécatl's analysis is the same as that of the missioners who defend human rights; pointing to the first years of the invasion he recalls,

> How much blood was shed! The blood of our fathers and mothers! And why? They know why: because they wanted to rule alone. Because they were hungry for foreign metals and foreign wealth. And because they wanted to put us under their heel. And because they wanted to mock our women and also our wives and maidens. And because they wanted to become owners of our lands and of everything which was our wealth. . . . [55]

That is exactly the same analysis which las Casas repeatedly made in his writings defending the natives.

The difference is that Tecpanécatl of the Náhuatl race, in the face of
the disaster of the invasion and the threat of extinction, accepts the new
God of the Christians, possibly because when they speak of that God as
the creator and as One with compassion he perceives a continuity with
the one and only supreme God, the Giver of life.

In similar fashion, the Mayan prophet Chilam-Balam opts to invoke
the God of life and justice (see discussion above). According to Miguel
León-Portilla, the Mayas, who are already familiar with the Christian
faith, know that it preaches love and peace, though their actions con-
tradict that message. The Mayas measure the practice of the Spaniards
according to their own doctrine:

> This is the face of Katún, the face of Katún of the 13th *Ahau*. The face of
> the sun will be broken, it will fall and smash apart over the other Gods
> who are present today. . . . They Christianize us, but they make us pass
> from one to the other like animals. God is offended by these blood-suck-
> ers. . . . [56]

In light of these references, it would seem that the victims have the
capacity to recognize the only God, revealed in Europe and in Latin
America and in many other cultures back to time immemorial. It is one
God, whose name is merely vanity when the practice of men and
women negate God's truth and justice.

It must be admitted that up to now the impression has been given
that the native people made allusion only to the "good side" of the foreign God; hence, the positive references to God in the foregoing testimonies. Between the lines it is possible to sense that they believe this
God will, in the end, accept them because this God is not "so different"
from their own God. In a certain sense, they maintained faith in two
Gods in the form of an alliance (cf. the words of Tecpanécatl above).

Nevertheless, there are other, more integrated ways of relating the
Gods. In the Náhuatl culture yet a further step is taken, in that not only
does it accept the Christian God, but it includes that God as part of its
own indigenous vision of the cosmos. That integration is taken to such
an extent that there is a live, religious continuity between the God of life
and the Christian God, which comes together under the figure of the
indigenous virgin of Guadalupe. That this harmony is the ultimate
result of bringing both Gods, Christian and indigenous, into one image
is evident in the well-known story called Nícan Mopóua, which tells of
the appearance of the virgin of Guadalupe to the indigenous man, Juan
Diego.

Mexican writer Clodomiro Siller has skillfully analyzed this integration. According to Siller, one important element of the legend is that Tepeyac, the mountain where the virgin of Guadalupe made her appearance,

> came to be a place where the Indian could express anything without exposing himself or herself to the charge of heresy. And, at the same time, her [the virgin of Guadalupe] name has been linked in the religious heritage to the ancient Tonantzin, the mother of the Gods, many of whose names have never been recorded.[57]

In another article, Siller further affirms that this Náhuatl story expresses the religious experience of the indigenous people insomuch as it gives life to ancient beliefs and accepts the new faith. It is a matter, he contends, of "the indigenous comprehension of their own living religious tradition in new circumstances of colonization and evangelization."[58]

The indigenous people had the capacity to recognize the God of life even in a culture that invaded them. It is we Christians who have not had sufficient wisdom and humility to recognize the God who is the Giver of life in other cultures that profess a non-Western, non-Christian faith. However, *that is our God* who is revealed to us in the Scriptures, who has revealed Self in the past and will always reveal Self in the history of every culture, since before the time of Abraham, whenever people cry out for justice or manifest in their lives communion, solidarity, love, liberation, justice, truth, faith, and hope.

That God challenges us in the present day through the indigenous and black victims of the invasion. Today, due to their ever-growing resistance to the history of the last five centuries, they become the "good news" for us *mestizos* and whites. Through them the Spirit of Christ, as well as the Spirit of Quetzalcóatl, are evangelizing us. All of us belong to one God, creator of life and the universe.

Part Two
Class Structures and Human Relations

4

FROM BASE COMMUNITY TO FOREIGN MINISTER

Autobiographical Reflections on Social Transformation and Political Power

Miguel D'Escoto

*I*t is possible to change the world and transform it into the caring community of brothers and sisters that God originally meant it to be. To participate in that creative activity is the only credible way to proclaim in practical terms our belief in the good news that God not only loves us but has adopted us as sons and daughters, and has done so not just in name but in reality. Therein lies the source of my profound hope for the world, despite the fact that I carry in my heart the pain of as many (if not more) defeats as I do successes in pastoral ministry and political action.

But long ago I learned to look beyond mere appearances so as to discover the possibilities for new creation in the most unlikely places. For instance, reflecting autobiographically, I surely would not have been the most likely candidate to become the foreign minister of a revolutionary government. Compared to the vast majority of people in my country I was born into opulence; in fact, my grandfather had been one of the richest men in Nicaragua. I was fortunate enough, however, to have a mother who exercised a deep moral conscience which consistently compelled her to rise above greed and self-interest. Early on she taught me that the gap which existed in the world between the "haves" and the "have-nots" was unequivocally unjust.

The Christian Brothers who ran the school I attended as a young boy also had a tremendous influence on me. And what I learned about religion in the classroom I immediately applied to the reality I saw around me. One enduring memory from that time is emblematic of my growing awareness: people in the streets of Managua looking for food in garbage cans. I regularly used to pass a particularly elite restaurant, the Terraza Club, where large garbage bins were full of leftovers from banquets held the previous evening, and nearly always I would see the poor sifting through the mounds looking for scraps that might feed their families. My nascent religious sensibilities cried out that such misery should not exist in a world where compassion was ever inviting us to a different way of being.

Those lessons were strengthened and confirmed by what I learned from poor campesinos who worked on our estate as gardeners and servants. At lunchtime I would often meet with them in the garden and listen to them relate the history of Nicaragua from their viewpoint at the bottom of the social spectrum. My family told me to leave them alone, but I was always too riveted by their stories. One of the gardeners was a Miskito who had come from the Atlantic coast. He spoke of the torrential rains that would come annually, destroying their small huts and crops; of the mining and timber companies that exploited their tribal lands; of rampant malnutrition and disease. It was in those conversations, though I was not so much conversing as listening, that I began to understand the roots of social inequity and structural violence. However, I soon discovered that voicing concern for the poor outside my own home was clearly unacceptable: I was called a communist for the first time at the age of twelve after sharing these ideas with classmates.

Like many young people of my social class, I was sent to the United States when I was fourteen years old in order to study at a parochial high school. Once there, I developed strong feelings of rebellion against my privileged socioeconomic position. In Nicaragua at that time we had referred to ourselves as *la sociedad*, the society. So, with cynicism I would defiantly pronounce it *la suciedad*, thereby changing its meaning to "dirt." It was not long, however, before I realized that even my bitterness was unwittingly a characteristic quite typical of my class roots. For hatred is a rare emotion for those who are really poor in Nicaragua; they have a great capacity to forgive even those who have caused them great harm and pain. It slowly dawned on me then that I did not actually hate the rich. But I knew that unless they changed, the suffering of the poor would go on unabated.

I had come to the United States with the hope of becoming an engineer. But the more I pursued that career, the more doubtful I became whether that was what my country truly needed in order to lift itself out of its misery. Though I was only seventeen years old, I believed that what we needed most was a movement of people within the church who were committed to becoming more authentic followers of Jesus. I eventually interpreted that conviction gnawing at my conscience as a call and vocation to the priesthood. Though I spent several ensuing years struggling over that decision—I had very much wanted to raise a family and knew that my vows would eliminate any such possibility—I eventually joined the Maryknoll order in New York.

My first foreign mission was to Chile, where I soon became involved with CENAPO, *Central Nacional de Pobladores*, or National Center for the Urban Poor, an organization that carried out community development projects in the urban slums of Santiago. CENAPO was attempting to explore ways that local unions might join together with other popular organizations in order to create a broad social base. It seemed to me that such a step was necessary in order for significant social transformation to take place, because in Chile, like most of the nonindustrialized countries of the Two-Thirds World, the unions alone are not a powerful enough force to effect meaningful change. Based on those experiences in the slums, I eventually started another popular organization that brought together advisors from a variety of professions—lawyers, urban planners, medical personnel, etc.—who put their skills to the service of the urban poor and to defend worker rights.

After several years working in that environment, I recall shocking my spiritual director when I confided one day that though I was quite fulfilled in my ministry, I was not quite sure if I still had faith. After taking me quickly aside to a private room where we could more confidentially discuss such a scandalous confession, he asked for an explanation. I related to him that I no longer *believed* in God. During my seminary training I had been taught that faith was believing upon the authority of the One revealing, and accepting that revelation as a gift because no human being could see or experience God's reality directly. I went on to explain that, in contradiction to that doctrine, I was indeed sensing God's presence quite clearly in the lives of the poor with whom I was working. Though my companions in the slums were often alcoholics, prostitutes, "criminals," and men and women with other serious problems, they were people who, allegorically speaking, were bare of any varnish. It was easy to see inside them and perceive God's presence with and through them. The Spirit of God, I realized, could be found in every human being, but in some people it is more difficult to uncover because they are too polished and sophisticated. I no longer had to "believe," for I could glimpse the reflection of God in history.

After many years of service in the barrios of Santiago, I was called back to the United States in order to take over the Maryknoll Department of Social Communications. During those years I participated in the production of *Maryknoll* magazine, collaborated with several colleagues to establish Orbis Press, and traveled to Maryknoll mission projects around the world. All during this period, Maryknoll was opening my eyes to the global marginalization of the poor.

Then, quite unexpectedly in 1976 came the call to help in the liberation of my country. The Sandinista Front for National Liberation (FSLN) sent representatives to ask if I would play a leadership role in a movement to channel the rising popular discontent that was sweeping across Nicaragua. Though I had respected the revolutionary front's commitment of bringing about social justice and political freedom, I originally told them that it would be extremely difficult for me to accept their offer because of my own deep moral convictions about nonviolence. But they refused to take no for an answer, arguing that they, too, believed that our country sorely needed a culture of nonviolence, but at that particular moment the war was fierce and the people's patience was exhausted. They said that they were planning to call for a general insurrection and needed my assistance to figure out how to proceed once the war was over.

Their persistence and persuasiveness left me exceptionally confused. On the one hand, I was deeply concerned about the problems that my involvement would inevitably cause the Maryknoll order, which by then I considered my family. I was worried as well how a "revolutionary priest" would be accepted by my superiors in the church. The painful thought loomed in my mind that I might even be expelled.

On the other hand, I could not help but think of that inevitable day of reckoning when we would all be called to give an account of our lives before the Lord. I could not imagine saying to God, "God, I refused to extend a helping hand to my country in its worst hour of anguish because I had to go on to Jericho for a very important pastoral meeting. I had my own religious agenda, so I walked around a people bleeding by the roadside of history." Deep in my heart, I knew that God would not accept excuses for not taking risks. I had to follow the example, not of the priest, but of the good Samaritan.

On that basis, I finally decided to become a part of the FSLN, clandestinely working to help them form a new government that could be put in place immediately upon victory. In the ensuing years I authored many of their communiqués directed against the dictatorial abuses of the Somoza regime. Taking part in that struggle was a profound religious experience for me. Never had I been surrounded by so many faithful people who were willing to give up their lives for their brothers and sisters.

LESSONS WE LEARNED IN THE REVOLUTION

The Nicaraguan revolution demonstrated that when a people are united they can overthrow a system, even though that system may be underwritten by the most powerful nation in the world. During the sixties and seventies most Latin American experts were of the opinion that the revolutionary overthrow of any government which enjoyed U.S. economic and military support was impossible (not that the current of opinion has changed much in the nineties!). Of course, social theorists most typically conceive of "revolution" as a band of armed insurgents who make it their objective to overpower an established military regime. The key variable which they regularly overlook in their analysis is the dynamic potential of a popular uprising. Without question, one of the primary reasons that the Nicaraguan revolution was able to succeed is that its leadership—even though it was critically divided—maintained the capacity to read the signs of the times and recognize a small window of vulnerability for a people's insurrection.

At the same time, though it may sound contradictory to the foregoing, we were eventually defeated by something that we did not expect: the depth of commitment that maintains the breach between the poor nations of this world and the wealthy, even if that obsession requires denying entire peoples their rights for self-determination and stifling any possibility of building authentic democracy. Specifically, we did not anticipate the intensity of the hatred and bitterness that the United States would direct toward us.

We took over a country that had been under U.S. occupation for seventy years, roughly dating from 1909—when the United States deposed duly elected Nicaraguan president Zelaya—up to the 1979 revolution. For some reason U.S. governments, both past and present, believe that it is in its "vital—*vitae*, as in life; a state indispensable for continued survival—interest" to control the political, social, and economic destiny of every country in Latin America. Having made that determination, right and wrong no longer hold weight; the law of the jungle dictates that the dominant power defends what it perceives to be its vital interest.

During the struggle to overthrow Anastasio Somoza, campesinos or farmworkers who knew that I was, for all intents and purposes, the "foreign minister" of the FSLN as an advisor to Daniel Ortega (indeed, soon after the 1979 victory I was commissioned by the new government to serve as the country's foreign minister, a position I maintained for the duration of the 1980s) would often ask me if I could recommend a book that would help them to understand why the United States "hates us so much and so desires to maintain a system that enslaves us." I would respond that they need not read a book in order to understand the attitude of the U.S. government, for their own daily experience with the *patron* or rural plantation owner, would give them a handle to understand its actions.

The *patron* visits the ranch perhaps only once a month, and then only to check out how things are running. Occasionally one of the farmhands will at that time request an audience with the *patron* in order to talk with him about a concern of critical proportions. Days in advance he would ask the chief steward for a meeting, and the farmhand would feel quite privileged if he was actually granted a meeting. On the appointed day, he would put on a clean shirt and approach the front steps of the house—of course, he would not think of entering—remove his hat, and voice his concerns as briefly as possible to the *patron*, then walk away grateful, not necessarily that anything was resolved but that at least he could now hope for an act of mercy. The entire plantation system depends on this style of relationship that is built on fear and subjugation. Put simply, campesinos must not be allowed to believe that they are equal.

Knowing that nearly all of the campesinos breathed the air of this environment, I would ask them to imagine what would happen if one farmhand decided to walk directly up the steps, greet the *patron* informally, using the second-person familiar, *vos*, walk directly into his house, and sit in his rocking chair while asking for a glass of juice. Every one of them would know that the *patron* would be incensed and immediately would order him out of the house with the harshest words, probably denouncing the farmhand as an *igualado*, one who makes oneself out to be equal with another, and fire him on the spot.

That is precisely what happened in our relationship with the United States. We walked into the White House and said *"Vos, we want to be friends."* And, of course, the answer was, "Who do you think you are? You are nothing but *igualados!*" It was taken as an insult that we wanted to base our relationship on one of equality. Evidently, it was deemed necessary that we would think of ourselves as lesser beings so that we would be docile. But instead we committed a heresy: we proclaimed our total belief and commitment to defending the principle of sovereignty and legal equality regardless of territorial dimensions and economic or military might.

These attitudes and fears are very deeply ingrained. That is why it is so important that the people of the United States are challenged to review those values that its government has listed under the rubric of "vital interests." Of course, that evaluation process will require not only political analysis but also spiritual vision. For the hierarchy of values that comprise the "vital interest" of the United States bespeaks spiritual sickness. The present value structure is a symptom of betrayal by the religious community, whose responsibility it is to raise the very questions of moral truths. If the values of "vital interest" are not challenged, then the possibility of change in Latin America becomes extremely unlikely.

I have often been asked what chance a small country like Nicaragua ever thought it had in trying to confront a military superpower. I always respond to that question with a second question: what future is there for a world of justice if countries like Nicaragua are not willing to stand up and refuse to burn incense before the imperial idol, falling on its knees and saying, "Your will be done because you have nuclear energy and have amassed great wealth"? The arrogance of the U.S. government perhaps can be compared only to that of the Vatican. Both institutions pretend to speak in the name of God while really believing themselves to be God. But we choose not to worship the idol because we recognize only one God, the God of Abraham and Sarah, Jacob and Rebecca, and the God of our Savior Jesus.

Another very important lesson that we learned during the course of our revolution was a quite unexpected one, though we now know that it is an experience we share with many other nations of the Two-Thirds World. For centuries, people in Nicaragua had worked very hard, yet they never really saw any improvement in their quality of life. In their minds, work became synonymous with punishment, at best something which they were condemned to do. In other words, work has never been understood as something rewarding for itself or for one's family, but was always done for someone else; they labored and labored so that someone else might become richer and richer. And after working for eight hours in the tropical sun, some campesinos would even go into Managua in order to sell their blood at a very low cost to a laboratory owned by Somoza and his cronies, who would turn around and sell the blood as an export item to First World countries. The Somoza regime was literally bleeding the people to death.

Given that background, it is easy to understand why liberation for the poor meant freedom from the chastisement of work. With the victory of the revolution the only thing that many workers wanted to do was take a holiday. A further complicating problem was the extensive disorganization of the workplace itself. Those who had served as stewards before the revolution were generally hated because of the cruel treatment which they had handed out to the workers. No Sandinista, then, wanted to fill that vital post in the early days of the revolution because they did not want to evoke the memory of the taskmaster from the past. And these elements only touch the surface of the complicated economic situation that contributed to low productivity during our initial years in government.

The vacuum of a work ethic, itself the legacy of the dictatorship, quickly became one of our major problems. In response, it was necessary to develop a novel pedagogy of work, complete with a Christian vision and understanding of its potential meaning and dignity. It took nearly eight years before we started seeing some significant positive changes in worker productivity—I thought it would take twenty.

Though we did learn many lessons in the midst of our struggle to shape a new and different society, we nonetheless slowly lost the confidence of many people who had once supported us. In that regard, I am also frequently asked if I lost hope when the Sandinista party was voted out of office in 1991. I can honestly say that I did not feel discouraged after the elections but saw the result as a new stage in the transformation process of our country. For people truly committed to social transformation should never merely desire to be in power but, rather, look for what role we can play in the creation of a truly just history. Opposition is a very important element in any political system, and there must be a revolutionary way to be in opposition that is different from the standard practice. The revolutionary way must take a patriotic and constructive path, because it would be unconscionable for us to wish that the ruling government would fail and that people would live in misery simply so that our popularity might increase. A true opposition party should be cooperating and participating in a political process that benefits its people in the present moment. The revolution continues, though we are now writing a new chapter. Maybe our role is less dramatic but it is just as significant.

FOLLOWING JESUS INTO A
SPIRITUALITY OF STRUGGLE

The foregoing "snapshots" and reflections briefly chronicle my irregular journey from child of privilege to lowly priest working in the slums to, somewhat miraculously, becoming the foreign minister of Nicaragua. I can humbly say that I have lived with, ministered to, and been converted by the margins of society, yet have also held private meetings with kings, queens, nearly every head of state in the world, and their foreign ministers. At the end of it all, my conclusion of what really matters in the world and what is essential for its transformation is quite simple: we must take the gospel seriously as a mandate for our individual and corporate lives.

The logic to which we have been called by Jesus is that of love. Though by no means irrational, it goes beyond reason to raise up a higher standard for our behavior. But therein lies a great dilemma: human beings are the only creatures that cannot fulfill their destiny by respecting the laws of their own nature. All other living beings most ably survive their environment by relying on their natural instincts. Likewise, if the nature of inanimate objects is respected, they too will fulfill their reason for being. For instance, gold is of such a nature that it does not corrode. Therefore, gold is used as a reliable filling for teeth; iron, on the other hand, given its properties, is not chosen for that function.

We even learn to respect the nature of those objects that we create. When designing an automobile, for example, a car manufacturer has numerous options, such as whether to install an air or water cooling system. Whoever buys the car is given a manual that describes the nature that the car has been given and how the owner should best take care of it. If one respects that nature one can likely expect a better performance and a longer life out of the car.

Human beings were created as rational creatures. However, if we choose to live by reason alone and make it the supreme norm determining our behavior, we will surely perish. Paradoxically, having been created as rational beings we were sentenced to sanctity and raised to the level of the divine, yet though creatures. In what traditional doctrinal language has called the Fall, we express the inability of the human race to hold this paradox together, giving way to the reason of self-interest over that of love.

In the life of Jesus, however, we see revealed what this life of sanctity requires in the actual realities of history. In him divine love became incarnate, offering to reason the image from which it was created. Paraphrasing the words of St. Augustine, "God became human so that humans could become like God." We henceforth are called to live in a way that will likely appear to the wise of this world as foolishness, the way of the cross.

When the soldiers came to arrest Jesus, Peter, seeking to defend his master at all costs, took out his sword and clipped off the ear of one of the soldiers. Jesus said to him, "Peter, you have been with me all this time and you have not understood. If I had wanted, I could call upon legions of angels to come to my aid, but that is not the way." Now today, 2,000 years after Jesus was born, lived, died, and was resurrected, we still somehow are not getting the point. The actual theology and practice of the Christian church, with its provisions for "holy" and "just" wars, arrogantly assert that we have learned new truths since Jesus that enable us to confront the religious and political sins of our time without having to experience Calvary.

The Nicaraguan people, like the people of the United States, made use of the just-war theory in the ideological legitimization of its revolution. However, immediately after the overthrow of Somoza, I believed and hoped that we could begin to follow the nonviolent path of Jesus. But, tragically, the war never ended; the United States organized the National Guardsmen into a fighting force of contras that would attack our people for most of the next decade. Yet, despite my personal convictions, I was not about to deprive the people of the option of bearing arms because (1) there was no other way for them to defend themselves, and (2) we Christians who have been mandated to testify to another way have never developed alternative models by our own example.

Though I have never personally taken up arms, I nonetheless make a sharp distinction between the force of the oppressor and that used by those who want to liberate themselves and their families from oppression. Despite all of the sophisticated weaponry that we now possess, the death that emanates from armed conflict is nothing compared to the murder that takes place every single day when millions of people die as a result of hunger and malnutrition. All of this in a world that has the economic resources and the technical know-how to prevent such death. That is violence.

Although within the church we might occasionally speak out against violence, most typically we only do so when the poor finally decide to fight back because their patience, as immense as it might be, is found to be wanting. It is then that we hear a self-righteous preacher condemn the violence of the revolution, all the while ignoring the institutional violence that has driven the poor to this type of reaction. Ironically, though we denounce the poor, it is we who are, in reality, the most violent because we cowardly accept the systemic violence that kills poor people around the globe every day. If we keep quiet in the face of violence, then we are accomplices because we assist in the maintenance and prolongation of that system. In short, the silent ones help to buttress that system by failing to denounce it.

I do not wish to disparage my brothers and sisters of faith who anxiously await the arrival of the Messiah, for I share their hope. But waiting does not simply imply inaction. In fact, it is the Messiah who is actually waiting on us. He arrives at our door and waits for us to open up and say, "Lord, come in and take over and use me." We have been made in the image and likeness of God the Creator and have been called to be co-creators with God, not merely spectators. This is an unfinished world and God is inviting us to put the finishing touches on it. The Messiah comes every day that we invite him to use us in this life. Therein can be fully understood Jesus' dictum, "I came to bring fire on this earth," for it is the power of this zeal that brings justice and community.

There is a political lesson to be learned here as well. I do not believe in that conception of democracy which merely defines it as the *opportunity* for the people of a society to participate in the process of making decisions on those issues which affect them. That is a prerequisite for democracy, but not democracy itself. It is indispensable that the people of a democracy are actually responsibly *participating* in their society, which is more than simply having the opportunity to participate.

We can change the world if we allow ourselves to be taken possession of by God, becoming instruments of God's peace and accepting the crucifixion that may come as a result of saying constantly, like Mary, "Be done to me according to thy word." When Christ implores us to change the world, together with that mandate is a demand to change the very means or methods employed to bring about that change. His life and death present a clear, unified message that we are to discard the conventional, traditional methods and "take up the cross," to be willing to say every minute of our life that we are ready to give our bodies to the service of building community. Christ has not come for nothing; either we take him seriously or we perish.

It is essential, then, to create a culture of nonviolence wherein people learn that there are ways and means to get things accomplished without violence. But in order to create a culture of nonviolence we must first dig deep down within our own roots in order to fashion a spirituality of nonviolence.

Only a eucharistic spirituality has sufficient resource to keep the society moving and developing toward a nonviolent culture. An unbending commitment to offer ourselves to others in the service of love is an inextricable element of the mystery we discover in the celebration of the

Eucharist. The central significance of the sacraments is revealed when the priest takes the bread and the wine and announces, "This is my body and this is my blood, which is offered so that all might live." When we say these words it is not as if we are talking to an old, forgetful God who must be reminded that Jesus offered his life on the cross; God need not be reminded of that by us. In the celebration of the Eucharist what we are saying is, "This is *my* body and this is *my* blood that I offer, together with Christ's body and blood, to be accepted as a sacrifice for God's kingdom." They are not to be spoken, then, from a point of neutrality or with confidence grounded in the unlikelihood that we would ever be called to suffer. When we say them we express our commitment to enter concretely into that passion in history.

Eucharistic spirituality, then, is a spirituality of struggle that is bound to the redemption of the world. The world will only be saved once we are willing to be brought to Calvary as a consequence of acting in defense of those who are treated in an unbecoming manner. It requires not only that we abstain from the use of oppressive force, but that we also unequivocally and openly denounce whatever separates men and women from the fold of humanity. Those who seek to become disciples of Jesus of Nazareth, therefore, embrace nonviolence as it is understood in this broad sense.

When I hear committed people say that they have no hope for a better world, I am not entirely disappointed, because we should not have hope if we think that we can carry out the struggle relying solely on our own resources. Our hope is not in one more meeting, yet another resolution, or perhaps a rousing demonstration, no matter how much wisdom and inspiration can thereby be generated. Our hope is Jesus Christ. When he takes over our life, we are able to move mountains.

In Nicaragua the month of May represents the end of the dry season. The earth is dry and thirsty and the foliage is burnt and dying. Women are telling their husbands that the store of corn and beans from last year's harvest is coming to an end. The farmers themselves are preparing the earth, trying to assess the right time to plant the seeds so that they will not be in the ground too long before the rains come. All the while, all are asking themselves, "Will the rains come on time this year? Will we have enough? Or will there be too much rain so that we will have to battle the floods?" It is a time of anguish, a time of expectation, a time of preparation, and a time of hope. So may be understood a Nicaraguan adage that is typically spoken when someone is especially longing for an event to come to pass, "I am waiting for it like the waters of May."

We must follow the example of the farmers. We are to prepare the soil for the arrival of the just one, Jesus, so that new life may come to a world so sorely in need of it. And when that happens, high-tech warfare and arrogant power no longer intimidate us; quite unexpectedly, they will crumble in the face of a people united and committed to living the mystery of the cross. We must therefore have the courage to live in a state of constant, uninterrupted availability to sustain whatever might be the consequences of standing up in defense of brotherhood and sisterhood. Once we do that, we will then be more committed to building our family in a way that excludes absolutely no one under the loving care of God. May God help us to prepare our hearts so that life-giving waters may sprout into Christ all over the world, signaling the beginning of the spring that we so earnestly await.

5

UNCOVERING A CIVILIZATION OF CAPITAL, DISCOVERING A CIVILIZATION OF WORK

Ignacio Ellacuría

*T*he struggle in Latin America today is not directed against what happened five centuries ago in the conquest of our continent. More importantly, we seek to recapture the experience of what happened then so that we may say, first and foremost to North Americans and then to Europeans, inasmuch as they belong to the same Western Christian civilization, that their present behavior toward Latin America and the rest of the Third World has not, in general, changed very much.

The Western powers seek to conceal the reality of their actions toward the Third World. In other words, though our reality is fundamentally determined by domination and oppression, that truth is being covered up by a beautiful ideological cloak. The consequent image of reality is nothing but a façade, and it is imperative to unmask it. During the last five centuries we have experienced, among other things, the domination of our peoples, cultures, languages, and religions. Therefore, in a manner consistent with our historical commitment, the appropriate action for us to take in response to the last five hundred years (and for all those years yet to come) is to practice liberation.

It is not necessary dogmatically to assert that nothing good has resulted during the course of five centuries of unrelenting domination. Though it would be easy to conceive the process of domination and liberation as two completely different pictures, one in color and the other in black and white, reality is never so clear and unambiguous. Nevertheless, what we cannot deny or pretend to ignore is the fact that after five centuries other countries are still acting toward Latin America today in a manner reminiscent of Spain and Portugal at the time of the Conquest. I repeat, this reality must be unmasked.

THE "DISCOVERER" IS ALWAYS AN OPPRESSOR

What really happened five hundred years ago to establish this interdependent relationship between the rich and poor nations of the world, a relationship that continues to the present day? First, the conquistador, or dominator, became discovered; in the "discovery" of the "new world" what was actually discovered was Spain's true identity, as well as the true character of Western culture and its church. They became the discovered ones, they were the ones stripped bare without even realizing it, because in their actions toward the Third World they carried out an act of concealment, not one of discovery. In truth, then, it is the Third World which discovered the negative and most real aspects of the First World.

Given that background, it would be very interesting and fruitful if, after five centuries, the Third World were now able to hear a confession from the First World. But that, naturally, is not likely to happen. For that reason, we believe that if the prophet (who in this case is the Third World) does not tell the truth to the First World, it will not be capable of seeing and discovering its own reality and, to the contrary, will continue telling the Third World what it must do.

At the beginning of the Conquest, the conquistadors said that they were setting out to the Americas in order to turn the indigenous people into Christians. But it is obvious that they did not go for that reason; it was a monumental lie. However much one may seek to justify their motives with the best theological rationalizations and however much some sincerely may even come to believe those justifications, the truth is quite different. Spain went to America in order to dominate, to conquer, to extend its power and its sources of wealth. From that moment forward the sociohistorical structure of Spain was unveiled (since it was previously hidden) as a powerful human force motivated by the persistent search for wealth and power. That, in reality, was what moved those individuals who came to Latin America. At the same time, it must be said that the sociohistorical structure of Spain was above all determined by an overarching expansionism that sought the growth of its power and its policies through an imperial political regimen (one does not speak in vain of the Spanish Empire).

The conquistadors journeyed to the "new world" accompanied by an ideological (or "ideologized") cargo, represented above all at that moment by the Roman Catholic Church, which legitimated their actions. Since it is true that a series of humanizing values were brought to the Americas, it must be noted that among the scores of people who went there were some who arrived with an intention and behavior contrary to the principal dynamic of the aforementioned process. But it is also true that these values were always subordinated, both collectively and nationally, to the effective attainment of what was actually being sought: wealth and power.

Also today, on a global level, it can truthfully be said that the First World approaches the Third World in this same manner and with these same intentions. And once again it comes dressed in ideological clothes which seek to conceal, in a "beautiful" way, its real intentions. The powerful nations of our day tell us that they come to the Third World in order to make us "wealthy" and in order to turn us into a "democratic" people. However, hidden behind these "generous propositions" is a very distinct political and economic project. To discover and unmask the ultimate truth of that project it is not necessary to look inside the borders of the dominating nations of the West themselves, but to look outside their borders. It is there that the ultimate consequences of the Western project, the maximum representative and bearer of which is the United States, are manifest.

Up to a certain point, the United States is able to act essentially in a democratic fashion within its borders while always maintaining an antidemocratic position on an international front. As a result, the democracy which it defends is false and deceitful, and can by no means be considered a universal value. The real truth of its political, economic, and cultural system is most clearly demonstrated not by virtue of the profits which that system enjoys, but by virtue of its need to conquer and dominate in order to maintain its power structure.

These claims could be illustrated in many different ways. To give one example, is it really credible to contend that the United States was concerned that there might be democratic elections in Nicaragua during the decade of the eighties? The truth is that it could not have cared less. If Nicaragua had been a special ally of the United States, it would have totally been allowed to have any political regime it so desired. In actual fact, then, as far as the capitalistic world is concerned a "democratic" regime is, for a variety of reasons, a political regime which best corresponds to and serves to defend the interests of capitalism.

Another illustration can be drawn from El Salvador. During the official negotiations aimed at peaceful solutions to end the civil war, the guerrillas made known their willingness to participate in elections as long as they were given a specified period of time in which to prepare adequately a list of candidates. The government rejected that offer, arguing that the Constitution stipulated a period of five years between presidential elections and, therefore, a postponement of the additional three months that the guerrillas requested would make the elections unconstitutional.

Fortunately, in this instance the Salvadoran church spoke a very prophetic and significant word: "Peace comes before the Constitution." That message, however, was considered by the "constitutionalists," the "legalists," and the "democrats" as some type of heresy. Lying in the background of all these legal entrapments of the Constitution, the real problem revolved around the fear of the powerful and the oppressors. Seeing that the proposal of the FMLN could represent a danger to the U.S. political project and to that of the ARENA party—who believed that they would win the next elections—they withdrew from the negotiations and declared, "We do not accept that proposal." The fact of the matter is that they were not looking for a political solution that actually responded to the necessities and the will of the people, but were once more simply pursuing a conquest of power.

THE "DISCOVERY" OF THE CHURCH

The previous section treated the reality of the last five centuries. It cannot be denied that the church was an important accomplice in the unfolding of that conquest. If one does not say that the church, with its missionary and evangelistic zeal, mapped out the plan for "mission America," it at least must be said that it legitimized that project as it was conceived by others. That legitimation did not always and in every place have negative consequences; on many occasions the church's activities actually improved the existing reality. And at times the church did very significant things to combat the process of domination and devastation.

Certainly there were church figures—above all from the religious orders—who put service to their faith above service to the crown, a concern for evangelization above interests which have no valid relation to Christian beliefs, and the defense of the indigenous above legitimation of the exploiter. Already at that time the preferential option for the poor was practiced, and that not just on an infrequent basis. Though it cannot be said that such an option was ever assumed by the entire church, or by the entire hierarchy, or by all of the religious orders, neither was it something occasional or merely of convenience.

In any case, it is probably most accurate to say that the church's participation in the process of conquest and colonization was always secondary and of an accompanying nature. It never took the initiative in what was being done. The primary initiative was always driven by economic and political interests. That fact reveals something quite profound: all ideology, once it becomes the justification for a series of historical actions, seeks to conceal the evil things while at the same time putting forth a good façade. The need to maintain this cover of goodness may be utilized actually to accomplish good things. For that reason the empire brought the church with it to legitimate its project, and the church, by and large, gave the Conquest a "good face."

Therefore, when reference is made to the church it may be said that many good things were discovered about it, but also some very serious bad things, such as its propensity to identify with the powerful and wealthy, an element of perennial temptation for the church, and its subtle tendency to prefer and prioritize the institution over its mission, another recurrent temptation. For the most part, the church allowed itself to be carried along by the following rationale: "We cannot at this moment realize the mission which corresponds to our true nature, that of announcing the reign of God in conformity to the message of Jesus, because by doing so we would put in danger the institution of the church and that, above all, must be saved. When the time is right, we will be able to carry out our true mission."

The film *The Mission* provides an interesting illustration of this historic question of mission in relation to institution, be it the country which led the charge toward colonization or the institution of the church itself. A few critical questions are raised by the movie: Why, in actual fact, were the Jesuits expelled from the indigenous settlements in Paraguay? Their mission was both an announcement of faith and a concrete realization of that faith in the midst of history. So why was the order to retire from that mission given by the Roman See and by the supreme authorities of the Company of Jesus? There can only be one answer to both of these questions: the mission of the Jesuits in the indigenous settlements of Paraguay was putting at risk the universal institution of the Company of Jesus.

Turning to the present as well as to the past, the church in Latin America continues to struggle with the temptation of prioritizing the institution over its mission. For example, we are faced with that challenge at the University of Central America José Simeón Cañas (UCA) in San Salvador. Quite often we are inclined to save the institution rather than realize our mission. It is also true, however, that we have many times put our institution in the dangerous position of being vulnerable to those who threaten to bomb or shoot at us. For instance, when I recently left El Salvador there was a bomb planted next to the university. Therefore, I sent a note to the newspaper announcing that I had left the country so that they would not explode a bomb on my companions while I was not there.

I do not thereby mean to say that we are endangering the institution to any great degree, though we have on several occasions risked at least a little. Once we published a book in defense of a teachers' strike, a position that cost us nearly $200,000 because the government had previously warned us that they would take away our subsidy if we came out publicly in defense of the strike. Though we were very aware of the reality of what we would lose and how that would weaken the institution, we nonetheless fully supported the strike. We are not going to be quiet simply because they target us with bombs.

In this context, it is also important to point out that the church in El Salvador has never taken any assistance from the U.S. Agency for International Development (AID), because its money is corrupt and has been used in a cunning way either to disseminate war in El Salvador or to carry out U.S. policy. We could have at our disposal millions of dollars from that agency in order to do a lot of good things, but the fact that we preach and enact our liberating mission among the marginal and popular groups means that the agency would take the money away from us in a second.

I would like to offer one final example. In the area of theology we have experienced, in another way, basically the same temptation: to offer a Christian reflection and praxis which is not grounded in the history and culture of the Latin American context. Any Christian theology that does not become historical or inculturated within its local context will become oppressive. In that respect it must be said that the widely discussed "theology of liberation," which for better or worse we have sought to create in our continent, is a Latin American reading of that Christianity that came to us weighed down with European "baggage."

It will be repeated yet one more time so as to summarize the hypothesis that has been developed thus far: with the arrival of the first Europeans (headed by Spain and Portugal) to that area which today is known as Latin America, a discovery was made. But those who were discovered were those who carried out the Conquest. What became known was the violent concealment and rape of the indigenous people—including their cultures, their religion, and their languages—who already lived there. They covered up what they had done and they did so violently. That profound concealment created, among other things, a "new culture," a "new race," and a "new religiosity."

In that light, it is imperative today to discover what was concealed, that is to say, to discover the potential from which a real "new world" might arise, and that not as a repetition of the "old world" but one that would be truly novel. But is that really possible? Is it simply utopian? Does the problematic legacy of our "old world" really have a solution?

PROBLEM IN THE SOUTH, SOLUTION IN THE NORTH

In a remark that might seem somewhat prophetic and paradoxical at the same time, it may be opined that the United States is much worse off than Latin America. The United States has a solution, but it is a bad solution as much for itself as it is for the rest of the world. Latin America, on the other hand, does not have any solutions, only problems. But however painful that may be, it is better to have problems than it is to have a bad solution for the historical future.

It is evident that Latin America has a terrible problem: the whole continent is a problem. Presently, the great challenge lies in resolving that problem, but not with the solution that the United States offers. Those statements are not intended to mean that everything the United States possesses and offers is evil and negative, but simply that the solution that it offers, seen as a whole, is not good. It can be judged as such on the basis of an absolute Kantian principle: any solution that cannot be universalized to all the world is not a human solution. Hence, if it does not serve humanity, it is a bad solution.

If the entire world maintained the levels of consumption (of meat, electricity, gasoline, etc.) that the U.S. consumes, the earth's existing resources would be exhausted within twenty years. From a point of view that is concrete, measured, ecological, and global, that is not nor ever could be a solution. In most cases, it is a solution for those and by those who are satisfied and proud. Meanwhile, what is left for Latin America and the rest of the Third World is a tremendous problem.

A popular Castilian phrase is yet another way of meaningfully expressing this daunting problem: "they have turned him into a Christ." In effect, the First World has turned the Third World into a Christ, into a "crucified people." Nevertheless, it may be repeated once again, no matter how painful it might seem it is better to have a large problem than to have a bad solution for that problem because, however inexplicable it may be, our faith tradition announces that among a people with problems, among a "crucified people," is where Christ is actually present and wants to be.

A CIVILIZATION OF CAPITAL AND
A CIVILIZATION OF WORK

Viewed from the perspective of faith, there exists an enormous potential to resolve the Latin America problem, though the solution is much easier to state in abstract terms than actually to implement. The problem revolves around the fact that the dominant civilization in the world today is the civilization of capital, and that is as true for the East as it is for the West. It is the civilization of capital that shapes our world and that turns nearly four-fifths of humanity into "Christ."

It is imperative to struggle against this dominant civilization and in favor of the construction of a new reality: a civilization of work. Since this is such a tremendous challenge it is necessary to understand it well. It is vitally important that the destiny of all humanity not be ruled by the internal laws of capital, for these laws are not just immoral but are amoral, bringing about a certain force that drags everything down that becomes entangled in it. It is not capitalists that make capital, but capital that makes capitalists and pushes them to do what they are doing in the countries of the North. The definitive issue here is not whether capital is in private or collective hands; though that is an important point to distinguish, it is not fundamental. What is fundamental is that both economic orders are civilizations of capital. It goes without saying that capital, left to its own development, moves along producing a mountain of things that are not only useless and deceptive for humanity but that also oblige the major part of humanity to live in dire straits.

For those reasons it is necessary to struggle for a civilization in which work moves history, but not that type of work which is done to produce capital, but work that is done to enable humanity to develop. That same message is conveyed in the Vatican's encyclical *Solicitudo rei socialis*, in which work is clearly given priority over capital: it is the measure of whether a political and economic order may be judged just or unjust. Whenever the force of capital predominates over the force of work within an economic order, that order is unjust, and it gives shape to a sinful structure which generates every other sin. To the contrary, whenever the force of work predominates over the force of capital within a civilization, it reflects a truly Christian inspiration.

The struggle for that "novelty" in El Salvador, which is the country I know best and for that reason to which I will refer, has arisen with tremendous force through a violent process, led by a revolutionary guerrilla movement. Though I am not a blind and uncritical supporter of that movement, since its posture has significant problems as well, it must at least be recognized as a force that was born in protest to invasion, colonization, and the oppression of the Salvadoran people.

I have always maintained that violence is evil. But I also think it is clear that there are some practices of violence that are worse than others. Every act of violence is evil, but on some occasions it may very well be that violence is inevitable. In that sense, liberation theology has insisted that the gravest form of violence, and the root of every other kind of violence, is structural violence, that is, the violence of a civilization of capital which keeps the vast majority of humanity in biological, cultural, social, and political conditions that are absolutely inhuman. The civilization of capital is the most basic form of structural violence. Therefore, to say that liberation theologians defend violence or that they promote violence is wrong. In reality, liberation theology is that theology which has most systematically denounced structural violence. Of course, nobody accuses the structural order of being "violent" since it just seems to be the normal state of affairs, a reflection of the established order, etc. But it is the most basic violence that we all must struggle to eradicate, if at all possible through the most minimum use of violence.

It is certain that the most common response to structural violence has been revolutionary violence. Of course "revolution" need not be equated with "violence." But at times, as has been the case in El Salvador, the guerrillas have taken up arms in order to fight against what they consider to be structural violence. To make violence into a cause, or to make violence into an ideal or a thing good unto itself, is certainly not Christian and most likely is not ethical either. But the central problem continues to be at what point it may be determined that such violence is inevitable. Once again, revolutionary violence in itself is evil, though perhaps many times it becomes inevitable.

In that context, we try in El Salvador to fight first against structural violence, utilizing every nonviolent force at our disposal. The institutional work of our university is thereby converted into a battleground against the country's structural violence. In essence, our work is based in the creation of those conditions that will make possible the liberation of the majority of our people who are oppressed. To that end we direct, with greater or lesser success, the potential of our university.

From that stance we relate to other groups, like the guerrillas, who battle against structural violence in other ways. Practically speaking, I myself have held some long and very critical conversations with one of the most well-known of the guerrillas, Commandante Villalobos. In one specific situation, I told him that the action that the guerrillas had taken in the murder of several mayors was absolutely intolerable, seen from the Christian point of view, and counterproductive, seen from the political point of view. I also told him that other actions which the guerrillas had been carrying out, like putting bombs in the homes of military personnel and in gas stations, in the hope of stimulating a popular insurrection (or as they later came to call it, a "social explosion") also seemed to me, given the actual conditions that existed in the country, a serious mistake.

We have struggled to ensure that the FMLN minimizes the amount of damage they do to the least number of people possible. When we obtain a declaration from its military command promising that they will not harm civilians, we believe a great advance has been made. We are now going to see if we can advance a little further in order to end the war through the negotiation process that we have launched.

But at this moment, despite the fact that I believe that armed struggle does not have much of a future in El Salvador, we cannot ask the FMLN to stop its war against the army nor ask them to stop carrying out acts of sabotage. What we can say to them is that it is necessary to negotiate and that it is necessary to search for peace because the path of violence only reproduces itself in El Salvador. Our struggle and goal, then, is to stop the war and to end the structural violence while minimizing the damage that every type of violence causes within our country. We believe that putting this plan into action is much more pacifist than violent.

In the midst of this struggle we have been able to discover what it is, at root, that motivates us. In El Salvador and in all of Central America the same things continue happening that transpired five centuries ago. A few foreign powers, allied with their internal elites, have set about shaping a civilization of capital while covering up the truth of what is really happening by pitting ideology against ideology. This describes our present situation.

Certainly in our present situation in El Salvador there has been and continues to be a seed of liberation which exists both within the popular majorities who have not lost their hope and within the church. It has cost a great deal of blood to maintain the life of that seed. Many priests, religious men and women, and lay people have been murdered. They, too, are part of the legacy of a church that over the course of five centuries has left not only bad seeds in Latin America but also seeds of struggle, having shed fertile blood on behalf of a humble people. Put simply, they are our martyrs.

Within the mark of this hopeful struggle for liberation, which is also full of martyrdom, it is essential to recall the memory of the exceptional case of Archbishop Romero. I remember that each time a priest was killed in El Salvador he said, in a spirit of resignation, yet quite hopeful at the same time: "How sad it would be, in a country where such horrible murders are being committed, if there were no priests among the victims!"[1]

Romero taught—although he was not given much opportunity to speak because he was killed before his time—that the preferential option for the popular majority and for the poor of the earth should be a fundamental element in the action of the church and in its preaching. And if there ever was a person who, in reference to the discussion above, had no fear of putting at risk the institution of the church in the way it carried out its mission, it was Archbishop Romero. Naturally, all of the powers of this world withdrew their support from him, threatened him, and attacked him even to assassination.

But the martyred blood shed in El Salvador and in all of Latin America, far from demoralizing us or driving us to despair, infuses us with a new spirit of struggle and with a new hope for our people. In that sense, if we are not a "new world" nor a "new continent," we are clearly, in a way that can be verified (though not necessarily by outsiders), a continent of hope. That is an extremely meaningful sign of a novel future compared to other continents who have no hope. The only thing that they really have is fear.

6

THE ECONOMICS OF ECCLESIA

A Poor Church Is a Church Rich in Compassion

Jon Sobrino

*W*ealth and poverty are contrary and mutually exclusive realities in the Scriptures, the former condemnatory and the latter salvific. The true church, therefore, ought to be shaped by poverty and by an opposition to wealth. At the same time, the ultimate truth of the church, as well as its identity, proceeds from its mission, and in that regard poverty and wealth must be seen in relation to that which facilitates or incapacitates that mission.

In the context of massive global suffering, the mission of the church can and should have its nucleus in the practice of compassion.[1] Consequently, it is more than just a play on words to say that a church wealthy in earthly goods bears forth a church poor in compassion and a church poor in earthly goods bears forth a church rich in compassion.

THE PRINCIPLE OF WEALTH AND THE PRINCIPLE OF POVERTY

The realities of wealth and poverty will be analyzed in this essay not so much as categorical realities, thereby miring ourselves in the interminable discussion of how much one church or another may possess in order to be defined as rich or poor. They will, rather, be viewed as two distinct worlds within which a church may insert itself. Above all, then, wealth and poverty will be treated as core principles of reality, that is, as those realities which are to be found at the beginning of an ecclesial process. But not only the beginning as a point of origin, but also that which remains present in the long run, providing direction to ecclesial process and giving shape to all of its elements.

To introduce the subject it may be helpful to reflect on one of St. Ignatius of Loyola's meditations known as "the two kingdoms," which is included in his *Spiritual Exercises*.[2] Though it is certain that the meditation is directed toward the individual so as to enable him or her to walk toward his or her own perfection, the meditation can also be very easily adapted to the mission of the church. It seems very useful to look at it that way because St. Ignatius focused on that theme which will most interest us in this essay: the character of the "principle" behind wealth and poverty.

In effect, St. Ignatius presents two paths, each with three steps, that are open to the Christian. One path is put forth by the forces of evil, the other by Jesus. But both paths, wealth and poverty, have a source that intrinsically gives them a direction for the entire journey. Wealth leads to the vain honors of this world, which leads to pride, which in turn leads to every other vice. Poverty leads to being disgraced and scorned, which leads to humility, which in turn leads to every other virtue. These two paths are formally presented as antithetical and antagonistic, to such a degree that to follow and advance in one of the paths it is necessary to act in a manner contrary to the other.

It can be seen how these principles, once they are made historical and approached from within the reality of today's world, which is predominantly impoverished and suffering, may be applied to an analysis of a rich church and a poor church. The path of evil begins with wealth and, from an evangelical (that is, rooted in the gospel) point of view, is on that account ipso facto the absolute negation of following Jesus; for the church this fact clearly signifies that it is the wrong path.

In a world predominantly poor,[3] wealth intrinsically causes the church to distance itself from the real world, to disembody itself from it, and to feign not to understand it. A rich church is, first of all, a church that has failed to become flesh in a world predominantly poor and is, therefore, a "fairy tale" church; in that sense, it is unreal. Not only is it then not a "Christian" church, since it does not follow the poor and humble Jesus, but it also is not a "human" church. In the first case it cannot be a sacrament of Christ and in the second case it cannot be a sacrament of humanity, even though both elements are mandated by the Second Vatican Council's document, *Lumen Gentium*. In sum, a rich church has no identity and no Christian relevance.

Furthermore, once it has fixed itself in the elite and sinful world of wealth, the church ceases to be earthly, incarnated, and instead becomes worldly, established, as St. Ignatius warns, in the "privileges" of the world. From there it falls into pride, once having turned into an oppressor church, and then to "every other vice"; that is, it participates in the chief evils of present-day humanity, evils that may be described in two ways:

1. The world of wealth is imbued with idols and by necessity grounds itself in them; to become wealthy inexorably means to enter into a relationship with them. The most powerful temptation is to worship them, a notion quite compatible not only with nonreligious ideologies but also with religious ones. Idols demand victims in order to survive, and to worship them means to provide victims to appease them. Thereby is revealed the primary evil of the principle of wealth: to bring forth death. Recall that in Johannine theology the Evil One is a "murderer."

2. Simultaneously, idols seek to remain hidden, to conceal themselves, even to misrepresent their very essence ("There will come a day when everyone who is brought before the tribunals will think that they are giving glory to God"). What is even more scandalous, idols essentially find it necessary to generate deception in order to improve their concealment. Recall, once again, that in Johannine theology the Evil One is also the "liar."

Within the world of wealth, the fifth and seventh commandments ("Thou shall not kill" and "Thou shall not steal"), which defend life and the basic means to live it, are massively and structurally violated, as is the eighth commandment ("Thou shall not bear false witness against your neighbor"), which addresses the fundamental attempt to conceal a violation of God's will.[4] To be in the world of wealth is already in itself "de-Christianizing" and dehumanizing. But a worse consequence yet is that the church then enters—whether it knows it or not or wants it or not—into a sinful dynamic which establishes it in a relationship with the chief sin of the world, that of causing death. Be it active or passive, through action or omission, it participates in that sin at least on a structural level.

The path of Jesus, on the other hand, begins with poverty and, from an evangelical perspective, should also be the starting point of the Christian church; a historical vantage point indicates as well that poverty must be the place of the church.

In a world that is predominantly poor, the church ought to be in poverty simply so that it may be real, to avoid communicating the painful impression of unreality and irrelevance, as happens when it merely seeks to offer intentions. Once again, it is essential that the church become a real organism within a world of poverty. Archbishop Romero graphically addressed this issue with these discerning words: "I rejoice, brothers and sisters, that our [Salvadoran] church is persecuted precisely for its preferential option for the poor, and for seeking to become incarnate in the interests of the poor." And in an even more chilling message, Romero said: "How sad it would be, in a country where such horrible murders are being committed, if there were no priests among the victims! A murdered priest is a testimonial of a church incarnate in the problems of the people."[5] Though the content of these pronouncements sets our hair on end, the message itself is of interest: it is fundamental that the church, before anything else, places itself in the true reality of the world. It is not a matter of intentionality, nor of pure factuality—that is, to be where one already is—but it is a call to be actually present in the most profound moments of reality. Hence, while the reality of this world is one of poverty, the church cannot situate itself in any other realm.

By virtue of its own internal dynamic, poverty leads to what St. Ignatius calls being "disgraced and scorned." In doing so, poverty resolves for the church the grand problem of being adequately in the world (of the poor), while not sinfully being of the world (of the rich), to be earthly without being worldly. Reality itself demonstrates, while leaving little room for doubt, the truth of that notion by spawning a defamed, threatened, persecuted, and martyred church. Poverty thus brings the church to be like Jesus and to "appease" the highest good—which is antithetical to the worst evils of wealth—which is propitiated by Jesus and demanded by the reality of the world. In light of the above, the principle of poverty may be articulated in two ways:

1. In opposition to idolatry, the church's incarnation within poverty brings it to defend victims, denounce idols, and announce the God of life. As its inheritance, the church then becomes a bearer of the *euangelion*, the good news (and the good reality) for the poor of this world. If the Evil One is a murderer and deprives people of life, the poor church brings forth life, and life more abundantly.

2. In opposition to lies and concealment, poverty brings truth into the light. As its inheritance, the church then becomes light in the midst of darkness, and truth in the midst of deception. If the Evil One is a liar, the poor church is a bearer of truth and light.

THE NECESSITY AND DIFFICULTY
OF THE CHURCH'S ELECTION

The central realities of wealth and poverty are key in distinguishing between a true and a false church. But to consider poverty and wealth as "principles" of a process—"in such a way that there may be three steps," as St. Ignatius insists—it further helps to verify if there actually is such a thing as a rich church or a poor church. If the church comes upon privileges and establishes itself in their enjoyment, that church allows itself to be governed by the principle of wealth, whether it admits it or not. Worse yet, that church fully participates in the sin of that world within which it has established itself. Inversely, if the church is "disgraced" by the sinful world and establishes itself within the oppressed world, that church has allowed itself to be governed by the principle of poverty. Most importantly, that church fully invests itself in the eradication of sin from the world.

The conclusion to all of the above is clear: the church ought to become a church of the poor and be governed by the principle of poverty. But to affirm such a fundamental principle, two important things still need to be clarified. The first is obvious: to be in poverty is to come to poverty in opposition to wealth.[6] At this point the question arises: What is it that has sufficient power to place the church in a position of poverty and keep it there? Second, as essential as the principle of poverty might be, it ought not to be considered merely the principle which gives structure to the church from within, but must also be put at the service of its mission.

Historically, what has enabled a solution to both of these dilemmas is the practice of compassion. The church must be in poverty because that condition will enable it to practice compassion; in turn, its practice efficaciously leads the church into poverty and continues to impoverish it. Surely other motivations as well might lead the church to become poor, above all the model of Jesus; but the material conditions of poverty are essentially what best unleash compassion. Put in simple terms, a poor church is inherently more compassionate, and a compassionate church is inherently poorer. What then is a compassionate church, and what is the principle of compassion by which the church should be governed?

THE PRINCIPLE OF COMPASSION

It is difficult to arrive at a clear understanding of the term *compassion*[7] because its articulation may connote ideas which are good and true, but inadequate and even dangerous: a feeling of compassion is accompanied by the risk that one may not analyze what has brought about suffering itself; the alleviation of individual necessities is accompanied by the risk of abandoning the transformation of structures; providing protection for victims is accompanied by the risk of paternalism. Hence, so as to avoid the limitations and misunderstandings which may be brought to the notion of "compassion," it is best not to speak simply of compassion as such, but of the "principle of compassion." So Ernst Bloch refers not simply to "hope" as one thing among many categorical realities, but of the "principle of hope."

It is well known that the source of the salvific process lies in God's loving action: "I have seen the oppression of my people who are in Egypt, and have heard their cries against their oppressors, and know their sufferings. I have come to liberate them" (Exod. 3:7f.). The term one may want to use to describe God's action here is to a certain extent secondary, though it could most adequately be called "liberation." What is most important to emphasize here, however, is the form of that movement toward liberation: God hears the cries of a suffering people, and for that reason alone decides upon a liberating action.[8]

So conceived, God's action of love may be called compassion. It must be emphasized, however, that: (1) it is an action, or more exactly a "re-action" to the internalization of the suffering of the other, which reaches to one's own heart and gut; in this specific case, it is the suffering of an entire people, inflicted unjustly and reaching to the most basic levels of existence; and (2) it is an action motivated solely by that suffering.

Internalization of the suffering of the other is, then, the principle which guides a response of compassion, and this, in turn, becomes the principle which shapes all of God's actions. Several remarks might clarify this statement: (1) This principle is not only to be found at the beginning of the salvific process. It is a permanent and fundamental feature of the entire Old Testament. Throughout, one may find God's partiality for the victims—not dependent on any action on their part but existing solely by virtue of their condition as victims. The Old Testament recounts God actively coming to their defense and God's will that they be liberated. (2) Springing forth from the internal logic of the Exodus came the demand for justice in other particular historical contexts and the denunciation of those who create unjust suffering. (3) By means of the Exodus, and not simply coincidental to it, and by means of subsequent actions of compassion, the very character of God is revealed. And (4) the fundamental demand on the human being and, more specifically, on God's people is that they renew God's compassion in their own actions toward others and thereby enter into a close relationship with God.

If it may be said, paraphrasing Scripture for a moment, that the absolute divine principle "is the word" (John 1:1), and by means of it creation transpires (Genesis 1:1), then it may also be affirmed that the historical, salvific, absolute principle "is compassion," and it is constantly sustained in the salvific process of God.

The primordial compassion of God becomes historical in the practice and message of Jesus. Jesus' "compassion for the crowds" [*misereor super turbas*] was not a merely occasional attitude in his life but one that shaped his entire life and mission, shaped too his vision of God and the human person, and brought him to his final destiny.

When Jesus wishes to present the model of the complete human person, he tells the parable of the good Samaritan. It is a solemn moment in the Gospels; it reveals a profundity far beyond the mere curiosity of knowing which of the commandments is most important. In essence, the parable seeks to articulate what it means to be a human being. The complete human person is the one who saw an injured man on the road, responded, and assisted him in every way he possibly could. The parable does not say what the Samaritan was thinking or indicate the ultimate purpose of his action. The only thing it says is that he did it "moved by compassion."

The complete human person, then, is one who feels in one's own gut the suffering of the other; in the case of the parable, it is suffering unjustly inflicted. Internalization of suffering is done in such a way that it becomes a deep part of the self, thereby becoming the primary, ultimate, internal principle behind one's action. Compassion, as a response, is the fundamental action of the complete human person. So conceived, it is not one thing among many other human realities but that which clearly defines the human person. On the one hand, it is not enough to characterize human beings so, because a human is also a being who knows, hopes, and celebrates. On the other hand, it is absolutely necessary, for in the eyes of Jesus, to be a human person is to respond with compassion. If one does not do so, that person has, at root, perverted the very essence of what is means to be human, as happened in the case of the priest and the Levite who went around the man lying in the road.

Compassion is also the reality that the Gospels employ to characterize Jesus, a figure who regularly healed others with the petition "have mercy [*misericordia*]" and acted because he felt compassion for people. Likewise, God is characterized in terms of compassion in another key parable: the father goes out to meet the prodigal son, and when he finds him sad and half-crazed, he is moved to compassion, responds, gives him a hug, and organizes a feast.

If one may describe the human person, Christ, and God by reference to compassion, then without a doubt it must be something quite fundamental. It is love, one may say in harmony with the entire Christian tradition, as is already known. But it is vital to add to that notion that it is a specific form of love: a love manifest in a praxis that arises from unjust suffering inflicted on the other so as to eradicate it, and seeks no other reason for doing so beyond the fact that the suffering does indeed exist.[9] Nothing else exists prior to compassion in order to motivate it, and nothing exists beyond compassion so as to reject it or relativize it. According to Jesus, without it there would exist neither humanity nor divinity.

These affirmations may be appreciated in at least a simple way when Jesus presents the Samaritan as the consummate example of one who fulfills the law of loving one's neighbor. Nowhere in the narration of the parable does it suggest that the Samaritan assists the one injured on the road *in order to fulfill a commandment*, however lofty that might be, but simply because he was "moved to compassion."

It is reported that Jesus healed, and on several occasions it is shown that he was troubled because those whom he healed failed to demonstrate gratitude. However, nowhere does it suggest that Jesus healed in order to receive gratitude, or so that they might realize his unique truth or divine power. Quite simply, all that appears is that he was "moved to compassion."

It is related that the father receives the prodigal son, but nowhere is it suggested that the father does so in order to achieve something of deeper interest, for example, that the son might confess his sins and put the father in charge of his life. It only says that the father is "moved to compassion."

Compassion, then, is what comes first and what comes last. Its exercise is not merely to be classified as a so-called work of mercy, though it also can and must express itself so. It is something much more radical: a fundamental attitude toward the suffering of the other, carried out with the conviction that to respond to the unjust suffering of another is to deal, without possible escape, with being itself.

The parable of the good Samaritan also demonstrates that when compassion is found wanting, as depicted in the response of the priest and the Levite, historical reality is exhausted. Though this is frightening enough for Jesus, the Gospel writers also show that he understood historical reality as being shaped by active, uncompassionate forces that injure and kill human beings, while also threatening and killing those who are governed by the principle of compassion.

Jesus places the healing of a man with the withered hand before the observance of the Sabbath because he was compassionate, not because he was a "liberal." His argument was obvious and defenseless: "Is it lawful on the Sabbath to do good or to do harm, to save life or to lose it?" (Mark 3:4). His adversaries, described in terms clearly antithetical to Jesus—for example, "their hardness of heart" (v. 5)—not only are not convinced by his argument but actually place themselves in opposition to him. The narration closes in terrifying fashion: "The Pharisees went out and immediately conferred with the Herodians against him, how to destroy him" (v. 6).

Whether the arrangement of this passage be considered anachronistic or not, what it fundamentally demonstrates is the existence of compassion and "anti-compassion." As long as compassion is reduced to feelings or "works of mercy," it is tolerable. But when it is elevated to a principle and the Sabbath is subordinated to the eradication of suffering, then the uncompassionate react because it reverses the values of their oppressive world. As tragic as it may seem, Jesus was executed for practicing compassion in a committed fashion until the very end. Compassion, then, is a reality which comes into existence in spite of and in opposition to those elements which are uncompassionate.

Despite that fact, Jesus proclaimed: "Happy are the compassionate [*misericordiosos*]." The reason Jesus offers in the Gospel of Matthew seems to be recompense: "for they will receive compassion [*misericordia*]." But there is also an intrinsic reason that more profoundly expresses Jesus' message: whoever lives according to the principle of compassion will realize the depths of what it means to be a human being, and so become more like Jesus—the *homo verus del dogma*—and more like God.

Therein may be understood the theory of happiness that Jesus offers: "Happy, blessed, are you who practice compassion, who are pure of heart, who work for peace, who hunger for justice and are persecuted for it, who are poor. . . . " These are scandalous but illuminating words. Jesus desires that humans be happy, and the symbol for that happiness is a table shared one with another. But while in history the "great banquet" of the reign of God fails to appear, it is necessary to practice compassion; and that, says Jesus, produces joy, happiness, and contentment.

The foregoing reflections may help to clarify what is meant by the "principle of compassion." Compassion is not the only activity exercised by Jesus, but it was the source of his actions and shaped his life, his mission, and his destiny. At times in the Gospel narratives the term *compassion* appears explicitly, and at other times not at all. But, with or without the term, it is always present in the background of Jesus' activity on behalf of the suffering majority, the poor, the weak, those deprived of dignity, and all others who move him. And those deep feelings shaped everything that made up who Jesus was: his knowledge, his hope, his actions, and his celebrations.

Jesus' hope lies with the poor who have no hope; to them he announces the reign of God. His praxis of healing, expelling demons, and accepting sinners is carried out in favor of the oppressed, the least, and in opposition to the oppressors, whom he unmasks and denounces. His "social theory" is guided by the principle that one must eradicate massive and unjust suffering. His happiness is to sit down at the table with the marginalized. His vision of God is of a God who defends the least and shows compassion to the poor. His fidelity to God is what lies on the other side of the coin of a commitment to practice compassion despite the risks and attacks that result from doing so. He teaches the destitute to pray to God as a child talks to a parent.

Compassion is the genesis of the divine and the human. It therefore ought to inform every dimension of human life, that of understanding, hope, celebration, and, of course, praxis. Each one of these dimensions is autonomous and will be shaped and guided by various fundamental principles, though compassion supersedes all of the rest. Lest this seem like nothing but pure speculative revision, turn to the decisive passage found in Matthew 25: Whoever practices compassion, regardless of what one practices within other dimensions of human reality, "has been saved," has come to be the complete human person for all eternity. The judge and the judged stand before compassion, and before it alone. The criterion used by the judge is not arbitrary, for God has demonstrated how to respond with compassion before the cries of the oppressed. The lives of human beings are determined by their response to those cries.

THE POOR CHURCH AS A CHURCH
RICH IN COMPASSION

The principle of compassion must be effective in the church of Jesus, and its pathos must be what informs and shapes it. The church, insofar as it truly is a church, must therefore reread the parable of the good Samaritan and hear its message with the same expectation, with the same fear and trembling that accompanied its first telling by Jesus. Perhaps the church ought to be and do many other things, but if it does not become immersed in the compassion of the parable and, as a result, allows its key principle to pass it by, then everything else will become irrelevant and possibly even dangerous.

Compassion is what today, more than anything else, essentially places the church in poverty. If it allows itself to be governed by the principle of compassion, the church will follow the steps that unleash the principle of poverty and that will lead it, in the language of St. Ignatius, "to every other virtue." In the language of systematic theology, compassion will lead it to become the true church. Of course, one cannot make an exact parallel between the analysis of the principle of compassion that has been offered in this essay and St. Ignatius's analysis of the principle of poverty. Nonetheless, a broad connection exists between the two, and both realities, poverty and compassion, are mutually empowering.

The church's fundamental struggle is adequately to incarnate itself where it ought to be. Formally speaking, that place is the world; and within the world that place is, speaking materially, the reality of poverty. By definition, the practice of compassion is what draws the church outside itself and leads it not just to any world—for example, to the world of culture or to the world of arts and sciences, however important they may be—but to poverty, a world of the highest priority. It is there, whether that place be physically or geographically coincidental to the realm of the church or not, that the church meets the one injured on the road. From there as well can be heard the clamor of those humans, who, as in the words of the song crafted by the oppressed African American community in the United States, cry out: "Were you there when they crucified my Lord?" That message alone is worth more than a thousand pages of ecclesiology.

The proper place of the church is to be in poverty, and it is compassion that effectively and existentially moves it to reside there. If the crucified ones of this world are unable to move the soul of the church to get outside itself and to confront the crosses upon which they hang, what force is there that will make the church take the "first step" toward poverty? We can talk till eternity about how poor the church itself should be, yet in pursuing that path the cynic need not take one step. But if the church practices compassion at least one thing becomes clear: it has moved outside itself and, at the same time, has begun walking toward poverty, the place where it ought to be.

How crucial this is may be illustrated by reference to an actual example. It is well known that it is not easy for the institutional church to move outside itself, much less to enter the world of poverty, but neither is it easy for the so-called progressive church, nor for those "progressive" individuals within it. Certainly, it is just, necessary, and urgent to demand, as the progressives do, for human rights and freedom within the church, more than anything on the basis of ethical grounds. Both human rights and freedom are signs of fraternity, and therefore signs of the reign of God, and without them the church cannot be credible in today's world. But it is important to remember that the focus is still on the internal affairs of the church. Prior logic should lead one to question what the rights of life and freedom may be in the world outside the church. This latter focus is governed by the principle of compassion and serves to "Christianize" the former concerns, but the inverse is not necessarily true. A "compassionate Christianity" may be progressive, and in Latin America it should be, but a progressive church is not always compassionate.

The internal humanization of the church is urgent, but its priority must be focused outside itself, from the vantage point of "the road" upon which the injured one may be found. It is also urgent that the believer, the priest, and the theologian reclaim their legitimate freedom within the church, a freedom that is presently restricted. But it is even more urgent to reclaim the freedom of millions of human beings who simply have no resources that might help them to survive poverty or to live in the face of repression and who are not free to ask for justice or for a simple investigation into the crimes of which they have been the object.

The foregoing example illustrates the difficulty that the church, even its most progressive elements, has in incarnating itself in poverty. When the church moves outside itself so that it may walk on the road where it will meet the injured ones and, once moved by compassion, stays on that road, it becomes a "decentralized" church, a church of compassion and a church of poverty.

In our world "works of mercy" are applauded, or at least tolerated. What is not tolerated is a church shaped by the principle of compassion, a church led to denounce the assailants who produce victims, to unmask the lies that provide a cover for oppression, and to inspire the victims to move toward liberation. In other words, the assailants who live within an uncompassionate world tolerate the healing of the injured, but they do not tolerate their "true healing," nor tolerate the struggle aimed to prevent the victim from once again falling into their hands.

When it falls into their disfavor, the church, like any other institution, is defamed and persecuted ("disgraced and scorned"), which verifies that it has allowed itself to be governed by the principle of compassion and is truly poor. At the same time, the absence of these same threats, attacks, and persecutions verify that the church has not allowed itself to be governed by the principle of compassion and is truly wealthy.

The committed practice of compassion, like moving beyond mere assistance to the defense of victims from their assailants, will cause the church to be called a "Samaritan." Though the term sounds quite good to us because it is now identified with the model of a compassionate person, it is important to remember how awful it would have sounded in Jesus' day. It was precisely for that reason Jesus used it, so as to emphasize the superiority of compassion over religious conceptions and to attack those religious leaders who did not display compassion.

The same continues to occur today. The assailants, who despise compassion, call those who practice it every name imaginable. In Latin America they are called subversives, communists, liberationists, or atheists. More recently, after the events which have taken place in Eastern Europe, they may be called, in a softer tone, ingenuous, anachronistic, or out of fashion.

If anything is clear in the world today it is that the practice of compassion leads to the loss of a good reputation, and is certain to lead to "disgrace and scorn." A good church continues to be called, pejoratively, "Samaritan." But not only that; when the church practices compassion in a committed fashion, until the very end, and denounces assailants, then it is touching the idols. That they are "the forgotten idols" (as they are insightfully called by J. L. Sicre) does not mean that they are gods who have already been overcome, for they are quite present and active in our world, even though carefully concealed. Idols also respond to the reality of the world, and in so doing submit the church to the worst disgrace and to the supreme impoverishment, death itself.

It is not easy for the church to remain compassionate once attacks come upon it, but if it is able to do so, it moves to another step that St. Ignatius calls "humility," what today is conceived of as the inner freedom to love and defend victims in a distinctively disinterested way. The freedom for compassion up to the final consequence was exemplified with total clarity in the life of Archbishop Romero. By his actions he brought upon himself painful personal and intraecclesial conflicts, put at risk his prior prestige within the institutional church, put at risk his reputation and his position as archbishop, not to mention putting at risk his very life. He also put at risk the institution itself, something that is even more difficult to do and even more infrequently done. Due to Romero's commitment to compassion, key elements of the church were destroyed—the radio station and printing house of the archdiocese, high schools and universities—and the most important symbols of the institutional church were decimated: priests and those in religious orders, catechists and delegates of the word were captured, expelled, and murdered.

The Salvadoran church was humiliated, estranged from anything even approaching "pride" or power that is based on wealth and earthly privilege. But this humiliation also brought it to an interior freedom, to the truth, to grace, or as St. Ignatius suggests, to "humility." In the face of the attacks and the destruction of the church, Archbishop Romero said to his afflicted audience: "When they destroy our radio station and murder our priests, know that they have not done anything evil to us." And in the presence of his own death, he announced:

> I have frequently been threatened with death. I must say to you, as a Christian, that I do not believe in death without resurrection. If they kill me, I shall rise again in the Salvadoran people. I am not boasting; I say it with the greatest humility.[10]

Such an attitude demonstrates that the practice of compassion and the disgrace suffered because of it may serve as purification, bringing the church to humility and definitively distancing it from pride. From there, St. Ignatius insists, the church is brought through three steps to "every virtue" and distanced from "every vice." To pass from one step to the next, however, is not done mechanically; for that reason St. Ignatius speaks of "being induced." But it is also true that within each step lies the intrinsic dynamic that leads to the following one. Applying this to the present topic, a church that allows itself to be governed by compassion in a committed way ends up being a true church or, at least, a church more true to Jesus than others.

A church committed to compassion, which has journeyed down its road to the end, gains a light by which it may more clearly see what it must be and do. Most of all, it arrives at the conviction that its fundamental principle is truly that of compassion, and that with which it began it must sustain always. That church also clarifies the content of its central task: "how to say to the poor of this world that God loves them" (Gustavo Gutiérrez). Additionally, it realizes the necessity of making that loving word of God historical; in other words, how to historicize and prioritize compassion. Though this aspect has already been discussed above in reference to the principle of compassion, it may also here be illustrated in relation to the attitude of the churches toward historicizing and prioritizing compassion.

In every time and in every place there exists many types of wounds, both physical and spiritual. Though their magnitude and depth vary by definition, we must react with compassion so as to heal them all. However, the church should not fall into the hasty universalization of every wound as if every cry is of the very same expression, nor should it invoke universalization solely in order to justify the lofty affirmation of works of mercy (which are, on the other hand, certainly of value). All human suffering deserves absolute respect and demands an answer, but that does not mean that there may not be some manner of prioritizing the wounds of the world today.

Undoubtedly in every local church there are specific wounds, both physical and spiritual, and all of these must be healed and bandaged. But since the church is one and catholic, it must, above all, look at these wounds on a more global level. Quantitatively, the greatest suffering on this planet of more than five billion people is, and continues to be, poverty, which brings with it indignity and death. And this massive wound appears much more radically in the Third World than it does in the First World. Though it may be widely known theoretically, it must be repeated that merely by virtue of the fact of having been born in El Salvador or in Haiti or in Bangladesh, human beings of these countries have much less life and much less dignity than those born in the United States, Germany, or Spain. That reality is today's fundamental wound, which means that we must affirm, as it is put in Christian language, that the wounded one is the very creation of God.

This global wound is the central wound for every church simply by virtue of its very magnitude, but also due to the responsibility that all local institutions share for their continued existence, be they governments, political parties, armies, labor unions, universities, or churches. If a local church does not attend to that global wound it cannot say that it is being governed by the principle of compassion.

That does not mean that a church should not attend to more local wounds, such as the presence of the so-called Fourth World within the First World (for example, the homeless), or other specifically First World crises like egoistic individualism and an obtuse positivism that deprives people of feelings and faith. It is necessary to respond to all of these things with compassion yet without passing what is primary to a secondary level. It must be asked if the First World's insensitivity and cultural malaise toward the global wound arises, consciously or unconsciously, from its shared responsibility for having created a planet predominantly injured by poverty and indignity.

That reflection is not obvious, though it seems to be true. It will not be shared, with conviction, in many churches for the fundamental reason that nothing is evident to those who do not have a pure heart with which to see the truth. To arrive at the truth—one of the other virtues signaled by St. Ignatius—it is necessary to assume a proper subjective attitude. But, speaking methodologically, a proper subjective attitude requires material conditions that can facilitate an honest subjectivity. What actualizes the possibilities of a subjectivity needed to see the truth, then, are the material conditions of poverty and the committed response of compassion. In plainer terms, it is much easier for a church to be enlightened regarding the true reality of humanity once it has responded to the one injured on the road and has suffered defamation and the even greater humiliation of martyrdom for having done so. The committed practice of compassion enables one "to see" the truth. When compassion is absent, truth will not be seen with ease.

What has already been anticipated by Scripture now becomes actual reality: in the suffering servant there is light, in the crucified one there is wisdom. But in order to gain light and wisdom, one must place oneself next to the servant and next to the crucified one. And if, beyond simply being present, one survives the cross, its light illuminates the truth that much more. The conviction that the worst evils in this world are injustice and oppression, since they create poverty, cause indignity, and rupture fraternity, will then become fundamental and unmovable; and so will it become clear that the central mission of the church is to place its faith in the service of the liberation of the oppressed. The church will also thereby become convinced that the practice of liberation will illuminate its faith.

The light that arises from the practice of compassion is only a sign, though a fundamental one, that the church has arrived at the "other virtues." As Ignacio Ellacuría used to say, the truths of liberation theology cannot fundamentally be traced to the fact that its theologians have more knowledge than others, but simply to the fact that they are in the proper place. By allowing itself to be governed by the principle of compassion the church allows itself to arrive at the proper place, and once it has arrived there, it will have more light.

What has been said so far is only one example, though an important one, of "the other virtues" at which the church arrives when it practices compassion in a committed way. Quite briefly, others may be mentioned: Once it is rooted in compassion, the church's faith becomes a faith in the God of those injured on the road, the God of the victims, the God of life. Its liturgy celebrates the life of those who have no life, the resurrection of the crucified. Its theology is *intellectus misericordiae* or intellectual compassion; liberation theology is nothing more and nothing less.[11] Its doctrine and social practice represent an anxious desire to offer, theoretically and practically, effective paths toward justice, and the willingness to journey down them. Its ecumenism grows and prospers in the midst of the crucified peoples who, like Christ, attract everyone toward it; history demonstrates that this is so.

It is vital that the church respond with compassion in order to become the true church of Jesus. That reflection is not mere speculation but is based on real observations of a Salvadoran church that has adopted the principle of compassion with absolute seriousness. It cannot be overemphasized, however, that it realized that potential not merely by means of intentional voluntarism, nor merely through fidelity to a text, be it past or present, sacred or profane, but through the practice of compassion.

In closing, two brief reflections will be made regarding the fullness to which the church may be brought through the practice of compassion. First, compassion is a beatitude; hence, a church that truly feels compassion is a church that experiences joy, and because it has joy it is able to demonstrate it. In that manner, the church may communicate *in actu*, in word and deed, the announcement of the good news, which not only is truth, but which also produces joy; that message is almost completely forgotten by the church. A church that does not convey joy is not a church of the gospel. However, it is not a matter of conveying just any kind of joy but that which is declared and distributed in the Magna Carta of the Beatitudes: compassion.

Second, a church characterized by compassion becomes significant in today's world, quite specifically because it has credibility. The credibility of the church depends on various things. In democratic and culturally developed areas of the world it is above all important to take into account the exercise of freedom within the church and the rational exposition by which it gains respectability. However, from a global perspective (which includes the countries of the First World) maximum credibility proceeds from a committed compassion, precisely because that is what is so absent in our world today. A compassionate church is at least credible, while an uncompassionate church will look in vain for other ways to attain credibility. Among the agnostics, the unbelievers, and those who are simply bored by Christian faith, a church of compassion at least makes the name of God respectable and ensures that God will not be blasphemed by what it does. Among the world's poor it inspires acceptance and gratitude. A church of compassion, then, becomes significant in today's world in a manner mandated by God.

Everything that has been expressed in this essay is nothing more than a reaffirmation of what in another language, according to the very declarations of the institutional church, is known as the church's charge to practice an option for the poor. Hence, what has been said here is nothing new, though perhaps it has contributed to an understanding of the radicality, the priority, and the ultimacy of that option. In theory everyone today is in agreement that the church ought to be a church of the poor. This essay has sought to illuminate the natural link binding poverty and compassion and to suggest that existentially the best way for the church to put itself into the difficult world of poverty is to respond with compassion. A poor church reaches out to be fully compassionate, and a compassionate church is moved to be poor.

7

TRANSNATIONAL CORPORATIONS AND INSTITUTIONALIZED VIOLENCE

A Challenge to Christian Movements in the United States

Mark Lewis Taylor

I saw them bury a dead child
in a cardboard box
(This is true, and I don't forget it.)
On this box there was a stamp:
"General Electric Company—
Progress is our Most Important Product"
—Luis Alfredo Arango,
in *Papel y Tusa*
Guatemala, 1967

*I*n the Guatemala of 1991, you could still see Mayan peoples proceeding to bury their dead children in small boxes, not all, of course, so startlingly stamped with a corporation label. An equally striking juxtaposition occurs if you happen to be driving a main highway to see what Guatemalan newspapers report daily: tortured and mutilated adult bodies, sometimes rolled into a ditch, lodged against wooden poles stretching upward to display the goods of corporate giants: Shell, Coca-Cola, Bank of America, Mitsubishi.

What would it mean for theology to think about the connection between a dead child and General Electric, between tortured bodies and transnational corporations (TNCs)? Can it be done without producing only the dismissable rhetoric of jeremiad and hyperbole? In this essay, I attempt that exercise in thought, beginning with a Guatemalan encounter of violence. Then in the second section, I identify the interwoven dimensions operative in that encounter. A third section presents "abstraction" as a key dynamic in the institutionalized violence embodied in transnational corporations. Against the backdrop of this approach to "corporate evil," the fourth and final section then seeks to present Christian movements as a kind of "corporate grace," issuing in strategic practices of resistance and hope.

GUATEMALAN ENCOUNTER: VIOLENCE AND A BLUE-CHIP INVESTMENT

Let us juxtapose the discourse of two voices from recent Guatemala: the voice of Nobel Peace Prize recipient Rigoberta Menchú, a Quiche Mayan woman now in exile, but still struggling against the poverty to which her Mayan people are subjugated; and then the voice of Fred Sherwood, one of hundreds of U.S. businessmen who have operated in Guatemala.

Menchú has related her story in detail in a book entitled *I, Rigoberta Menchú: An Indian Woman in Guatemala*, widely read in Guatemala, but for a time banned there, and recently ridiculed by right-wing thinkers in the United States because it has been placed into the Stanford University curriculum track called "Europe and the Americas."[1] Menchú's text offers a look into the life of this Mayan woman and her community. Some salient features of her story are these.

She has decided that in contemporary Guatemala it is not worth being a mother because, as her own mother told her when her siblings died, to be a mother is to know that half your children will die of malnutrition. Menchú lost a younger brother to illness when her family, accustomed to the cooler Guatemalan highlands, was forced, as many Mayans are, to work the hot coastal plantations. She also watched another brother be tortured to death by the Guatemalan military for his participation in labor union organizing. Her father, a member of an organized group of campesinos, participated in a January 1980 march on Guatemala City to demonstrate at the Spanish embassy for peasant rights, only to die there when Guatemalan security forces opened fire on the embassy.[2]

Most revealing, perhaps, is the story of her mother's torture and death by the military in the Guatemalan highlands. Menchú's mother organized women in many areas of the country other than her own, lecturing and strategizing with them at specially called meetings. She was particularly committed to harnessing poor women's anger and bitterness so as to channel them into hope-filled, organized resistance. Often this organizing could appear to be, and often was, in fact, supportive of the labor union activity in which Menchú's brother and father had been involved before their deaths. Such labor union activity regularly invited accusations of being "communist" as a prelude to torture and death.

The story of her mother is a painful one, told in wrenching detail in Menchú's autobiography. Menchú testifies to knowing in detail the fate that befell her mother. It included not just kidnapping on April 19, 1980, as she was returning from organizing work, but multiple rape, starvation, beatings, close confinement in a pit, facial and other bodily dismembering, revival by serum injections, more rape and torture, then being left still alive under a tree, guarded by a permanent sentry, to a slow death from wounds that festered with insects and larvae over days. "After that my mother was eaten by animals; by dogs, by all the *zopilotes* [vultures] there are around there, and other animals helped. They [the army] stayed for four months until they saw that not a bit of my mother was left, not even her bones, and then they went away."[3]

Hear now the voice of Fred Sherwood. The following interview with him occurred in September of 1980, the same year that Menchú's father, older brother, and mother were killed. Sherwood is an ex-president of the American Chamber of Commerce in Guatemala and a "leading spokesman for the North American business community."[4] In 1954 he flew with the CIA-backed air force that supported the overthrow of a Guatemalan government that had challenged United States business interests. Since that time, Sherwood's investments in Guatemala have grown with the nationwide encouragement of practices that allow foreign corporations to establish business in the country.

> *Sherwood*: I've got 350 [workers] and I saw the commies try to take it over. . . . They came in and, organizing from the outside, they hit us like a ton of bricks. . . . It was done to factories, [like] this Coca-Cola plant. It's commies! They talk about labor leaders, labor leaders. Sure they were labor leaders but they were commie labor leaders. Just like in my place. They came in and they fell on us, and honest to God, we were all on our knees. And they had it all organized. They met on Sunday. Sunday late, Sunday night.
>
> *Question*: They called the workers together?
>
> *Sherwood*: Well, just fourteen of them. And the workers were not to blame. They're just poor dumb guys that they got together

[and] convinced. . . . The workers were not unhappy. The
commies came in and made them unhappy. . . .

Question: The State Department says that the government hasn't been
doing enough to deal with the death squads. Do you think
that's reasonable?

Sherwood: Hell, no. Why should we do anything about the death squads?
They're bumping off the commies, our enemies. I'd give them
more power. Hell, I'd give them some cartridges if I could,
and everyone else would too. They're bumping off enemies,
which are also the enemies of the United States. Why should
we criticize them?

Question: Do all the U.S. businessmen feel the same way?

Sherwood: Of course they do. After all, they're trying to stop them from
doing business. That's all in the world the commies want to
do. They want to stop the economic growth. . . . It's a hell of
a lot of violence going around. No one approves of violence, I
don't. But if it's a question of them or me, I'd rather it be
them. . . . We grew up on the basis of private enterprise. Private ownership of capital. . . . But these peasants, they don't
know how to run something. Really, I'm not downbeating
them, but they don't. They're dumb, damn savages.[5]

DIMENSIONS OF THE ENCOUNTER

The violation of Rigoberta Menchú's family members and thousands
like them is an obvious cruelty. Sherwood's 1980 words, viewed in the
context of people's suffering, are callous and heartless. I cited at length
the Sherwood interview, within the context of Menchú's story, to set
the stage for understanding the effects of TNCs in Guatemala. The argument will *not* be that all U.S. businessmen who represent TNCs in
Guatemala manifest Sherwood's viewpoints, though many do so to
varying extents or, at least, benefit from others' support of such viewpoints. Nor will I argue that all U.S. investments, or all TNC investment activities in Third World countries, always have negative impacts.

The juxtaposition of Sherwood's and Menchú's discourses will
enable me to describe the multidimensional scene of political and social
disruption within which TNCs have worked in Guatemala, which they
often reinforce, and from which they regularly benefit. This will enable
me to discuss in greater detail, in the next section, a key dynamic of "abstraction," which is crucial to the institutionalized violence in which
TNCs are often complicit. This dynamic of abstraction, however, can
be identified only after treating some of the complexities of the Guate-

malan encounter. The complexities do not mitigate the brutality; they increase our awareness of its depth and recalcitrance.

Let me order these complexities by identifying five dimensions of the tension between Menchú's and Sherwood's discourses. Each dimension features a structured relation, and transnational corporations (TNCs) contribute negative dynamics in each relation.

Guatemalan Economy/North Atlantic Economies

The first structural relation operative in the encounter is that between the Guatemalan nation's economic system and those of North Atlantic states (e.g., Germany, Japan, the United States) which have greatest control over the global economy. This is the distortion of *imperialism*.[6] Sherwood's affiliation as ex-president of the American Chamber of Commerce in Guatemala points to this dimension. The main link of the Guatemalans' economy to the global one has been through their relation to U.S.-based firms. As one who flew in 1954 with the CIA-backed air force that overthrew Guatemala's only real democracy, Sherwood is especially emblematic of this dimension, because that U.S.-backed coup was clearly a move to protect the landholdings of the U.S.-based United Fruit Company.[7] Since that time Guatemala has become Central America's largest economy, with a diversified cosmopolitan elite and a thriving group of TNCs consisting of over 200 U.S. firms. In the 1980s, Guatemala became a $400-million U.S. export market with direct investments valued at $300 million.[8]

This "largest economy," is, by almost any study, seriously flawed, even while transnationals find Guatemala a "sound and profitable place to invest." Throughout the 1980s, an already serious problem of poverty skyrocketed so that now 87 percent live in poverty, and over two-thirds in "extreme poverty" (cannot secure a minimum diet).[9] Combining infant mortality, literacy rates, and life expectancy, one study concluded that Guatemala has the lowest "physical quality of life in Central America, third lowest in all of Latin America."[10] Especially after World War II, but even more after the 1954 coup, Guatemala has had to adapt to U.S. transnational business. Early in the 1960s, for example, U.S. AID worked hard to create an institution known as FIASA (Financiera Industrial y Agropecuaria, S.A.), designed to integrate U.S. business interests with those of Guatemalan business elites. Indeed, through a combination of strategies, FIASA veritably created the Guatemalan bourgeoisie.[11]

Time and again, the initiative and domination of the U.S. transnational firms was exercised. In the 1980s, Bank of America, then the most powerful firm in Guatemala,[12] used largely U.S. AID loans to organize a consortium of fifteen U.S. agribusiness companies (LAAD) that, in turn, arranged with sixty Guatemalan businesses a system that regularly benefited the TNCs, which subcontracted local farmers to do the growing while retaining control over marketing.[13]

Moreover, at present, it is only the TNCs and allied local elites who are living well in Guatemala. This is partly due to recent "structural adjustments" advocated by the United States and stipulated by the International Monetary Fund (IMF). These adjustments benefited TNCs and local elites but they subjected the country to traumas like successive currency devaluations, raised prices for basic goods and services to "control inflation," imposed wage ceilings and "disciplines," dismantled protectionist structures, privatized state-run enterprises, canceled state subsidies for social services, and slashed public spending.[14]

While these debilitating adjustments are imposed by an international body (the IMF), it should be remembered that the IMF is dominated by representatives from North Atlantic nations, and that the United States is the country on the IMF board which has the most voting power of any single nation.[15] In addition, IMF headquarters is in Washington, D.C., where day-to-day staff activities are overseen by a managing director who has always been a European, and a deputy director who has always been a U.S. citizen.[16] The "structural adjustments" made in Guatemala at its people's cost are arranged from the North.[17]

It should also be noted that this imperialist relation is facilitated by the fact that the community of U.S. and Guatemalan businessmen[18] is perhaps the most tightly integrated in Latin America. According to Allan Nairn, through the American Chamber of Commerce, which Sherwood headed, and its Guatemalan counterpart, the Amigos del Pais, these businessmen undertake joint ventures, intermarriages, and political projects.[19] There are Guatemalans in the American Chamber of Commerce and U.S. representatives in the Amigos del Pais. The tightly knit integration is evident, for example, in the following connections: Bank of America, which in the 1980s was exceeded only by the Guatemalan government as a source of agricultural capital, was the only institution in the country permitted to make loans over five million dollars, giving it the inside track on all major projects. It was also the only corporate member of the Amigos del Pais, an organization that has lobbied for U.S. weapons sales to Guatemala. Bank of America's clients have included Guatemala's most powerful landowners, industrialists, and military elite.[20]

Guatemalan Elite/Guatemalan Laborers

From the period of the Conquest, Guatemalan society has featured an exploitation of labor: various systems of slave labor and forced labor. This exploitation is still in place, not only in the low wages that most Guatemalans receive, but also because almost any effort at bettering the laborers' situations can result in repression and death. This is evident in my opening encounter: all three of Menchú's family members found death through links to labor-organizing efforts.

This structural relation is the *classist* one and features repression by Guatemalan elites vis-à-vis Guatemalan laborers. Sherwood's various comments about "controlling labor" and his general disdain for it display the U.S. business community's quiet condoning of the oppression. Some U.S. spokespersons use harsher language. One businessman replied to the question of "How to handle a bothersome labor leader?" as follows: "Shoot him or eliminate him. Assassinate him. Murder him. Whichever is most applicable."[21]

The quotes from Sherwood and his business colleagues suggest the acceptance, if not outright support, of the death squads in repressing labor organizing for better wages and conditions. Such quotes do not prove widespread involvement of U.S. TNCs in support of the death squads; the involvement is nevertheless significant because death-squad support is evident among high officials of the chamber of commerce organizations for both the United States and Guatemala. Amigos del Pais, the group of Guatemalan businessmen with U.S. members, has been shown to be one of the private sector groups financing the death squads.[22] The corporate/worker relation as mediated by death squads has a long history, as evidenced by the decade-long worker struggle with Coca-Cola.[23] U.S. TNCs were implicated in the death squads not only by Bank of America's presence as a corporate member of Amigos del Pais, but also by the number of private U.S. investors in Guatemala who routinely collaborated with and justified the activities of the death squads.[24] It is little wonder, then, that when the Reagan administration wished to express its support of U.S. market interests in Guatemala, its "transition team" visited Guatemala in 1980 and developed close ties with ultra-right military and civilians linked to the death squads. The ultra-right party, the MLN, which almost all Guatemalans know to be associated with the "White Hand" death squad, donated to the

Reagan presidential campaign, and Sandoval Alarcon ("Godfather of the death squads" in Guatemala) attended Reagan's inauguration.[25]

The Menchú family deaths were not the only labor-related ones occurring in a country dominated by elites with ties to TNC interests. In all, 110 labor leaders were assassinated in that same year of 1980— roughly two per week.[26] These are just labor leaders; unknown are the deaths of countless others active in labor organizing. These deaths signal an overall repression of labor practiced in many ways. Allan Nairn summarizes the situation well:

> Guatemalan and multinational manufacturers, responding to the recession by seeking to cut wage costs, have been laying off their work force *en masse*, then rehiring temporary workers who will again be laid off in a few months. In this way, companies such as Alimentos Kern, a Riviana Foods subsidiary and a notorious practitioner of the layoff gambit, keep their workers at the lowest salary grades, preventing them from moving up the pay scale provided by the national labor code, and discouraging union organization. Unlike more capital-intensive investments in countries such as Puerto Rico, manufacturing multinationals in Guatemala are concentrated in low wage, labor-intensive industries. They depend on the country's depressed wage structure—where daily industrial wages range from $2.50 to $4.50 for their profitability.[27]

By 1988–89, interests of TNCs and of local elites in the private sector were the preferred interests in Guatemala. Under structural adjustment policies put in place by the administration of Vinicio Cerezo (1986–90), laborers are still generally the most exploited, with their wages held down, but not the prices.

Guatemalan Elite/Mayan Majority

The first two dimensions of the Guatemalan encounter with TNCs consist of imperialist and classist structural relations. Our opening event of violation, however, also harbors a dimension of *racism*. In Guatemala, as often elsewhere, suffering by class exploitation is compounded by an *ethnic oppression* inflicted on the Mayan people, who feature some twenty-two language groups and make up 55–60 percent of the total Guatemalan population. The ethnic discrimination was signaled in my opening encounter by the fact that those killed were Quiche Mayan, and also by businessman Sherwood's frequent characterization of laborers as "savages." Sherwood, like many Guatemalan elites, draws on ethnic oppression to disparage Mayans already repressed by class exploitation. Ethnic oppression, as compounding class exploitation, is registered by very tangible signals. By all indicators (life expectancy, infant mortality, malnutrition, illiteracy), statistics for the Mayan majority are far worse than for the *ladino* elite.[28] Since colonial times, the Mayans have had as their principal struggle the recovery of their land and resistance to the kinds of further evictions and expropriations that also have continued throughout the 1980s.

It should also be noted that the Guatemalan economy has been built upon coerced labor, but especially "forced *Indian* labor at the service of *criollo* and *ladino* landowners."[29] To this day, elites and the military who support them take advantage of the Mayans' harsh living conditions in poorer rural areas in order to coax or coerce them into providing cheap labor.[30]

It is this labor pool that, in part, makes Guatemala such a blue-chip investment for TNCs. In their advertising and expectations, the TNCs and allied elites rarely portray the Mayans as more than a "rich cultural heritage" or as major attraction for tourists. Of primary interest to the corporate culture is the "civilizing" of Mayans from their primitiveness, from their status as what Sherwood called "savages." This often means little more than enlisting them as laborers in growing cash crops, such as broccoli, for export. There is little appreciation for the cultural heritage of Mayan peoples when it comes to corporate development. In 1988, for example, the U.S. government embassy was helping to support the enlistment of Mayans to raise cash crops for export. A chief economic officer at the embassy, completely ignorant of the mythological, cultural, and survival value of corn and bean production for the Mayans,[31] concluded his remarks, "After all, any damn fool can grow corn and beans."

Corporate Power/Guatemalan Women

The intensity and viciousness of the violation of Menchú's mother signals another dimension that can best be described as corporate power functioning in opposition to Guatemalan women's lives. As in much of the Third World, the issue of gender is just beginning to be theorized in relation to class.[32] We can note here the dynamics of *sexism* in the encounter. Statistics that allow visibility to women's plight are hard to come by, but it is increasingly clear that in Guatemala in the 1980s, the number of women grew significantly as a percentage of the openly unemployed and underemployed.[33] In the better-paying industrial sector, men are greatly favored over women.[34] In the newer, "cheap labor" assembly plants (the *maquiladoras*), which seek unskilled workers to assemble parts of products that are finished elsewhere, women workers are often preferred "since their labor is cheaper, more dispensable."[35] TNCs and U.S. firms have expended great effort to create these low-cost assembly plants and to exploit cheap labor. In 1989, 95 percent of workers in textile *maquiladoras* were women, earning about 5 percent of what textile workers earn in the United States for comparable work.[36]

Susanne Jonas summarizes these and other aspects of women's situations in contemporary Guatemala: "There has been a decline in women's participation in productive sectors of the economy; the most modern and 'most capitalist' sectors (export agriculture and industry) are those where women have had least access to jobs."[37] Laurel Bossen stresses that "Both structurally and culturally, capitalism has brought about a redivision of labor which has relatively penalized women."[38] Add to this the cultural and psychological stress brought on by IMF- and U.S.-initiated "structural adjustment" policies of the 1990s (which weigh most heavily upon women, studies show)[39] and then we can understand why Menchú's mother would seek to respond to the "anger and bitterness" of Guatemalan women,[40] and why her death can serve as a concrete symbol of corporate wealth's antipathy to women's health and well-being.

Corporate Politics/Guatemalan Land

When corporate power works disadvantage and death for the Guatemalan poor—especially Mayans and acutely for women—can we overlook the obvious fact that vicious corporate politics entails the spilling of human blood upon Guatemalan land? Menchú's mother—left on the ground, tied to a tree, violated repeatedly on the land—symbolizes another dimension of this violative encounter: the blight upon Guatemalan land. In this, too, corporate power is implicated. *Environmental destruction*, to which I now turn, is bound up with the whole genocidal period of which the Menchú deaths were a part.

By the time of the Menchú family deaths, Guatemala's army itself had been converted into a veritable death squad. The economic devastation had swelled the guerrilla movements among Mayans and the poor, prompting the government's military to move against any and all suspected of supporting subversives. The land's villages and populations were bombarded and sent into upheaval. The government's tactics in the early 1980s and at intervals throughout the 1980s into the 1990s included techniques of depopulation, "scorched-earth" burnings, massacres of whole village populations, and massive forced relocations. Jonas summarizes:

> Entire sectors of the population (overwhelmingly Indians) became military targets, leading many scholars (as well as the U.N. and Catholic Church authorities) to identify these policies as genocidal. Falla called it genocide "in the strict sense," because it involved massacres of the elderly and children who did not yet have the use of reason and therefore could not be considered guerilla collaborators. The statistics are staggering: Over 440 villages were entirely destroyed, well over 100,000 civilians were killed or "disappeared" (some estimates, including those of top church officials, range up to 150,000); there were over 1 million displaced persons (1 million internal refugees), up to 200,000 refugees in Mexico.[41]

It is more than rhetorical flourish, therefore, to sum up this counterinsurgency campaign as a "scorched-earth" strategy. The blood of the assassinated is associated with a blight upon the land. Confirming the association is the fact that during its counterinsurgency campaign the military intentionally destroyed highlands and jungles, often burning forests to prevent guerrillas and refugees from finding cover.[42] Guatemala's land and environment paid an extraordinary cost in irreversible devastation; the devastation even modified patterns of climate and rainfall.[43]

If we recall the systemic connections between the interests of Guatemalan elites and U.S.-based TNCs, and that the military and other security forces constitute a diversified death squad for corporate cultural elites, then transnational corporate culture is implicated in the violation of those bloodied on Guatemalan land and in the environmental devastation of that land. The link between transnational corporate culture and the "scorched-earth" destruction is even more direct if we recall the extent to which U.S. corporate technology, imported either from the U.S. government or from its allies, has equipped the military and security forces. Further, to the extent that corporate cultures, as in the case of Bank of America, have granted loans to military officers to buy up large tracts of land areas for environmentally destructive development, TNC corporate culture is also implicated in environmental abuse.

In sum, there is little, if any, indication that voices within TNC culture were raised in outcry over the impact of their policies. There were few signs that there was much interest in finding out about possible connections to destruction. Surely there was no concerted movement to use TNCs' corporate and international power to halt the devastation. Fred

Sherwood's callous words might well be taken as speaking for TNCs in the 1980s: "It's a hell of a lot of violence going around. No one approves of violence, I don't. But if its a question of them or me, I'd rather it be them."

INSTITUTIONALIZED VIOLENCE AS ABSTRACTION

Transnational corporations embody a dynamic of "abstraction," which is crucial to each of the dimensions mentioned above. I here want to interpret institutionalized violence as "abstraction" because this notion enables us to articulate connections between the various distortions — not only between international imperialism and local class exploitation, but also between those and gender injustice, ethnic oppression, and environmental destruction. "Abstraction" then also becomes crucial for understanding the complex working of institutionalized violence on the way to envisioning, theorizing, and mobilizing Christian movements of emancipation that might create sustained structures of freedom from that violence.

The TNC depends on abstraction. I will distinguish, within a dialectic of abstraction, a *distancing* function and a *destructive* function. The distancing function has been discussed by a number of theorists, notably Karl Marx. More recently, Joel Kovel has identified it as "the nuclear mental operation of Westerners in its purest form." By means of this mental operation, "nature, which had been experienced in previous eras as an organic and direct unity, is abstracted and made remote from [people]."[44] Especially in the exchange economies of Western cultures, this distancing from nature, from the material, is strikingly evident in the development of money:

> Money itself has become progressively more abstract as the logos of the West has worked itself out in the modern era. The concept of money began as a gift of something valued in itself, and passed through a stage in which valued objects were bartered for each other. Soon it was focused onto objects useless in themselves, though still concrete; then it became more abstract, until shells, stones, gold, coin and paper have led to cheques and credit cards. Soon, as the rationalization reaches its end state, it will become pure number.[45]

The TNC traffics, often, in something like pure number, especially since the 1973 breakdown of the Bretton Woods agreement when money was "dematerialized," meaning it lacks a formal link to precious metals or to any other tangible commodity. As David Harvey notes in *The Condition of Postmodernity*:

The world has come to rely, for the first time in its history, upon immaterial forms of money—i.e., money of account assessed qualitatively in numbers of some designated currency. Exchange rates between the different currencies of the world have also become extremely volatile. Fortunes could be lost or made simply by holding the right currency during the right phases.[46]

This has given rise to what is now frequently termed "paper entrepreneurialism," profit making through creative accounting. In this, the transnational corporation has extraordinary power to excel, monitoring international markets and political conditions so that they can generate wealth from shifting currency values or interest rates, or from corporate raiding and asset stripping of other corporations.[47]

What better emblem of the TNCs' distancing function of abstraction than the physical locating of its bureaucratic paperwork in the skyscrapers of major cities, with very little face-to-face exchange with people in rural areas or urban barrios.

Intertwined with the distancing function, however, is the *destructive* function. Economic systems of pure number recycle abstract representations while "disgorging an endless supply of material things which, though more valued, are progressively less enjoyed."[48] The mere use of number for exchange purposes is not the problem, but rather the tendency of exchange transactions to be made according to abstract numbers that are not calibrated with knowledge of the cultural-material conditions within which real people live. In the case of the TNCs, therefore, their distance from people's cultural-material existence, in corporate cultures of abstracted exchange, deprives the distanced ones of material goods needed for survival. Conceivably, and this is often claimed by TNC executives,[49] TNCs might convey material goods and resources to those needing them. Such positive results do occasionally take place. There are benefits resulting from TNCs in Third World regions.[50] But empirical studies from Guatemala and elsewhere continue to show the generally negative impact of the TNCs,[51] and even a resistance by TNCs and supporting multilateral organizations, like the IMF and World Bank, even to care enough to monitor the impact of their economic decisions.[52]

The institutionalized violence of TNCs spins out of these functions of abstraction. Fascinated by science, the mystique of production, and "creative accounting," and fueled by desire for profit and acquisition, TNC cultures practice a seeming "hatred of nature," of the material—even while their individual members often sing praise to its beauties.[53]

The distancing and destructive functions form corporate culture's dialectical power of abstraction, and are evident in the practice and concrete legacies of TNC culture. Not only is there an abstraction from the poor (a destructive remoteness from them) operative in international imperialist classism and in local classisms, but the dialectic of abstraction is also at work in the other dimensions I discussed above.

There is, for example, an abstraction from the culturally different, such as the Mayans of Guatemala. Destructive remoteness from them means TNC culture tends toward a cultural racism. It is not only out of touch with Mayans' material needs and contributions, but it also knows little or nothing about Mayan worldviews, its alternative values, its own ways of mobilizing production and reproduction.[54]

It is also appropriate to speak of abstraction in the sexist distortion pertaining to women. Indeed, by reference to the murder and torture of Rigoberta Menchú's mother, and to the other women and mothers in Guatemala who bear the highest maternal mortality rate in Central America,[55] we can say that the TNCs' distancing from women and women's needs has accompanying destructive effects, thus implicating TNCs in a "matricidal" dynamic.[56]

Finally, there is abstraction, a destructive remoteness, from the land. The distance of TNCs from land issues and from people of the land, which also has led to environmental destruction, has already been referred to in the case of Guatemala. As Kovel puts it, the distancing and destructive dialectic tends to make land and its inhabitants into "an inert mass whose inner forms are to be pulverized into property." He continues:

> Land is not really a commodity, since it was not made by [people], but made them instead. Yet, in making it into a commodity from which endless wealth can be extracted, [people] have vented such aggressive energy upon it as to bring nature into abject submission. The submission is deceptive, since, as we are beginning to learn, nature so traduced by technology has its ways of recoiling.[57]

When nature does so recoil, then ultimately the members of corporate cultures are themselves often caught up in the vortex of institutionalized violence. Remoteness and isolation from humanity's cultural-material matrix, and from land and nature, take a toll upon those who abstract, as well as those from whom corporate powers abstract. In particular, the dissociation, numbing, and doubling that Robert Jay Lifton and others have discerned in corporate cultures—especially among engineers of nuclear weaponry—have a destructive impact on corporate actors themselves. The complex "corporate evil" spun out by the whirl of the distance/destroy dialectic of abstraction thus also catches up corporate oppressors themselves in its oppressive force. It should again be stressed, when discussing TNCs as implicated in a "corporate evil," that Third World countries themselves often seek to attract TNCs to ensure increases in flows of foreign investment.[58] Because of this and other analyses of TNCs in the global economy, there is great debate among political economists about TNCs based in wealthier "home" countries. TNCs have their advocates in these debates, their vigorous critics, and then also their so-called fairer evaluators, who seek to acknowledge the possibilities of both beneficial and harmful consequences for host countries.[59]

The political, economic, and social configuration of factors in Guatemala, in which TNCs have been discussed in this chapter, clearly supports the more negative reading. Note, however, the nature of the argument. The argument is *not* that all TNCs and their impacts are negative, but that they must be resisted insofar as they participate in the negative dynamic of abstraction. This may result in conclusions that the majority of TNC impacts are negative, for those studies of TNCs impacts that also analyze the values by which we label impacts "negative" or "positive" have made some of the strongest arguments for the negative reading. Archibald Alexander and Robert Swinth, for example, conclude their own careful study by warning that from the perspective of commitments to host countries' experiences of "peace, economic well-being, social justice, ecological balance, and positive identity," increases of TNC penetration into Third World host countries will have an increasingly unfavorable impact.[60] Such warnings can be heard full force, without overstatements that would overlook the positive contributions. What is crucial, however, is the dynamics of abstraction that pervades institutionalized violence of the TNCs.

UNLEASHING THE "THIRD SYSTEM": THE CONTRIBUTION OF CHRISTIAN MOVEMENTS

The pervasive institutionalized violence that TNCs often embody can work numbing despair once it is exposed and lamented. As powerful as this structural violence is, however, there do exist communities and dynamics of resistance and hope. In spite of the despair and ennui that knowledge of such violence can breed, in this final section I think in reliance upon the presence of such resistance and hope.[61]

Movements and the "Third System"

In considering the present global political situation, Richard Falk has distinguished three systems of political action. The "first system" is what this essay has characterized as diversified institutionalized violence. It is the system of power in governing structures of territorial states:

> in short, the state system, including its supporting infrastructure of corporations, banks, media; a system that is hierarchical, fragmented and in which war and violence are accepted as discretionary options for power-wielders and in which armies, weapons, police and military doctrines play a crucial role within and among states.[62]

A "second system" of power consists of the United Nations and various "regional international institutions." Falk sees this as basically an extension of the first system with only a nominal verbal mandate, decrying first-system violence, lessening hierarchy and fragmentation.

Notable achievements of the second system rarely occur without linkages to a third system. This is a system of power consisting of "people acting individually or collectively through social movements, voluntary institutions, associations, including churches and labor unions. . . . " It is the primary embodiment of new values, demands, and visions. Hence, it can be co-opted, subverted, and repressed by the first system (or sometimes by the second system, too).[63]

Christian movements are obviously not the only contributors to this third system; but they, like others in the system, make their contribution by prompting the second-system agents into normative initiatives with structural consequences. Christian movements' contributions may, as Falk suggests of the third system generally, often be latent, potential, or symbolic, but precisely as such they can be catalysts and tools for needed social change.[64]

In the following two subsections, I present the Christian movement as contributing a distinctive mythos of emancipation, and a set of strategic practices. I emphasize that for the third system that needs to be unleashed against TNC institutionalized violence, it will need to be a coalition of diverse religious and nonreligious communities. In fact, religious communities in North Atlantic contexts may often *not* be the most vital contributors, or, at least, they will require the goading of other contributors in the third system. If I here discuss the contribution of Christian movements, I do so to clarify the nature of that contribution for Christians, and to initiate, from the side of Christian vision, a coalition-building dialogue with other third-system practitioners.

A Mythos of Reconciliatory Emancipation

Christian movements are first and foremost movements for emancipation. They are a distinctive kind of freedom-making movement. To be sure, we know well how from its earliest times, especially when consolidated with Constantinian rule, Christianity has served up obstacles to freedom. It has licensed repression, implemented inquisitional terror, and still reinforces systems of the worst sort with the power of its religious myth and ritual.[65] The use of Christian language and cult in South Africa is a clear recent example.[66]

In its formative years, however, when Christianity is perhaps best described as the "Jesus movement" or "early Christian movement," the primary value was one of emancipation and liberation—in the senses of both *from* every kind of oppressive dynamic and also *to*, or *into*, structured communities that sustain emancipation. As also a Jewish movement, it drew from the Exodus and prophetic traditions a stress on a kind of freedom making, which, though worked by divine power, was nevertheless historical and human. Moreover, this movement of emancipation grew in the structurally dangerous time of imperial Roman domination and in a territory under especially ruthless, religiopolitical Hasmonean and Herodian rule.

There are, of course, the often-mentioned limits to how politically revolutionary one can present the historical Jesus movement. As Richard Horsley has emphasized, however, these constraints are no license for Christian scholars to screen out the political and emancipatory nature of the movement. Horsley well summarizes Jesus' position and the spirit of the emancipatory movement:

> Jesus would appear to have believed that God had already begun the political revolution even though it was hardly very far along. But in the confidence that it was underway, it was his calling to proceed with the *social revolution* thus made possible by God's rule, to begin the transformation of social relations in anticipation of the completion of the political revolution.[67]

Proceeding with the social revolution, therefore, it was fueled not only by the fact of oppression, but also by the sense that a sacrally enacted political revolution was already in motion. With this kind of fusion of grace and politics, the early Christian movement featured a unity of

spirituality and human action. The social revolution meant the thriving
of the movement especially among local peasant cultures and others suffering double taxation (local and imperial), increasing indebtedness,
and loss of land. At times, the movement exacerbated class conflict. It
moreover sought renewal through embodiment of a "new family." In
rejecting rank and prestige, its communal aims were more egalitarian,
seeking to be "an extended, non-patriarchal 'family' of 'siblings.' "[68]
Based on these many dimensions of the early movement, the Christian
movement may be understood as a multidimensional movement of
emancipation and has been interpreted as such by contemporary Christian activists and thinkers.

The key qualifier here is signaled by this very word, "multidimen-
sionality." Without forfeiting the primacy of its emancipation motif, it
seeks to unify a manifold of emancipatory needs. In this sense its emancipatory interest is "reconciliatory," that is, it seeks to make unity along
with, or in the wake of, making freedom from oppression. In the
present setting, this would mean insisting on emancipation that orches-
trates the claims of different groups (victims of class exploitation *and*
ethnic oppression, *and* gender injustice *and* homophobia and heterosexism, etc.). The reconciliatory qualifier also means that Christian
emancipatory action ultimately aims at a community that includes even
the enemy-oppressor. Thus, as in the liberation theology of Peruvian
Gustavo Gutiérrez, a "universality of Christian love" is extended even to
the adversary. Such "love of the enemy" is compatible with both a preferential option for the poorest and most oppressed, and with a sustained adversarial stance toward the enemy.[69]

Enough has been said of the nature of the Christian movement's
mythos of reconciliatory emancipation to enable an identification of the
strategic practices mandated by the crises of corporate culture's institutionalized violence. For theologians, the relevant point is this: the
praxis of Christian movements arises within an emancipative mythos
that envisions sacral power as having already set in motion the political
revolution that is capable of freeing Third World peoples from the institutionalized violence often embodied in the TNCs and other parts of
the "first system." It remains now to identify certain strategic practices
in which representatives of the Christian movement might now participate to embody a revolutionary praxis of reconciliatory emancipation.
The mythos of reconciliatory emancipation does not romanticize any
human structure or movement; but it does foster particular values and
hopes needed for mobilizing strategies of resistance and restructuring.

Against Abstraction: Four Strategic Practices

When considering the institutionalized violence of corporate culture, the practices of Christian movements especially need to move against and model alternatives to the distancing and destructive functions of abstraction. In this regard, four kinds of practice are strategic. They constitute part of Christian movements' contribution to unleashing the third system of coalitional forces needed for resisting first-system destruction.

First, Christian movements entail the local, on-site organizing of people in distress. There is enormous empowerment for resistance and hope just in this organizing, which hears the cries of specific people in need and then brings them together. The hearing and the gathering are significant even without considering the also necessary agendas that may later emerge.

I use the term *organizing* intentionally, to suggest an effort at the grassroots level that structures relations among the oppressed. In Third World settings, those most victimized by structural adjustment policies or TNC firm actions do precisely this: they gather together and organize, not only to lament together but also to strategize for survival and change. U.S. Christians need to organize among populations on North American terrain those whose cries of distress can be linked to abusive TNC policies. A prime example here might be those without health insurance coverage who, through organizing, can begin to see the links between their deprivation and the exploitative practices of medical technology corporations.

By the stress on locality, grassroots, and the concrete organizing of local groups, the Christian movement begins to construct a countervailing dynamic to corporate abstraction. The emphasis on the local is a dynamic resisting the remoteness and distancing function of abstraction in institutionalized violence. Christian movements cannot simply engage in high-level corporate policies to resist institutionalized violence. Such macrolevel policy-making is essential, as I will suggest below. But without redressing the distancing function of corporate remoteness, substantial change will be less likely to occur; or, at least, less will be known about which "high-level" changes are needed for the cultural-material needs of the people "below."

Second, Christian movements must nurture, move out from, and return to distinctive kinds of social interaction: communities of the face. As applied to Christian movements, this phrase comes from the philosophy of Jewish thinker Emmanuel Levinas through Christian theologian Edward Farley. These are communities featuring a kind of embodied relationality that constantly rehearses its members, at the level of the concrete, in a sense of "species-being" (awareness of "the universal face") and in a sense of the unsubstitutable distinctiveness of each being (awareness of "the particular face"). Both the more universal reminder and the particular presentation are developed from Levinas's meditations on experiencing the face in relation. The universalizing impetus emerges from the fact that the face always points beyond regional loyalties and obligations, and thus communities that heed the face are oriented to the species as a whole, indeed to all life forms.[70] The face, however, has a special particularizing power, too. "It is the 'infinitely strange' and 'mysterious presence' of something that always contests my projecting meanings of it. . . ."[71] Thus, communities of the face inspire at once a universal sense or "species consciousness,"[72] but also a sense of each individual's particularity. Though Christian traditions have regularly compromised with, had their ideals kidnapped by, proponents of regional loyalties, Christian movements taking their cue from the reconciliatory emancipation of the Christian movement manifest the universal and particular senses of the face. The species consciousness is crucial for effecting a collective emancipation from structural evil and institutionalized violence, while the sense of the particular in the face is needed for developing that "reconciliatory" posture that acknowledges the many different types of emancipation needed, and seeks to orchestrate their particular, often conflicting, claims.

Perhaps a concrete example of the power in communities of the face can be taken from reflection on the practices of interrogation and torture. Victims frequently report (among them Jennifer Casolo, a U.S. citizen not tortured but interrogated and threatened in El Salvador in 1989) that wielders of intimidation often prefer their victims blindfolded, their faces somehow obscured. This is because face-to-face encounter or eye contact tends to break down the dehumanizing process. Is it any wonder, then, also that members of corporate cultures in Third World areas rarely cultivate sustained, face-to-face contact with the rural or barrio poor? In the course of her own interrogation, Casolo connived to get her interrogator to remove her blindfold and this mitigated the harshness of the interrogation. Christian movements have as a second strategic practice, then, this search to be in relation as communities of the face, nurturing face-to-face contact, indeed celebrating this contact. As such, they are forging a hedge against the distancing and destructive functions of abstraction in which the TNCs and institutionalized violence excel.

Third, Christian movements cannot avoid the strategic practice of global networking and institutional formation. Crucial as are the above two strategic practices for resisting and providing communal alternatives, especially to the "distancing function" of institutionalized violence, the global structures of transnational corporate culture will not be halted without countervailing structures of international scope and complexity. Global corporate culture has achieved a systemic power that also has the "destructive function," and this requires a countervailing, structuring response. With theologian Friedrich Schleiermacher of the nineteenth century, we might emphasize today that a "corporate evil" requires acknowledging and activating a "corporate grace,"[73] and this requires global networking and institutional formation.

Throughout the Third World today is evidence that locally organized modes of Christian movement and communities of the face (for example, "base ecclesial communities") are engaged in global networking now, to establish working connections with Christians suffering exploitation by corporate cultures on all continents.[74]

These efforts are still largely on the level of theological discourse. Christian movements still need to embody themselves in struggles supporting political-structural transformation. Many Third World countries and thinkers are now questioning second-system correctives to TNCs, such as the voluntary code of conduct sponsored by the United Nations. This voluntary code of conduct for regulating TNC practices leaves Third World countries in little better position than before the code.[75]

Hence, meaningful structural resistance to TNC culture requires the formation of "Third World only" organizations (sectoral, subregional, regional, interregional) for controlling the TNCs.[76] This entails an enormously complex task of institutional construction. Of course, Christian movements are themselves not the locus of such institutional arrangements, but if such movements take resistance seriously they need to support and incarnate themselves to some degree in such efforts.

For U.S. Christians, the special challenge of this strategic practice of global networking and institutional formation is no less demanding. There already exist significant organized resistances. The World Council of Churches and various ecclesiastical denominations have, for example, denounced the merely voluntary codes of conduct, have called for lobbying and pressuring of corporation shareholders, denouncing oppressive corporate policies, organizing boycotts of corporation products, etc.[77]

All these are important, but what really needs doing and what many in the established churches of the North are often reluctant to do is to work for radical structural changes in the present system of the global economy. Christian movements committed to participating in the emergence of a "corporate grace" to counter corporate institutionalized violence would do well to seek alliance with any of the following exemplary kinds of organizations working for radical structural transformation.

1. There are a number of environmental groups which have launched major campaigns, several of which have contributed tangibly to the education of development groups, and have addressed the World Bank and the IMF on the entrenchment of poverty around the world. They have also very effectively used the media, computer technology, and political processes to challenge the power of international monetary organizations and multinational corporations.[78]

2. In addition to environmental groups, there are other nongovernmental organizations (NGOs) working throughout North Atlantic states, which have carried on a variety of important third-system operations. Exemplary have been the efforts of the Non-Governmental Liaison Service (NGLS, New York and Geneva) to monitor IMF and World Bank policies, to set up conferences simultaneous to IMF and World Bank annual meetings, and to pressure especially U.S. policymaking members of these organizations. Very significantly, the NGO movement has also been lobbying for legislation that directs the U.S. executive director of the IMF to promote staff and policies that make the board aware of the social and environmental implications of its policies.

3. Another kind of effort, perhaps a most important one, requires support of Christian movements. Since 1968, the World Order Models Project has been explaining the need for global structural change. Its recent work has focused on a Global Civilization Project (GCP) that seeks to mobilize scholars and activists of all levels and from different countries (the United States, the United Kingdom, Russia, Yugoslavia, Portugal, the Philippines, India, Japan, Egypt, and others). The effort is to organize a global civil society which, contrary to abstracting dynamics of destructive corporate culture, seeks a "rooted international society that emphasizes its normative moorings in law and human rights, and its practical urgency in relation to general peace and ecological sustainability."[79] The aim of the project is a "global constitutionalism" that seeks a reconstruction of international life by building international institutions, frameworks of legal rights and duties of states, and transna-

tional assemblages of third-system actors and groups to form an international "democratic base" for such global constitutionalism. These efforts require long-term international organizing. This is an effort involving diverse communities, many with no connections to religious groups. I suggest that for those in Christian movements, only this kind of effort ultimately allows a fulfillment of a kind of "corporate grace" able to heal the destruction wrought by corporate evil. Such efforts in global constitutionalism need to become a strategic practice of Christian movements.

4. Finally, strategic practices for global justice include a *celebration of the peoples' arts*. Strategic practices are notorious for fostering burnout, using up volunteers, and draining vision. That which sustains a dynamic Christian movement, perhaps any movement, is also a spirit of celebration and symbolic vision.

Christian movements may have a fundamental contribution to make to efforts to resist corporate cultures, because of their mythos of reconciliatory emancipation, and their rituals and liturgies of worship—sacred art forms, we might say, from which practice drinks from visionary power. Christian communities, however, even if they have a lively liturgical tradition—and often in North Atlantic Christendom they do not[80]—have regularly allowed their liturgies and art forms to become ecclesiocentric sedimentations that are abstracted from people in struggle. Such ecclesiocentric abstraction only reinforces the political-economic abstraction of corporate culture.

Christian movements in the United States need to find their way into relation with the arts of people engaged in struggle. This may mean including those art forms somehow in the regular meetings of Christian communities. More significantly, however, it may mean that representatives in Christian movements lead their communities into artistic movements already mobilized for structural change. This may mean participation of Christian movements in local arts and crafts, in music concerts, and in alliance especially with popular music developments which have the potential for yoking youth's desire in music to issues of structural change. Christian movements honor their own defining impulses when they see themselves in alliance with musicians—whether Public Enemy rapping that today "the Ku Klux Klan wears a three-piece suit," Bonnie Raitt giving concert proceeds to battered women's shelters, Jackson Browne singing against U.S. corporation and government involvement in Central America drug running, Bruce Springsteen saying "No thanks, mister" to Lee Iacocca's eight-million-dollar offer to buy his "Born in the U.S.A." song for Chrysler Corpo-

ration commercials and then singing for the Christic Institute instead,
Neil Young mocking the capitalism of the corporate-controlled music
channel MTV, or Michael Stipe of REM lecturing from the stage about
limitations in NBC's reporting because of its connection to the General
Electric Company. Whether we think of these musicians in the United
States or Chinese rock star Cui Jian in the 1980s, Chilean folksinger
Victor Jara of the 1970s, the experimental absurdist rock of *The Plastic
People* in Czechoslovakia of 1976, of Thomas Mapfumo's *chimurenga*
music in the Zimbabwe revolution or the musical-theatrical group Dos
Que Tres in Guatemala of 1989—in all these contexts popular music
played a key role in destabilizing tyrannies and repressive systems.[81]

Not only music, but all the arts are resources for the Christian movement and the unleashing of the third system generally. Maybe this is
especially true of poetry, about which Audre Lorde has said, "Poetry is
not a luxury, it is a vital necessity of our existence. It forms the quality
of the light from which we predicate our hopes and dreams toward survival and change, first made into language, then into idea, then into
more tangible action."[82]

Thus, I close with words from the Guatemalan poet Otto René
Castillo, who in 1967, along with his *compañera*, Nora Paiz, was captured, tied to a tree, tortured, and burned alive in Guatemala.[83] His
voice:

> From
> my bitter darkness
> I go beyond
> my own hard times
> and I see
> at the end of the line
> happy children!
> only happy!
> they appear
> they rise
> like a sun of butterflies
> after the tropical cloud-burst.
>
> I'm happy for the children
> of the world to come
> and I proclaim it
> at the top of my lungs,
> full of universal rejoicing.[84]

Part Three
Gender, Politics, and Personal Identity

8

KEEPING A CLEAN HOUSE WILL NOT KEEP A MAN AT HOME

An Unctuous Womanist Rhetoric of Justice

Emilie M. Townes

*M*y grandmother was a woman of plain talk and action. She loved the Lord, she loved her church, she loved her family, and she loved her people. Sometimes her people made her weary, but she never could give up on the people that made up the black section of Southern Pines, North Carolina.

Miss Nora lived to be eighty years old. And for a lifetime she has been teaching me: that you have responsibilities for yourself, you have responsibilities to your kin, you have responsibilities to your people, and only a fool would try to go it alone. What Miss Nora and Miss Rosie and Miss Montez and Cousin Willie Mae and Mrs. Hemphill and Mrs. Waddell didn't teach me, my parents and the other fathers and mothers who helped raise me took on as their responsibility.

Learn to learn; and when somebody or something makes you uncomfortable—trust the "dis-ease" and watch them or it closely. You have a right to question, you have a right to your dignity. You are a child of worth because you are a child of God.

I have learned to look at life as not only a joy and a blessing, but as a strategy. A strategy not to reify what is, but to challenge and push for what can be. To explore the rock principles of my faith and the faith of my ancestors and to allow my faith to guide me as much, if not more, than my intellect.

I begin with the experiences of the women—African-American women—who as a people constantly defy the norm by our very existence. Who as a people challenge dominant ethics by continuing to draw their breath and create future generations. Who challenge the notion of freedom and a range of choices being available to all. Black folk live a different life than the life so valued by dominant ethics. Ethical values from a tradition that carries within it the trickster, Brer Rabbit, haints, ghosts, voodoo, High John de Conqueror, and Jesus cannot be identical with the values of white society and its plantations, Puritans, witch trials, monopoly capitalism, multinational corporations, and the Christ.

Black women have been called matriarchs, sapphires, and castrators. This is due, in large measure, to the active role many black women have played in the support of children, husbands, and black society. Each of these groups has *assumed* black women's capabilities. This differs considerably from where the majority of white feminists begin. Historically, white culture has not assumed that white women were capable — capable of anything other than the roles of wife, mother, and housekeeper. None of these roles is bad in the abstract, but when women are confined or forced into those roles rather than free to choose those roles, oppression has begun.

A MEMORY OF TRAGEDY AND TRIUMPH

The challenge for the African-American woman as a moral agent is to create and then articulate a positive moral standard that critiques the elitism of dominant ethics at its oppressive core and is relevant for the African-American community and the larger society. From this tradition of tragedy and triumph, I turn to the writings of Mrs. Gertrude E. H. Bustill Mossell (1855–1948). Mossell wrote under the initials of her husband, Dr. Nathan Francis Mossell, but maintained a radical witness for justice and black women's image in the late nineteenth-century and early twentieth-century United States. She provides a valuable resource for contemporary Christian womanist reflection on the nature of justice and social rhetoric.

In *The Work of the Afro-American Woman* (1908), Mossell advocated that the home should be founded on right principles, morality, Christian living, heredity, and environment that promise good for the future. In this superb work, Mossell adroitly handled the social location of women in African-American culture while advocating for a wider range of possibilities for male and female interaction and roles. She offered her wisdom to newly married women and exhorted white women to join African-American women in a joint quest for the social and moral uplift of black people.

Mossell, the daughter of black Quakers who later became Presbyterians, was influenced by black evangelical Christianity and its demand for a disciplined person and a moral life-style. This religious experience enabled Mossell to balance competing demands and roles. In this extended mother-daughter dialogue, Mossell displays the womanist spirit of care and concern for self and for her people. She balances her strong political views, which point to justice, with an evangelical appeal to the Spirit and Christian values.

In the first chapter of *The Work*, Mossell presented a litany of witnesses to the active and integral role black women played in the uplift of the race. The fields of education, literature, journalism, medicine, law, religion, government, the World's Fair, business, the military, office workers, inventors, the arts, philanthropy, homekeepers, and seamstresses became a resounding yes to the work of black women. Mossell listed no fewer than 200 women, spanning the womanish stance of Ida B. Wells-Barnett to the revolutionary war soldier Deborah Gannet. These women formed a monument to the work black women did and could perform in the twin tasks of the uplift of the race and the advancement of women.

Mossell had the exceptional ability to provide piercing womanish social commentary while maintaining her role as wife and mother. She began her book with an optimistic spirit—that emancipation, higher education for women, and women's suffrage engendered a spirit of uplift for African-American women and the individual woman that had not been a feature on the U.S. scene. She was crystal clear in her advocacy for black women:

> The women of this race have always been industrious, however much the traducers of the race may attempt to make it appear otherwise. . . . The women of this race have been industrious but it is only in late years, that they have reaped the fruits of their own industry.[1]

Active nineteenth-century African-American churchwomen had a deep, personal relationship with God, Jesus, and salvation. The piety of these women was grounded in personal and social transformation to effect salvation. The reality of their religious and moral lives stands in stark contrast to the defamers' image or stereotype of African-American women as licentious, wanton, illiterate, or ever-smiling mammy.

Mossell took image and reality and crafted a new ideal. She redefined the nature and role of the mammy as positive (although somewhat romantic to contemporary ears). Rather than view her as a negative stereotype, Mossell's black woman eschewed individual success and showed:

> The marvellous loving kindness and patience that is recorded of the native women of Africa, . . . that forms the tie that still holds captive to this day the heart of the white foster child of the "black mammies" of the Southland was not crushed out by the iron heel of slavery but still wells up in their bosoms and in this brighter day overflows in compassion for the poor and helpless of their own down-trodden race.[2]

Her early womanist vision also created a wider range of possibilities for male and female interaction and roles. Remaining true to a traditional view of the roles of women and men:

> Man desires a place of rest from the cares and vexations of life, where peace and love shall abide, where he shall be greeted by the face of one willing to provide for his comfort and convenience—where little ones shall sweeten the struggle for existence and make the future full of bright dreams. Woman desires to carry into effect the hopes that have grown with her growth, and strengthened with her strength from childhood days until maturity; love has made the path of life blend easily with the task that duty has marked out.[3]

Yet Mossell's womanist ideal of health prompted her biting advice to newly married women (and perhaps those who had not yet given up on reforming their spouses):

> Keeping a clean house will not keep a man at home; to be sure it will not drive him out, but neither will it keep him in to a very large extent. And you, dear tender-hearted little darlings, that are being taught daily that it will, might as well know the truth now and not be crying your eyes out later.[4]

However, this frank advice is coupled with a traditional, if not stereotypical, view of men:

> The men that usually stay in at night are domestic in their nature, care little for the welfare or approval of the world at large, are not ambitious, are satisfied with being loved, care nothing for being honored. . . . A man who aspires to social pre-eminence, who is ambitious or who acquires the reputation of being a man of judgment and knowledge, useful

as a public man, will be often out at night even against his own desires, on legitimate business.[5]

Continuing her early womanist vision, Mossell did not maintain that women must always greet their spouses with a smile:

> Women must not be blamed because they are not equal to the self-sacrifice of always meeting husbands with a smile, nor the wife blamed that she does not dress after marriage as she dressed before; child-birth and nursing, the care of the sick through sleepless nightly vigils, the exactions and irritations incident to life whose duties are made up of trifles and interruptions, and whose work of head and heart never ceases, make it an impossibility to put behind them at all times all cares and smile with burdened heart and weary feet and brain.[6]

Notwithstanding, she held fast to a domestic ideal and believed that women should not allow the list of trials recounted by Mossell herself to deter women from maintaining themselves in some semblance of dignity and beauty:

> Wives should be kind, keep house beautifully, dress beautifully if they can; but after all this is accomplished their husbands may be away from home possibly quite as much for above given reasons. [She here refers to the aspiration for social preeminence.][7]

Mossell not only addressed African-American society, she also addressed the white women of her day:

> Hath not the bonds-woman and her scarce emancipated daughter done what they could? Will not our more favored sisters, convinced of our desires and aspirations because of these first few feeble efforts, stretch out the helping hand that we may rise to a nobler, purer womanhood?[8]

The color caste system among blacks did not escape her piercing eye. Her pithy observation and indictment of the paucity of black faculty at educational institutions devoted exclusively to training African-American students cut to the quick:

> Unlike other educational institutions, the preference (where it is possible) is not given to their own alumni. . . . The continued failure of these institutions to acknowledge this fact, to employ any considerable number

of colored men in the Faculties . . . has led the colored alumni, and many
friends of education, to feel that there is a *deep-seated cause* for this neglect
of colored graduates; and that the explanation lies in caste prejudice.[9]

She answered the standard excuses—black faculty would be unable
to secure funds from white patrons, the patrons would not be so liberal
with their funds if blacks control how it is spent, the time was not right
for such a move, blacks did not contribute significantly to the endow-
ment and should not have a voice, and blacks had a lack of confidence in
their race—with a shower of voices to the contrary.[10]

She ended with her own judgment on the matter. Mossell noted that
part of the problem was an attempt to ignore blacks socially. She argued
that if blacks became faculty members they would have to be treated as
other members of the department. This, Mossell believed, would never
be met with acceptance or accord. However, she was more disturbed
with the role of the black church in education:

> An odd feature of this caste prejudice is the strong hold it has upon the
> churches. . . . The State institutions all over the country are fast becom-
> ing free to all, and where the schools are separate . . . the positions are
> given to competent colored teachers; but the church, the denominational
> schools under its control, the Christian Associations, cling to caste prej-
> udice and sow the seed of distrust and unbelief in the heart of the black
> man.[11]

What emerges from Mossell's refined rhetoric is a resource ethic of
justice for contemporary Christian womanist praxis. Mossell's refined
unctuous rhetoric[12] is neither dystopian nor utopian. It is radical hope
in the midst of odious circumstance. Mossell's concern is to give both
an accounting of the reality of African-American life and the role and
work of women within it, as well as critique black sociopolitical structures. She writes to educate herself, the black community, other
women, the wider U.S. society. But most of all, she records the truth
for her daughters, who she hopes will grow into a pure and noble womanhood.

This radical act of truth telling—of reality testing and reality
challenging—is at the heart of a womanist ethic of justice. For as both
a people and as genders, African-American women and men have been
stereotyped, categorized, scrutinized, and dichotomized into a people
straining against the bonds of double-consciousness and triple consciousness. As a womanist ethic of justice emerges, it must be radically

rooted in the truth tradition and history of African-American life and witness. It cannot succumb to a praxeological framework in which all the women are white and all the blacks are men.

DESCRIPTIVE ELEMENTS OF A WOMANIST ETHIC OF JUSTICE

The task of the womanist ethic of justice is to move within the tradition descriptively yet jump for the sun so as to climb beyond the tradition prescriptively. An ethic of justice *must* be based on the community from which it emerges. For it can degenerate into flaccid ideology if it does not espouse a future vision that calls the community beyond itself into a wider and more inclusive circle. This circle is neither tight nor fixed.

Mossell's unctuous rhetoric is a model for the descriptive function of a womanist ethic of justice. Like Ida B. Wells-Barnett, Mary Church Terrell, Mary McLeod Bethune, and other black women dedicated to racial and gender justice, Mossell has a specific audience in mind—the next generation. She is well aware of the pivotal function of memory and remembrance in an ethical framework that emerges from an oppressed community. The struggle to move beyond double and triple consciousness is a confrontation with a history that is systematically and methodologically ignored. To recover the record of black women, the work of African-American women is a vocation of ornery patience and will.

All too often, black women must answer the questions—some well-intentioned, some not—Isn't this just another form of separating us? How are the lives of black women relevant to my world? Why am I blamed for something that I am not responsible for?

Awareness of Histories and Heritages

A womanist ethic of justice responds from its own well of history and sociopolitical methodology: we cannot bring together that which we do not know. For a unity forged on imperfection, romance, poor vision, limited knowledge, and fissured reconciliation will always benefit those who have the power and leisure to enforce and ignore differences. Unity as a teleological goal can be dangerous and life defeating, for it can overwhelm and neglect equality. Unity is only vigorous in an atmosphere that is unafraid of difference and diversity, an atmosphere that does not view difference as a barrier, but like the proverbial stew makes the aroma richer and provides greater sustenance for the work of justice.

The collective experience of black women, like the experience of any group, can inform and challenge the dominant worldview. African-American women must seriously consider a womanist analysis of society, culture, and history. For a black woman to forget her blackness is to deny a rich heritage that crosses the continent of Africa, moves in the waters of the Caribbean, touches the shores of South America, and is vibrant in the rhythms of Alice Coltrane, Miriam Makeba, Marian Anderson, and Sweet Honey in the Rock. She loses part of her very soul if she turns away from Zora Neale Hurston, Alice Walker, or Phyllis Wheatly. African-American women must continue to draw from the deep well of the lives of Fannie Lou Hamer, Cora Lee Johnson, and Septima Clark.

However, care must be taken neither to idealize nor romanticize African-American women. An even greater danger is to confuse collective with monolithic. Strength, determination, and steel will are part and parcel of black women's heritage. But this does not mean that this heritage is always healthy. She has been the breeder and the unwilling mistress. She has been the big mama and the prostitute. She has suffered in kitchens and borne child after child. She needs not only to celebrate her heritage but also to take a long, hard look at it.

Feminists have shown that exclusive masculine language and imagery are factors contributing to and undergirding the oppression of women. Womanists must investigate the relationship between the oppression of women and theological symbolism. Simply to dismiss the concerns of inclusive God language as a white woman's issue is to close the dialogue too soon. If we, as blacks, can identify God as black, then we can certainly explore other imagery for God. Indeed, we call God our doctor in the sick room, our lawyer in the courtroom, our bright and morning star, our bridge over troubled water, our wheel in the middle of a wheel. With such creativity and with such a rich testimony of how God is experienced, why stop at a masculine pronoun for God? Why confine leadership to gender-specific roles?

Traditionally, black women have been clear that it is the humanity of Jesus and not his maleness that is significant about his life and ministry, the crucifixion, and the resurrection. Jarena Lee's reply to Richard Allen's unwillingness to allow her to preach illustrates this:

> And why should it be thought impossible, heterodox, or improper for a woman to preach? seeing the Saviour died for the woman as well as for the man. If the man may preach, because the Saviour died for him, why

not the woman? seeing the Saviour died for her also. Is he not a whole
Saviour instead of a half one? . . . [13]

The dialogue on inclusivity will prompt a rigorous discussion on the
nature of gender. However, this cannot be the end of the discussion; it
must be the nucleus. Gender analysis and challenge are intricately
wedded to race and class analysis. The task of womanist justice is to
remain a thorny reminder that issues are complex. There is a world of
domination, subordination, equality, and just possibilities beneath the
veneer.

White feminist theologians must not be quick to move to a prescriptive stance on the nature of the church and society. They must be willing to wrestle with their sisters of color. It is not necessary for us to
agree on the nature of God, the centrality of Jesus, forms of spirituality,
or what constitutes good preaching. It is not a failing of feminist dialogue or womanist dialogue to disagree. Failing is to cease to listen to
one another when we disagree. Failing is assuming that if our sister
does not come to see what we know to be the truth from our experience, she has not heard us. The truth of who God is for us, how the
church affects us, how we choose to live out our spirituality is grounded
in our vastly differing experiences. The faith experience of one woman
is not necessarily the faith experience of the next.

Our paths to liberation differ. We must come to grips with that and
learn how to be comfortable about the diversity found in women's experience. We have to learn each other's cultures in an intimate way and
then seek to build the bridges needed for a just society. It is only then
that we can talk about solutions and remedies in a meaningful way. If
we seek to transform society, and not merely reform it, then we must
engage in education, awareness, acceptance, and challenge. Our witness
means risking our being misunderstood and hurt. It also means risking
that we will be heard and affirmed.

The crux of the matter is to increase our knowledge of our histories
and the myriad of ways folk have done analysis, responded to circumstance, visioned a future, and also failed to do so. The relevance of our
world views is more of a challenge than we admit or accept. True relevance implies a willingness for each of us to open our lives for uncompromising and meticulous introspection—but this introspection takes
place within the context of a group and a society. A monologue is not
enough, a dialogue is better, a chorus is wonderful, but a ring shout is
what a womanist ethic of justice seeks. There are no observers, only pil-

grims in the ring. Each has her or his story of faith and each must share it for the good of the body of faith.

Reflections on Place

The point that Gertrude Mossell raises for contemporary reflection is not whether the house is clean, but whether there is a house at all:

> I notice that it is only when my mother is working in her flowers that she is radiant, almost to the point of being invisible—except as Creator: hand and eye. She is involved in work her soul must have. Ordering the universe in her personal conception of Beauty.
>
> Her face, as she prepares the Art that is her gift, is a legacy of respect she leaves to me, for all that illuminates and cherishes life. She has handed down respect for the possibilities—and the will to grasp them.[14]

Alice Walker speaks of the black woman as artist. Her words also echo the African-American woman who seeks to minister, who seeks to be prophetic not only within her churches, but to society as well—who build a house to come home to. Often she is denied her right to be both black and a woman. Often she is told to choose between her selves, as if only half of her is enough to survive. But, as the artist who strives for the work her soul must have, so moves the black woman in the church.

All theologies of liberation are theo-ethical reflection on the assignation of place. They attempt, from a particular context, to critique society as well as the church and traditional theology. This critique is designed to be a more faithful witness to the kingdom or realm of God.

Feminist theology attempts to articulate this faithful witness through a call for the reimaging of the roles of men and women in the church as well as in secular society. It is inductive and based on praxis. The inductive approach taken by feminist theology, as opposed to the deductive approach of classical theology, stresses experience. Rather than deducing conclusions from principles established out of Christian tradition and philosophy, theologies of liberation begin with lived experience. The Gospel message is good news to people when it speaks to their needs in a concrete manner.

Feminist theology refuses to accept the place we either allow ourselves to assume due to social mores and strictures or to which we may be assigned by those same forces. The task before feminist theology is to name the particular sin and be able to articulate the universal dimensions of it. Feminist theology, at its best, attempts to be nonracist, nonsexist, nonclassist, nonhomophobic—including groups of the traditionally dispossessed.

As a womanist, I find that feminist theology gives me much to hold on to and celebrate. Its horizon is one that challenges and promotes growth for a whole society rather than a particular group. But the actual practice of feminism falls short of its vision. When issues of race and class challenge feminist practice, feminist theology and feminism, in general, are often found wanting. Feminism contains so much that speaks to the creation of a just society. However, even within postmodern feminism, women of color and poor women cannot fully embrace the feminist agenda or must radically redefine and refine it structurally and methodologically.

The practice of feminism causes many black women to sigh in exasperation and anger. A monocausal focus on gender renders feminist theory and feminist theology suspect. Growing numbers of feminist theorists and theologians have reached an awareness that such shortsightedness is bad theory and even worse praxis. However, the challenge remains to do more than state one's social location as a badge of particularity. Universal reason and ubiquitous knowledge tempt us to move from guarding against talking in generalities to creating new categories of otherness with little to no acknowledgment that the other is embodied.

There is a major methodological flaw: incomplete praxis. The action and reflection that are key to any liberation theology are deficient. The reflection done in much feminist theology is either not inclusive (or haltingly inclusive) of the experience of black women (or any woman of color), poor women, and lesbians. Time after time, black women and white women clash over such traditional notions as God, Jesus, the nature of the church, and spirituality.

We clash because there is a basic lack of knowledge about black worship, black history, and patterns of black social interaction. There is a yawning chasm of acceptable comprehension of black experience and writings and little or no mention of African-American women writers, critics, theorists, or just plain folk. Attempts to appropriate African-American women and men's experience for descriptive and methodological cues have been done with sincerity, but remain inadequate. The responsibility rests on white and black women to get to know each other's worlds better and not simply to rely on interpretations or cursory glances to supply the information needed to build bridges and create a more just society.

Incomplete praxis permits the ignorance, the naïveté, the divisions between black and white women to exist. Class issues must be dealt with on an intentional basis. By and large, class differences mean that while most black women are dealing with survival issues, most white women are dealing with fulfillment issues. Neither is more noble or more desirable. Both mean hard work and the necessity to fight a system that is happy to keep us where we are. But class differences are important, for they mean that fundamentally black and white women begin in different places. There is no judgment placed on this; it is simply to recognize a fact and begin to explore how that fact changes how we view ourselves, our analyses, our struggles, and our agendas.

Feminism that is authentic is more than a further extension of tokenism to include more women in existing social structures. Feminism that is authentic seeks to transform radically the social structures and human relationships within those structures. Like womanism, the agenda of authentic feminism includes relationships of student and professor, clergy and laity.

An authentic feminism is mindful of differences as well as commonalities. Feminist theological reflection must include the internal struggle of feminists and womanists as we wrestle with race, class bias, age, differently abled, homophobia, and beauty. Human liberation cannot be achieved by the elimination of any one form of oppression. Real liberation must be, to borrow a phrase from Anna Cooper, broad in the concrete — it must be based on a multidimensional analysis. We have to stop talking at one another or across one another. White women need to move past guilt into reflection and black women need to move beyond anger to contemplation.

At a minimum, black women must deal simultaneously with race, sex, and class in their analysis of the black church and black society. Black women choose solidarity with black men on the issue of racism. We also choose to struggle with black men about their sexism. We have learned all too well that the uplifting of one segment of the black community does not immediately ensure the uplifting of the whole. Sojourner Truth pointed this out poignantly:

> There is a great stir about colored men getting their rights, but not a word about the colored women; and if colored men get their rights, and not colored women theirs, you see the colored men will be masters over the women, and it will be just as bad as it was before. So I am for keeping the thing going while things are stirring; because if we wait till it is still, it will take a great while to get it going again.[15]

A womanist ethic of justice does not seek to assign blame; rather it calls us into a radical accountability with one another. It is hard work to listen to a history and a tradition that has not been a part of dominant discourse. There are those who respond to such a revelation with guilt, shame, and anger. Rather than explore the emotion of the response, too often the rational impulse takes over and the result is a denial of the invitation to justice. And the response is one of feeling blamed or held responsible for the sins of the forebears. A womanist ethic of justice again makes the appeal to history and tradition and asks the question: How can an authentic ethic of justice be separated from where we have been and who we have been to one another? The contemporary scene did not emerge from a vacuum; it evolved from and in history and is immanently contextual. That context has its moments of brilliance and its seasons of mourning. We cannot divorce ourselves from the totality of our history and expect even a glimmer of efficacious justice.

PRESCRIPTIVE ELEMENTS OF A WOMANIST ETHIC OF JUSTICE

The prescriptive elements of a womanist ethic of justice must be as relentless in its analysis as it is inclusive in its recovery of history and sociopolitical analysis. A womanist ethic cannot be content with a justice that addresses only a particular person or group's wholeness. A womanist social ethic must embrace all segments of society if it is to be thorough and rigorous. We must continue to push ourselves into a critical dialogue that presses the boundaries of our humanness. Race, sex, and class analyses are crucial. But we need to challenge the ageism (of both the young and the seasoned), the homophobia and the heterosexism, the myriad of issues around accessibility, our own color caste system, and the Pandora's box around issues of beauty. The work we are about is not only eradicating an unjust white social order that names us "less than." It is about the ways that we help that system find new ways to deem us children of a lesser God.

The black church and much of black theo-ethical thought have their own peculiar form of patriarchal oppression. They reflect the same patriarchy of society at large, but they are also imbued with the dynamics of racism of the dominant white society. Hence, black women must deal not only with the negative effects of racism, but also with black men's own virulent form of sexism as well.

There are no shortcuts to curing the complexity of problems a womanist ethic of justice faces. It is better to take the long, hard, steady route—in which a womanist ethic explores the individual and the African-American community. The route is forged from the knowledge that womanist ethics not only seeks to understand white folk, but also needs to be in a dialogue for understanding and solidarity with the various tribes of Native Americans, with Hispanic and Asian American cultures, in fact carrying on a search for understanding globally. As Marian Wright Edelman says so well, justice is neither cheap nor quick; it is a hard, ongoing process.[16]

A womanist ethic is unapologetically confrontational. The root meaning of confront is "to face together." Implicit in this is a relationship between equals. There must be mutual respect for the dignity of others, a willingness to engage in dialogue, and an awareness and acceptance of diversity. If one thrives in a power dynamic that places one over and against rather than with, all prophetic voice is lost. We must learn to trust and respect the gifts God has given us to speak the truth and act through our faith. Black women need not apologize for naming injustice for what it is or for challenging the black church and the church universal to live into more of what it is called to be.

Another prescriptive element in a womanist ethic is coalition building. Our partners are those folk who are committed to the struggle against oppression and who understand the need to act as well as reflect and analyze. Few social problems, and certainly not the multitude of social problems that face the contemporary black church and African-American society, can be solved with a single strategy. Hence womanists, like the church and folk we love and critique, must move beyond ideological boxes and obtuse language.

My mother is the dean of a small, black liberal arts college in the South. She, like her mother, believes in plain talk. She can be erudite if the situation calls for it. But she prefers coffee to cappuccino, hamburger to beef Wellington, and an amen to existential angst. She reminds me, keep it plain.[17] For if those who have been chosen to lead in the life of the church cannot make it plain, we fall victim to elitism. We must translate the vision of the reign of God in ways that make sense to our people. If we cannot make it plain, we will not only be elitist, we will be irrelevant.

A womanist ethic of justice names the particular sin and can then articulate the universal dimensions of it—the universal is *manifested* in the particular but not exhausted by it. An unctuous rhetoric of justice is more than a vague concept of civil rights in a racist and misogynist system. It moves beyond tokenism to a radical transformation of social structures and human relationships within those structures.

An unctuous womanist rhetoric of justice learns to find and listen to the stories and the traditions before offering a prescriptive agenda. It does not assume the universal in the particular if there has been no critical reflection on the scope of praxis utilized. It involves a self-critical inclusivity and seeks clarity in thought, speech, and action. This is crucial in an epoch that features ambiguity, confusion, and the latest political spin. It is rooted in the present as it draws its knowledge from the past and its strategy for the future.

BUILDING A HOUSE INTO A HOME

Our future is made with human hands and the liberating promises of God through Jesus Christ. Justice is beyond history; it is not limited to the realities and limitations of this world. The divine future breaks into the present with each thorny act of unctuous justice. However, African-American women and men cannot ease into the arrogance of self-made men and women. Such notions are bad architecture and bespeak inane and incomplete social analysis. The womanist agenda for justice recognizes and relies on the gospel message of justice, and not one crafted solely from human desires and idiosyncrasies.

The task of the black church in building a house to come home to must take gender analysis seriously. The essential space the black church can provide is one which welcomes *and* challenges. As much as a womanist ethic of justice challenges feminists to clarify their claims about womanhood, it also challenges African-American men to address sexist rhetoric and actions.

Within the church and without, African-American women and men are competing for life. This competition is a cruel wager on scarce resources in a hegemonic culture and social structure. Playing this wager means settling for an imposed hierarchy in which only one gender's concern is addressed at a time. The result is a praxeological disaster and an endangered community. A community affirms the worth of the people who are in it and invites others to join it because it offers life and health. To set up a hierarchy of needs based on femaleness and maleness is shortsighted and discriminatory. This lives out the model of the white power structure and the white version of Christianity that condones oppression.

If we are to model justice together, as female and male, then the descriptive and prescriptive elements of such a justice must be scrutinized with utmost care. As womanists we must listen to our stories, our experience, before we try to shape the new creation. Such care-filled listening, construction, and reconstruction are mandatory in a rigorous praxis. A rigorous praxis is at the heart of an unctuous womanist ethic of justice. However, the tunes are sung not only by African-American women. Peoples of all colors have a word to say to us. Rather than commit the modernist sin of universal presumptions of knowledge and reason, womanist descriptive evaluation seeks to listen to the plethora of voices as we discover our own voice in the ring shout.

This means that class analysis must be a part of our tool kit for justice. Such analysis cannot remain descriptive. It must critique and offer a new vision for African-American society and the black church. The impact of the rise of the United States' black middle class in the 1870s has not been studied with precision by African-American people of faith.[18] Race analysis has so dominated inquiry and rhetoric that class and gender issues are assumed as mere appendages to justice. The incomplete praxis and inadequate reflection which has marked feminist theory and ethics is evident in black theory and ethics as well.

Failure to analyze and strategize with class consciousness will doom all our efforts to mediocrity if not defeat. It is imperative that we begin to address the peculiar dynamics of a class within a class. African-American society has its distinctive features, which cannot be explained by using the descriptions of hegemonic culture. Collapsing all African-American experience into the "black experience" is the worst kind of modernist turn.

Self-critical inclusivity is mandatory. The challenge of womanist ethical discourse and action is to guard against using the masters' tools to dismantle a supremacist house: arrogance, universalism, progress, grand cultural narratives, renovation, domination, subordination. Rather, the womanist house of justice challenges these elements of the house. This challenge is not done without acute awareness that the cultural narratives and cues we learn from birth may tempt us to create new systems of domination and subordination. The task remains for us constantly to evaluate goals and standards in light of the gospel understanding of justice. This justice is dynamically revelatory. We must know justice, a justice which is always within our grasp and just beyond it.

If we truly have the truth, then we sing while we build this house. We sing with passion, for passion is what distinguishes us as Christians. We sing when the times of life are failing. Sing when folks tell us we have no gift for singing. Sing when someone has taken the sheet music. Sing in the midst of joy and laughter. We sing using heart and soul. Sing using mind and intellect. Sing using witness and faith. As African-

American womanists, we sing because there is a song inside which must be let go. As the song of justice is sung, a house is being built. Such a house is not forged on arrogant despotism or militant indifference. This house is one of faith and hope. One in which a history of the rude "grandiloquence" of proclaiming the discovery of a continent and civilizing it, while millions fell victim to physical and cultural genocide, is not seen as a marker for celebration but for repentance and reparation.

We must have clarity in our speech, action, and thought. The world we live in, and the church we seek to minister in and to, thrives on ambiguity and confusion. These become the measuring tape and the leveling edge for a house of sin and destruction. In a time when poor educational systems are obscured behind debates on the pathology of the underclass, and AIDS is described as a crisis in the United States while some Third World countries see it as only one of many in a cacophony of epidemics, clear, direct, informed words of justice and analysis are crucial.

We are building a house of justice, a liberation community. We must live in the present and strategize for the future because our sisters and brothers are dying. This charge cannot be taken lightly. The responsibility my grandmother taught me and the accountability she modeled remain a testament of hope and justice in the midst of loathsome events. Our ability or even willingness to be present and to work with others from our own resources is often devalued. The notion that success is measured by economic gain or spectacular productions camouflages the real success of moral action: persistent, faithful action. Action that is neither flashy nor extraordinary. It is the common action of the very amazing routine—patience, hope, faith. There is value in a womanist will to see the extraordinary in the ordinary, to celebrate the small acts of justice that lead to the cataclysm of redemptive hope.

Above all, this is a house of faith planted in God's liberating and reconciling love. This challenges us to faithful reflection. Such reflection holds within its gaze and hermeneutical circle the other elements of the house of justice: particularity, inclusivity, passion, clarity, strategy. This social agenda is also a theo-ethical one. The genius of womanist reflection is that it understands that all that it attempts arises from God's call and claim on our analysis. This is dangerous business. History is littered with those who have claimed God's prerogative, only to commit evil and inflict suffering. The womanist ethic of justice must be unctuous to hold on to its sanity and its consecration. If this ethic fails to remember the seduction of egotism, it will devolve into another form of hegemony. It will have no tools to build a house of justice or a way station of hope.

No, a clean house will not keep any of us home; it won't drive us out, but it does not assure that we will choose to spend our time there. If African-American women and men of faith content ourselves with issues of style and form—at the neglect of substance and a hefty devotion—we will have pristine, sparkling, inconsequential churches that will be empty in both body and soul. For the people are crying for a full gospel, while we are busy debating who can and can't serve, who gets which church, the color and texture of the sanctuary carpet, which store to buy the altar candles from, who has the biggest church bus, and who has the best sermonic whoop. A clean house is not the point, but instead whether we have a house to begin with *and* whether there is anything there to come home to.

The place *we* choose to situate ourselves through our analysis of who we are as oppressors and oppressed must be one honed from the hard work of being open and honest and acting to change what is divisive among us. Building a house is only the first task. Intrinsic in this enterprise is a deep and abiding care for the people. An unctuous womanist rhetoric of justice cannot slide down the slippery slope of theory and prescriptions at the expense of the lives of children, men, and women. Our methodological musings and praxeological constructs must be centered on justice and life. The next generation and this generation are too precious to allow us to dally with navel gazing and academic posturing. And centering on justice and life—this is what loving the Lord, loving the church, loving our families, and loving the people is all about. Thank you, Miss Nora.

9

RESISTANCE AND THE TRANSFORMATION OF HUMAN EXPERIENCE

Ellen K. Wondra

*T*he intent of white feminist theory and practice has been the liberation of all women into full humanity. The contributions of white feminism in this direction are many and significant. However, white feminism's laudable intent has been distorted and limited by its proponents' historical and ongoing failure to engage concretely and systematically the very interstructuring of race and class with gender, upon which much feminist theory insists. That is, white feminist theologians have ignored the differences difference makes in the experience of women of color and white women.[1] This failing is, in part, a result of the social location of white feminism within interlocking structures of gender, race, class, and sexual orientation. It is also a failing that white feminism may overcome—indeed, must overcome—as it moves toward its own liberating vision.

Among other things, this essay is an attempt to move beyond an analytic framework of domination on the basis of gender to a framework of interstructured and interactive realities of domination and liberation. Thus, this essay allows Euro-American interests in meaning, epistemology, and metaphysics to interweave with liberation interests in reflective and transformative wisdom arising from the concrete praxis of struggles against oppression and for the liberation of the whole of human existence. I begin by specifying the location and significance of white North American feminist religious thought in terms of a view of reality as interstructured. I then discuss the formal understanding of experience that is operative (but largely implicit) in white feminist theology in order to indicate how this interstructuring effects similarities and differences in consciousness and experience. Next I look at the phenomenon of resistance as one concrete theme that can be found in multiple locations of struggle against domination. I will suggest that the resistance of the subjugated has a transcendent element to which various liberation theologies point. Finally, I sketch briefly how resistance understood as both historical phenomenon and transcendent reality may be elaborated within the properly theological considerations of Christology.

WHITE FEMINISTS: DUAL LOCATIONS OF PRIVILEGE AND OPPRESSION

In theology, white feminists have formally defined patriarchy as a "pyramidal system and hierarchical structure of society in which women's oppression is specified . . . in terms of race and class."[2] But white feminists' studies have often focused primarily if not exclusively on the struggle against male domination. In this sense, white feminist theology has presumed to speak for all women while listening only to the experience of white women, and it has sought to define the rules and agenda for the struggle against sexism in a way which both ignores and suppresses the just claims of women of color and perpetuates the racist orientation of the dominant culture.

The irony of this concealment is striking: white feminist religious thought begins, after all, with a critique of the insistence of patriarchal thought on the universalization of the experience of a privileged few. But more, the concealment and suppression of issues of race and class means that white feminist thought and practice have failed to work effectively toward overcoming the alienation between women of color and white women, and between poor and working-class women and middle- and upper-class women, in North America and in the rest of the world. Indeed, to the extent that white feminism has subordinated race and class to gender, it has unintentionally perpetuated other legacies of domination.[3] Thus, a primary tenet of white feminism—the solidarity of all women—has been undercut by white feminists themselves.

As white feminists seek a new vision for religious thought and practice as specifically liberating, it is imperative that the concrete location of white feminism be recognized. In the first instance, this means consistent recognition of patriarchy not as primarily a system of domination based in sexual or gender dualism, but as an interlocked "pyramidal system and hierarchical structure of society." That is, "Patriarchy defines not just women as the 'other' but also subjugated peoples and races as the 'other' to be dominated."[4]

Such recognition makes it plain that not all oppressions are the same. Further, some who are oppressed because of the patriarchal construction of gender stand to benefit from patriarchal constructions of race and class—as do white middle- and upper-class women—at the same time that the concrete suffering of others is increased and modified, such as the suffering of women of color and of poor women of any race. Rendering white feminist analysis more complex need not, however, result in fragmentation, competition for the dubious distinction of being "most oppressed," or paralyzing guilt and self-abnegation. Rather, reframing white feminist analysis so that it focuses on connection and alienation through similarity and difference leads to more effective transformative action in solidarity with others. Such action empowers more thoroughgoing and adequate analysis and more fruitful theological reflection, which has the power to nurture hope and enliven further action.

It is imperative that the ambiguity of the social location of white feminism be faced without flinching. This ambiguity is itself twofold. First, white North American women are members of both dominant and dominated groups—by race and class (internationally as well as nationally) in the first instance, and by gender in the second. Therefore white feminists must continuously find concrete ways to divest themselves of the power and privilege conferred by their race and class, at the same time that they construct for themselves a liberated sense of self and community that transforms domination on the basis of gender.

The placement of North American white feminist theology in locations of both privilege and oppression further suggests that this theology engages concerns of both contemporary Euro-American theologies and those of the liberation theologies of peoples of African descent and of Latin America, Asia, and Oceania. That is, white feminist theology is engaged in searching out and presenting the nature and meaning of women's experience of oppression and liberation into the full humanity that patriarchy systemically denies. It engages in this search through concrete sociohistorical struggle (as do all liberation theologies) *and* through thoroughgoing criticism and reconstruction of assessments of meaning and truth discovered through experience (as do Euro-American revisionist and narrative theologies).

WOMEN'S EXPERIENCE OF
SIMILARITY AND DIFFERENCE

For the thoroughgoing critical moments of white feminist religious thought, the depth and extent to which patriarchy is embedded in Western religious traditions pose the problem of nonbelief in the claims of these traditions. At the same time, feminist critical agnosticism and nonbelief are also evoked by the history of both Christian practice and Christian theology, which have designated women and members of other subjugated groups as not fully humans–that is, in some critical senses as nonpersons–even while teaching the dominated to resist domination and hope for liberation.

White feminist theological *construction* has emphasized women's experience as the basis of resolutions of problems of the meaning and truth of human existence. With other revisionist theologians, feminist Christian theologians such as Patricia Wilson-Kastner and Marjorie Hewitt Suchocki argue that reflection on experience–and for them specifically women's experience–is part of the human drive toward transcendence, which links humanity with the divinity that is its source and goal. At the same time, and with other liberation theologians, feminist Christian theologians such as Rosemary Radford Ruether and Carter Heyward insist that the praxis of liberation–and for them specifically the praxis of the liberation of oppressed women–gives rise to an eschatological vision that pulls the transforming future into the present.

In both approaches to feminist theology (as is the case on the larger theological scene), there is an understanding that truth is always mediated by the context in which it is disclosed, concealed, and recognized. Such mediation means that any disclosure or recognition is always also a concealment, that all views are both particular and partial, and that any context generates distortions of vision and understanding as well as clarification, liberation, and the seeds of transformation.

In such a situation, where truth is acknowledged to be mediated by the contexts of experience, the term *experience* needs careful definition, particularly if issues of the conjunction of gender, race, and class are to be fruitfully engaged in theology. In the North American context, and perhaps especially among white Protestants, appeals to "experience" would appear to fall into two broad categories: one overly universalized, and one overly privatized and individualized. For thirty years and more, North American theologians working from white feminist, womanist, African-American, and economically marginalized contexts have critiqued the ways in which the casting of "common human experience" as *materially* universalizable (as in pride as *the* universal sin) makes normative the concrete experience of only a privileged few.

At the other pole, references to experience are all too often appeals to a privatized and internal view of reality, which is privileged precisely because it is individual and even unique. Such appeals not only block critical engagement; they also contribute to the relativization and fragmentation of discourse and action, leaving little room for establishment of a genuinely *common* language or well-being.

At both poles, the descriptive and prescriptive understandings of the human and of human relation to divinity are less than adequate. Some aspects of existence are concealed by false universals, other aspects are misrepresented, and the whole is distorted. Among the consequences of such suppression and distortion are the generation and perpetuation of unjust relations among humans, and the limitation of human encounter with the divine as it is mediated through human cultures.

The appeal to "women's experience" in white feminist theology refuses to see these two alternatives as the only available options. In the first place, feminist theory identifies Woman—that is, the putative essential female human being—as a cultural concept rising from patriarchal systems and structures. Any form of biological or philosophical essentialism (what women *are* as such) posits an abstract universal that masks the particularity and contextuality of the experience described, usually at the expense of the experience of differing, less powerful groups.

However, within the confines of patriarchal society, shifting the basis of conceptualization from what Woman essentially *is* to what women *do* (including what they think and feel) cannot stand. All practices are pervaded and distorted by multivalent and interstructured systems of domination. Further, mere description of what *is* without critical analysis (which requires some notion of either alternative or ideal) cannot fuel or direct concrete or theoretical movements toward liberation and transformation.

One of the primary constructive tasks of feminist theory has been, then, to provide an adequate articulation of women's experience, a project which "modifies or fractures the constructs that left [women's] lives out of account" in the first place; that is, a project which modifies theory itself.[5] And among the elements of theory modified or fractured are the definitions of subjectivity, consciousness, and experience, all of which arise out of and reflect patriarchal, androcentric practices and modes of thought.

Like other movements of resistance and liberation, feminism relies on a form of conscientization for the development of analysis, plans of action, and solidarity. The corporate, critical, and self-critical exploration and reflection on women's concrete lives which feminists name "consciousness-raising" provide significant epistemological bases for new, interactive, and processive understandings of the human subject, of consciousness, and of human experience. The epistemological claim inherent in practices of conscientization is that reliable knowledge arises out of a corporate situation of mutual engagement, reflection, analysis, struggle, and transformation in which the marginalized and suppressed "hear each other into speech." The knowledge emerging in this way is taken to be reliable, even while subject to modification through further reflection and analysis. A second claim is that even the deep-seated effects of domination and suppression may be overcome within just such a corporate context of critical reflection and action.

This epistemology is, in turn, based on a complex view of the human subject. Feminist theorist Teresa de Lauretis suggests that subjectivity is grounded neither in some human core or essence unaffected by the changes and chances of existence, nor in subjects' material conditions. Rather, subjectivity is constituted "by one's personal, subjective engagement in the practices, discourses, and institutions that lend significance (value, meaning, and affect) to the events of the world." Experience is then defined as "a complex of habits resulting from the semiotic interaction of 'outer world' and 'inner world,' the continuous engagement of self or subject in social reality."[6]

The emphasis here is on the social as well as the personal construction of reality: "practices, discourses, and institutions" are human products that organize material conditions in particular ways, giving them their significance and providing suggestions of how they are to be perceived, interpreted, and understood. Such constructs include sociopolitical systems, economic arrangements, cultural and religious institutions, and linguistic structures. They also include constructions of gender, race, class, and sexuality, which serve further to place individuals' and groups' lives and aspirations within social reality.

The human subject is thus understood to be socially and historically constituted through her involvement in multiple communities of discourse and practice, and human consciousness develops and changes within the limits of historical identity and humanly construed concrete situations. At the same time, the subject's agency within her situation reconstructs both the situation itself and her consciousness of it:

> Consciousness is not the result but the term of a process . . . , a particular configuration of subjectivity, or subjective limits, produced at the intersection of meaning with experience. . . . [D]ifferent forms of consciousness are grounded, to be sure, in one's personal history; but that history— one's identity—is interpreted or reconstructed by each of us within the horizon of meanings and knowledges available in the culture at given historical moments, a horizon that also includes modes of political commitment and struggle. . . . Consciousness, therefore, is never fixed, never

attained once and for all, because discursive boundaries change with historical conditions.[7]

Obviously, then, the many particular dimensions of any subject's individual situation have formative significance, and produce great varieties of experience. Human experience is nevertheless common in its most basic processes and structures rather than in its content. Each and every human subject is constituted by the interaction of internal and external worlds; what differs is the concrete elements of those worlds, and how particular elements in all their concreteness are interrelated in value, meaning, and significance. Under the terms of this view of experience, the subject is historically and contextually formed, conscious, and critically and self-critically reflective. And the subject exists as a subject within a community or set of communities likewise formed. Thus, when either meaning or experience changes–as both do with changes in their constituent parts–consciousness itself changes.

The concrete content of *women's* experience, writes de Lauretis, can be sought "in that political, theoretical, self-analyzing practice by which the relations of the subject in social reality can be rearticulated from the historical experience of women,"[8] particularly when this experience is deliberately understood as pluralized by factors of race, class, and sexual orientation, as well as specified by gender. Experience thus specified is the appropriate source for feminist, womanist, and *mujerista* theory and practice because, as an ongoing critical and self-critical process, it resists the forces of domination. That is, it breaks the silences and suppressions that are a consequence of patriarchy, interrupting patriarchal domination, disclosing the participation of women in all areas of human existence, and revealing the social and historical construction of all experience.

Feminist theology, while standing in agreement with the general view of the structure of experience I have outlined here, attends as well to its specifically religious elements. Religious experience is never unmediated or entirely direct. Rather, its immediacy is always mediated by the structures, processes, and contexts in which religious experience occurs. Therefore, as consciousness changes, so does religious experience. Women's understandings of their own humanity and their hopes for liberation are prompted, distorted, suppressed, reinforced, and transformed by their encounter with the divine as that is mediated through the many dimensions of their existence, including the spiritual, ecclesial, and theological. As Rosemary Radford Ruether put it in her 1984 address to the American Academy of Religion:

The patriarchal distortion of all tradition, including Scripture, throws feminist theology back upon the primary intuitions of religious experience itself, namely, the belief in a divine foundation of reality which is ultimately good, which does not wish evil nor create evil, but affirms and upholds our autonomous personhood as women, in whose image we are made. . . . [Feminist theology] is engaged in a primal re-encounter with divine reality and, in this re-encounter, new stories will grow and be told as new foundations of our identity. . . . It allows the divine to be experienced in places where it has not been allowed to be experienced before.[9]

The experience of liberation thus decreases the mediation of patriarchal symbols and structures–both traditional and contemporary–and opens up the possibility of a re-encounter with the divine, which validates the feminist experience of conversion from alienation and transformation toward wholeness.

Defining women's experience in the manner I have indicated (including its religious dimension) has the distinct advantage of opening into the emerging discussion of difference as a central issue for feminist (and for all) theology.[10] To understand experience and consciousness as suggested here is to recognize that the varieties of women's experience are irreducibly interstructured on the basis of gender, race, class, and sexuality; and that the fundamental characteristic of this interstructuring is domination and subordination. When patriarchy is understood as that system of domination and subordination which constructs race, class, and sexuality as well as gender on hierarchical lines, it becomes evident that, while women may have in common some elements of experience on the basis of gender, their experience as women will also differ as their race/ethnicity and class locations differ. Nevertheless, their experience is connected, because the elements which constitute experience are tied together in relations of conflict, domination and subjugation, mutual support, and overlapping struggles for survival, liberation, and transformation. Thus women's experience is at the same time different and similar; and the interplay here makes it possible for persons to understand and learn from each other's differing concrete experience without suppressing the differences and conflicts of their historical existences.

RESISTANCE AGAINST DOMINATION

Such differences and similarities can be also thematized to disclose previously concealed aspects of human historical existence, and to assist in reconstructing our understanding of the human person as historical subject. One such theme, found in reflections from many widely differing groups who have in common historical experiences of massive suffering, is that of resistance.[11] This phenomenon connects the struggles for existence of the dehumanized with the very structures of human experience, and therefore with humanity as such. The phenomenon of resistance also demonstrates how human persons may surpass the limitations of their existence even while living within them. This phenomenon thus illuminates the ways in which liberation theologies are reconstructing the notion of transcendence, a notion that has been shattered for Euro-American philosophy by the very instances of massive and unjust suffering from which these theologies emerge.[12] Such events radically and relentlessly refute the presuppositions and primary orientations of both thought and faith by exposing those flaws and deficits in both that render them incapable not only of preventing such a horror, but even of comprehending it.[13] Thus, events of mass human suffering precipitate paralyzing crises of meaning, even as they are always already crises of human existence. For all involved, the temptation to despair is compelling.[14]

However, an even more compelling hope of overcoming and mending this shattering and its accompanying despair are provided by one thing: those most fully assaulted by logics of destruction and domination resist their own dehumanization. Resistance–understood as the retention, maintenance, and recreation of even "a shred of humanity" in the midst of massive and pervasive dehumanization–breaks the logic and effectiveness of such destruction, and so reconstructs the subjugated as full human subjects. Such resistance is a direct confrontation with the overwhelming horror of dehumanizing assault. This confrontation grasps the meaning of such assault, despite the logic of destruction which conceals that meaning, and appropriates that experience in order to struggle concretely against it.[15] Resistance, in other words, confronts and endures finitude in its most extreme forms, thus allowing those in resisting communities to surpass, in both action and reflection, the humanly produced limitations which, even so, may continue to entrap them. Thus, resistance is a way of being in history, a generative interaction of both "inner" and "outer" worlds which reconstructs human consciousness, human experience, and so human subjects. When understood from the perspective of those who are subjugated by dehumanizing logics of destruction, resistance is part of the dialectical movement of historical liberation, from domination to transformation. Resistance involves "overt, flesh-and-blood action and life."[16] Within the contexts of dehumanization, the aim is survival precisely as human. Here, the fundamental moral question is not "Why did so many succumb?" but "How did even one survive?"[17] When the moral question is framed in this way, authentic resistance—authentic life—may incorporate action whose present transformative consequences are readily apparent. But, given the pervasive and persistent nature of systemic dehumanization and subjugation, resistance also entails "both the accommodation necessary to survival and the creative defiance that lays the groundwork for change in the future."[18] Resistance in the present and the "dangerous memory" of resistance in the past may empower the subjugated to know both that they are unnecessarily afflicted[19] and that they have the capacity to participate in the alleviation of their affliction and the transformation of its causes. Through resistance, those subjected to dehumanizing forces are able to participate in the creation of more humane possibilities for themselves and others.

Resistance to dehumanization thus discloses and develops previously neglected aspects of human being in history, and generates hope for further transformation, not only for the resisting victims, but for those who remember them. Through resistance, thought and practice, ruptured by the effects of domination, are mended. Thus, resistance and reflection on it reconstitute the human subject, even in the midst of massive unjust suffering.

Further, as resistance mends and motivates the human capacity to engage the very conditions of existence, resistance reveals anew the connection of human being to ongoing history and the transcendence toward which humanity strives. It is the victims' sense that they are "under orders to live" that spurs them to confront the powers which would destroy them.[20] These "orders" spring from human subjectivity itself, but they also manifest an Other who is present and who draws near to those who claim their humanity, even in the face of death-dealing domination. The experiential conviction that "I have a living Avenger and that at the end he will rise up above the dust,"[21] that "God knew what it was like to be a woman who was raped,"[22] that "Neither the slavers' whip nor the lynchers' rope nor the bayonet could kill our black belief"[23]–this conviction witnesses powerfully to the unbreakable relation between humanity and the divine, a relation whose continuation is desired and sought on both sides. For when a shred of humanity is maintained and mending the ruptures of history becomes possible, what is disclosed is the resistance of divinity itself to ruptures of the connection between history and transcendence that are consequences of domination.[24]

A CHRISTOLOGY OF RESISTANCE AND TRANSFORMATION

For Christians engaged in struggles for liberation, the suppressed history of the resistance of both humanity and divinity to domination is decisively re-presented, clarified, and validated in Jesus the Christ. In the Christ, Christians see their own authentic existence as it participates in the existence of God. Yet Christology has been problematic for white feminist theologians. The particular location of white feminist Christians has assisted us in developing cogent and exhaustive critiques of the use made of Christology to support domination.[25] But white feminist theology has at times faltered as it attempts constructive proposals for Christology, in part because white feminist theologians have been unable to enlarge and modify their framework to attend to issues of race and class as well as gender.[26]

Understanding Jesus as the embodiment of resistance can vindicate and connect feminists' and others' efforts to resist and transform domination in a world that is still ruptured and fragmented by massive and unjust suffering. Jesus' own refusal to participate in the perpetuation of systems of interstructured subjugation and privilege provides an empowering history of the possibilities of resistance and its transformative effects, even in the midst of complex, ambiguous, and seemingly intractable systems of domination. The fact that Jesus himself occupied an ambiguous social location — standing to benefit from gender and ethnic arrangements while suffering on the basis of class and nationality — yet was able to live a life characterized by mutual regard and cooperation manifests how the human and divine join together in solidary presence for the comfort and liberation of the subjugated.

Jesus' life in a time of concrete anticipation of the reign of God manifested his own "lively expectation of the coming of God's kingdom" as an historical era of peace and justice[27] built on the expectations of renewed relation with God. Jesus' vision emphasized the reign of God as already manifest in the midst of human struggles for personal and social survival, wholeness, and healing. In words and deeds, Jesus proclaimed God's reign as a Jubilee, the "conquest of human historical evil; the setting up of proper conditions of human life with God and one another here on earth within the limits of mortal existence."[28]

In his own relations with those around him, Jesus directed his attention to relations of domination and subjugation, resisting the dehumanizing actuality of these relations by living a life characterized by mutual regard and cooperation. His intimate and immediate engagement with others empowered them to heal and free themselves, and thereby to enter more fully into the human community and into their own humanity. His lifting up of the lowest and their social roles as exemplary models proclaims a radical redefinition of leadership as mutual service, in which none is master and all serve each other. In his inclusive interactions with others, Jesus challenged even those whose lives and choices were severely limited by sociohistorical circumstances to risk engagement, resistance, and transformation. Thus, his example of the transformation of hierarchical power into mutual cooperation witnessed against that internalization of unjust power which leads to reversal of unjust relations rather than to their transformation. Jesus also relentlessly criticized "the love of prestige, power and wealth that causes people to seek domination and lord it over each other,"[29] and encouraged those in positions of power and wealth to renounce their privileges for the benefit of the poor and marginalized.

Jesus' life, then, manifests and proclaims the actuality and possibility of an authentic humanity that engages the conditions of human existence, and that actively and effectively resists their dehumanizing elements at individual and social-systemic levels. In himself, Jesus embodies the possibility and actuality of the new, thereby changing the experience of those around him. This embodiment also provides both the hope and the reassurance needed by others in order to follow his example. In this way, Jesus' advocacy and embodiment of the transformative reversal of prevailing social roles opens up further possibilities for the in-breaking of God's reign in the context of human existence. In the Christ, what it means to be fully human is decisively disclosed, and movement toward that full humanity is encouraged and enabled. For those marginalized and subjugated by systems and structures of domination, Jesus is the Christ because he is the manifestation of the transformation of humanity in the struggle to resist domination. Thus, Jesus' life vindicates and re-presents the fullness of authentic humanity.

Through Christ, Christians find the dialectic movement from domination through resistance to transformation both vindicated in history and connected directly with the existence of God. That is, the Christ is also the definitive re-presentation of the only God who saves. The transformative qualities of Jesus' relations with others reveal that God is love made evident in justice.[30] This love heals and raises up the lowly, manifesting God's presence with the suffering and the dominated in their struggle for survival.

God's love is also manifest as judgment in Jesus' call to repentance and to the renunciation of the privileges of power and wealth embedded in systems of domination. Jesus' resistance to the exercise of authority for its own sake, in both social and religious arenas, manifests God's freedom and power to break through human pretensions and destroy human idols in order to make all things new. Jesus' resistance also reveals divine power not as dominating, but as self-expressive and self-giving, coming into creation in the multiple forms of love, wisdom, and just power. Through Jesus, God's love can be seen to be the self-expression of God's being, which is inherently relational and so directed outward. The self-expression of God in Jesus extends God's creative engagement with creation, revealing what God has been doing from the beginning.

The meaning of Jesus' life is confirmed in his death and vindicated in his resurrection. In suffering an ignominious and agonizing death, Jesus maintains both human and divine solidarity with the suffering and with victims of domination. Jesus' suffering and death are a voluntary pouring out of self for the sake of others whose suffering is not voluntary. Jesus' suffering and death also reveal God's presence as always fully and relentlessly present as fellow sufferer in the midst of human tragedy.

Jesus' resurrection proclaims that death is not the final word about human existence and God's transforming involvement with it. The resurrected Christ reveals redeemed humanity free of fragmentation, and part of the whole of creation rather than alienated from and destructive toward it. At the same time, in the resurrection, God definitively resists and overcomes the evil consequences of sin, and promises that this mending will be extended to the entire cosmos. The resurrection of Jesus reveals the power of God's love to be stronger than death.

Jesus embodies and begins a new order; but he does not complete it. Jesus shows us "ourselves as we are meant to be."[31] Those who follow Jesus are called to embrace and actualize this reality in lives of resistance, liberation, and transformation. Such lives, like Jesus' own, manifest "God's activity in conjunction, partnership, friendship with humanity."[32] That is, they manifest "Christ in the form of our sister" and brother.[33] The concrete reality of the reign of God is always emergent as new possibilities emerge in human existence, and as human experience and consciousness respond to these possibilities.

For Christians, then, Jesus is the Christ in that he is the decisive representation of an authentic humanity which resists domination and transforms it toward mutuality and just cooperation. He is also the personification in history of the divine self, the definitive re-presentation of the only God who saves. The incarnation of God in Jesus the Christ is simultaneously revelation of what has always been the case *and* the resistance by the afflicted to the dehumanization that seeks to overwhelm them. In his own resistance unto death and resurrection, Jesus vindicates the enduring if concealed and distorted reality of such resistance. His life, death, and resurrection are both promise and prophecy of the greater future fulfillment and transformation in which such resistance participates proleptically.

In biblical and traditional terms, Jesus is both Wisdom and Logos, the self-outpouring of the divine in human reality. He prophetically and eschatologically embodies the movement of creation toward the divine, and the divine movement toward creation. Jesus' manifestation of the liberating and saving relation between humanity and divinity is also a proclamation of the future into which creation is being moved by divine initiative and human response. Yet, under the finite conditions of historical existence, the fullness of that recreation always lies ahead, in the promised future in which God reigns in a new and renewed creation of harmony, peace, and justice.

10
LOCATING MY THEOLOGY IN SACRED PLACES

Bill Smith

*T*he Blues is not just a music that sings a sad song. The Blues is a culture, a tradition, a people. The Blues is seeing and facing pain critically, with truth. The Blues is finally having to face and live with the reality of the consequences of history. The Blues is living in the Here. The Blues is yesterday today trying to be tomorrow. Many Queer/Gay men of color come out of the Blues tradition (if not the music, then the life) and intrinsically understand the Blues.

The Blues is a way of living, walking, talking, crawling, fighting through the anger and pain caused by the conditions of living, without trying to mask them or hide from them. The Blues is a way of consciously living through the reality of your history with whatever tools of transcendence are at your disposal. The Blues is a way of naming the devilment you be going through. The Blues is a gate to Immanuel, a gate to transcendence and transformation.

I am spiritually and existentially drawn to the Blues, drawn to juke joints, drawn to liberated gay urban spaces for my spiritual ecstatic encounters with the Holy. I am drawn to the fundamentally, literally forbidden; drawn to the impure; drawn to the most viscerally human for my expressions of communion, for the loss of and rebirth of my self in Spirit. When the band goes home, when the last call comes, when it's time to catch the cab home, it is then Blues Time. Blues Time is the time of the Cross, the time spent in struggle with whatever would prevent Spirit from concrete realization.

I am drawn to spiritual and theological reflection when the feelings of freedom, relationship, celebration of life, unrestricted physical and aesthetic creativity experienced in the world of ecstasy are denied, repressed, and restricted. I am drawn to relationship, for witness and companionship in the struggle to reclaim the "Rule" of the Holy for every moment of my waking life. This be the "grist for the mill" of the Blues.

I am drawn to work with words in my efforts to live in Blues Time, to understand why I always have to leave Eden to enter the world that is organized systematically to exploit and exhaust the strength, the intelligence, the feelings, and the spirit of the poor in behalf of the rich. Blues Time is the residence of the human condition.

The human condition is the struggle against the forces that would deny us life. These forces themselves are products of previous struggles for life free of oppression. These forces arise out of the fear of and resistance to the change and the difference that is rooted in habituation and addiction to the familiar. These forces have many names; among them are domination, oppression, repression, subjection, despotism, imperialism, sexism, racism, heterosexism, suppression. These forces employ many strategies: murder, theft, control, appropriation, exploitation, lying, cheating, manipulation, coercion, "conventional wisdom." These forces act through every institution of culture and society.

Blues Time makes the human condition personal, real personal, unescapedly personal, unanswerably personal. From the position of the oppressed, oppression often appears to be ontological, essential, a fact of being. It is with the development of critical awareness that other responses occur.

CONFESSION AND LOCATION

No!

I was not there when the foundations of the earth were laid, nor do I know who fixed its dimensions, nor who stretched the measuring line, nor can I command the morning to come, nor do I know the depth of the deepest reaches of the sea. This cooling rock of many rocks floating in space with all its mysteries, including the development of my human being—it is quite beyond my capacity to fathom the origin of its genesis. What I can do is study this human being responding to Here and the history of that responding.

No!

I did not create this Here. This Here is a product of many forces beyond my understanding. But this Here is what I've got to respond to. I've tried wishing it away/praying it away/planning it away/designing it away/writing it away/working in every which way for it to go away, and it still is here with all its misery and despair. I cannot stop my awareness of the exponential increasing of not only human suffering but also that of other life forms.

I cannot stop babies from shooting up/beating/killing/making babies. I cannot stop police/soldiers/presidents/businessmen from butchering/maiming/raping/torturing children/older adults/the innocent. I cannot stop the pain/"dis-ease"/horror/terror I feel every day I walk out the door/drive up streets/go to work/talk to friends/make love. I cannot stop this Here from going on. I see the genesis of its tomorrow.

No longer do the false hopes of democracy/revolution/development/consumption let me off the hook. I am really Here and it doesn't go away. I cannot dream it away/sleep it away/cry it away/smoke it away/drink it away/eat it away/buy it away/love it away. I cannot even forget it away because it is Here, and Here is the progeny of the fathers and it will not fade away. And I do not know why Here was made this way but as long as I live Here, to be truly alive, I have to accept and acknowledge all of this pain and despair that makes Here Here. This is the 'awe-full-ness' of my freedom. Here is where I must confront the reality of my being and all that which would deny me the awareness of the task or the means to accomplish it.

No!

I cannot see happiness as synonymous with freedom, although sometimes there is a convergence, nor can I see the struggle to claim one's freedom as particularly heroic, although there are heroic moments. Nor can I see freedom as a task everyone chooses to accept; Esau sold his birthright for gruel, and things seem to have turned out alright for him in Edom. Nor can I see attempting to escape the realities of Here as becoming any less costly. Being Here costs. It costs our lives, and we cannot escape that truth; trying to escape exacts greater costs. It costs us our innocence; Eden taught us that. The price for escaping from the struggle of Here/Right Now always is our freedom, because all freedom is the struggle for truth, empowerment, relationship, and transcendence Here/Right Now.

The feeling of having escaped Here/Right Now is always temporary. We always come back Here. The only exit is our death, and the peace of that death is not contained in slavery. Slavery is a living death where any moment you might be brought back and have to face yourself Here. The costs of accepting slavery are increasing, and the costs of freedom are the painful acceptance of the costs of Here. I accept the fact, hence the responsibility, of my freedom, which demands I confront Here and all that which would deny me an awareness of my birthright, freedom, and task.

No!

I don't have many tools, only where I have been/what has happened to me/what I have learned/where I am now/what is happening to me/ what I am learning. I must use these tools to discover what is Here and how this Here came about. I must deconstruct the fact and how of my Here here. I must stare into the desperation of my feelings of abandonment/rejection/molestation/rape/my color/my sexual identity/my difference/my alcoholic, crazy family/my own craziness/my alienation/my crimes of commission/omission/my desertions of traditional duty/my drug and sexual attempted escapes from Here/my refusals of love/my denials of my and others' need/my failures of imagination/my spiritual doubting/my acceptance of guilt/my too easy acceptance of ideological explanations of what might be called the "Holy."

I must deconstruct these, feel each element of these histories, learning that this Here is a shared construction not only of the fathers but of myself also. And in this deconstruction, I realize that our sins are the primary constructive building blocks of the world, that the Blues/Cross are the means, the how of how I can get to the truth of the despairing genesis of our Here. In fact, we must embrace the Blues/Cross to begin to realize the fullness of freedom. It is out of the dreck of yesterday that today and tomorrow are created. No matter whose good dream we follow we break someone's heart.

THE NATURE OF "GOD"

Who is this "God" of whom it is claimed creation came? Can this be the same "God" from whom it is also claimed my comfort, my support comes? Like Job I am confused.

Who and what is this "God" that the Church has historically placed at the service of the State and the rich, this "God" who would have the dispossessed and oppressed bow themselves in humility and obedience, in collaboration and complicity, in fear and in ignorance to systems of exploitation and degradation? Is this the same "God" who was discovered and encountered by African slaves, who had been kidnapped to make Europeans rich and prosperous in the New Jerusalem, the "God" that inspired these Africans to resist, to endure, to escape, and to rebel? What is this "God" that is claimed for purposes of both domination and liberation?

As a Gaymale of mixed heritage, a person of color, reared in African-American culture, an orphan, working class, with a memory of childhood incest and peer rape, and a future of HIV infection, a Queer, I am drawn to resolve this spiritual contradiction that feeds my Blues Time. And I am not an exception in my community.

Even were I not to name myself as a Christian, the contradictions of these conflicting ideas of who and what "God" is shape my life in the most intimate and most political ways. My health, my civil rights, my economic well-being are, to a large extent, all shaped by the collective understanding of who and what this "God" is and what this "God" considers appropriate human behavior.

As I understand christian history, the contradictions between a "God" who demands sacrifice for the sake of the ruling classes, the Temple Priests, owners of the means of production and the State, a source of fear and awe, and a "God" who is an indwelling spirit that comforts, inspires, and sustains one in the midst of despair, a cause for joy, are part of the nexus of Christianity's beginnings in the Hebrew Torah. This struggle is archetypally represented in the Gospels' Jesus stories, with the balance of the New Testament a midrash on the outcome of that struggle. This Hebraic-Christian archetypal struggle over conflicting ideas of what a "God" is, as well as the attempts to reconcile the inescapable contradictions, are a primary core of the Christian biblical "story"; in fact, it is also the reason for its writing. Further, this struggle serves as a metaphor for the uses of the "holy" or "spirit" in the struggles between the oppressed and the oppressor.

The ruling classes claim that "God" authorizes the distinctions between purity and impurity, sin and sinlessness, obedience and sacrifice, favor and disfavor. They justify their rule through the Church, the First Estate, by means of that authorization. Those who struggle for empowerment reclaim "God's" presence and power on their behalf and attempt to rename the distinctions of the ruling classes.

The biblical metaphor of the struggle between the "God" of the oppressor and the "God" of the oppressed is useful as a base for the development of a common language between myself and other Christians struggling against oppression and for the development of relationships that create spiritual bonds in that struggle. However, the biblical metaphor of the patriarchal "God" as authority must be recast to be of use Here to my community. Beverly Harrison speaks of "God" as "our passion for justice."[1] Carter Heyward speaks of "God" in terms of "mutual relationship."[2] I accept Matthew's Immanuel, "God with us" (Matt. 1:23), as the embodied incarnational source of our individual and collective ability to transform reality; it is this same representation of "God's" presence that is celebrated by Mary in the Magnificat (Luke 1:46-55).

THE TASK AND METHODOLOGY OF THIS LOCAL THEOLOGY AND PRESENCE OF THE HOLY SPIRIT

My experiences and my relationships mark my spiritual journey. I find this is not unusual in the communities from which I come. It is from these sources that the tasks for my theology are drawn. It is in answer to collective community needs felt personally that I experience call. It is in the struggle to realize materially and in everyday life what is experienced in the spiritual ecstasy of the dance, music, sex in the liberated spaces of the emerging Gay/Lesbian/Queer community.

We are an emerging community, created out of the ongoing, dynamic social construction of sexuality and the evolution of industrialism. Our community and identity come from relationships born of struggle: struggle with ourselves, struggle with our families, struggle with the Church, struggle with the State, struggle with the health care system, struggle with death. Our community is bonded from these struggles. Our community, like the Jesus community, creates family out of these struggles, creates culture from these struggles, creates love from these struggles, creates truth from these struggles, creates and discovers healing in these struggles.

Our community is a people who were born out of the oppression and repression of our sexuality, our ways of talking, walking, being in relationship. We were born out of the denial of our existence as legitimate human beings. Our sexual and behavioral individualities were made into a psychological and criminal category. Out of that category we emerged as a people fighting for liberation. Emerging as a people, we created communities.

The first order of theological business for our emerging community is critical analysis of the spiritual and concrete conditions of our oppression. Once these conditions are understood and named, once we have faced our Here, our yesterday turned into today, our Blues, the task then turns to employing the technologies of the sacred, the fields and avenues of the transcendent—in Christian terms, the sacraments—to transform our today into the resurrection of tomorrow. The Blues, another word for Crossroads, for the Cross, is the place where the struggle for liberation takes place. Blues Time is when the struggle takes place. Blues Time is when revelation occurs.

Immanence and transcendence are the existential experience of the Holy Spirit, the desire for transformation of the Here of oppression, emerging from the concrete experience of suffering, and reaching into the not Here yet of liberating imagination, to inspire, shape, change this Blues of yesterday today into the hope of tomorrow. This communally experienced feeling is a spirit born of the crucifixion of the pain of daily life of the oppressed. It is Immanent and is called "Immanuel." Its reaching into the Not Yet Become with the intention of transforming the Already Here is a hope in the liberating power of Transcendence.

CHURCH AND SACRED SPACE

For this Queer, like many other Gaymen of color, Church is not my only place of spiritual renewal and celebration. Being a Christian is only part of the process I employ in my struggle to extend liberated space and time. It is the lessons and means of the Blues, the full-get-down-funky feeling of the Blues, the mean-sweaty-holler-stomp dance of the Blues, the echoes of African spiritual tradition where sexual ecstasy brings you into the communion with deepest spirituality that is the Blues.

It was one of my foster fathers who called me into the Blues; he was a musician. He called me into the music of W. C. Handy and his "St. Louis Blues." And it is the Blues that taught me how to explore Gay/Queer holy space and discover more than a promise of full liberation. It is the Blues that brought me to the door of resurrection and rebirth. The Blues is the dissonance that remembered the sexuality, sensuality, fecundity, the rebelliousness of African spirituality that the African-American church, with its stress on purity, tried to forget. The Blues and its institutions became the refuge of those called impure by the African American church, those called criminal, those called sinful, those called slothful, the sexual but unmarried.

It is the Blues, with its tradition of sanctuary for the impure, those whose sexuality fell outside of the church door, that serves as my inspiration and model. Gay/Queer dance spaces are liberated spaces, spiritual playgrounds for a community in transformation. Like the Jesus community in its formative stages, like the Blues People of the "juke joints," we are refugees of the purity codes of the Temple/Church, seeking liberation from life-denying restrictions. These liberated spaces are where the immanent becomes the transcendent, and they are defined by our denied spiritual/sexual needs. They are primordial spaces created as sanctuary from the ever-encroaching tentacles of "civilizing society," tentacles that seek to domesticate all human experience. They are shadow spaces transformed into a place of revolt against that domestication; a place of exploration of the nonrational; a place to release and eroticize the brokenness of spirit, of heart; a place of psychic renewal; a place of nonsocial hierarchy; a place where all of it gets played out; a place requiring serious initiation and training in order to survive; a place not for the innocent, the naive; a place of phantoms, demons, and angels; a place where the denied spirits have play. They are playgrounds where the spiritual power of sexuality is both immanent and transcendent; where reality is deconstructed to serve the needs of the erotic imagination; where social roles are exchanged, magnified, or reversed.

Because everyday social identities act as barriers for entering this space and sense of transcendence, identities become categories of consciousness. Rituals, tools, and agents of transformation of consciousness, like different forms of "drag," dancing, cruising, and sexual conversation are gateways to the other side of this sexually repressive domain and into our liberated underground territory. The Blues tradition would recognize these spaces as kindred. They are kindred as are the spaces of the Jesus community (early Christian churches), kindred to people breaking class, cultural, sexual, gender boundaries and seeking spiritual liberation.

Spiritual liberation is necessary for and the base of the imagination for material liberation. In these spaces, the technologies of the sacred, art, music, oral and written literature all express the needs and struggles of the community seeking the transformation of oppressive conditions. A Gay/Queer positive ministry would be a ministry that expresses, respects, and utilizes the experience and witness of these forms, a ministry that empowers and helps in the enabling of the community to use the insights and gifts of these spaces to create freedom-making activity in the Blues Time of the concrete jungle world we live in.

THE BIBLICAL METAPHOR

My cultural background called me into being a Christian, that same African-American background which had come to claim the European "God" as its own protector and liberator. Malcolm X called me into a critical evaluation and awareness of the African-American, "colored" churches' self-hatred of Blackness. James Baldwin called me into awareness of the awesome price that the church's hatred of homosexuality exacted.

It is in the critical examination and evaluation of our experiences and in the context of struggle for mutuality in relationship that an understanding of how the Bible's texts and our relationships within the church can shed light on our struggle for liberation. Part of a *Gay/Queer of color* Christian theology, a theology of particularity, is the sharing of critical biblical hermeneutical skills and resources, which include socio-historical, anthropological and literary, and politico-economic analytic tools with the community. Critical biblical analysis is necessary to relativize the text so that the concretely useful liberative information may be revealed. Because we are not included in the Bible, like African-American womanists, we must also reopen the canon to include our presence and our struggle, to include our Blues, the written and oral accounts of our experiences in struggle.

The Church, its Scriptures, and its Traditions make up what may be called the biblical metaphor. In the struggle against oppression, the question must be asked: Is the biblical metaphor of the struggle between the oppressed and the oppressor for power over human organic creative energy a useful tool in the struggle to create liberated space and time? If it is, in what way(s) would it be most useful? These questions must be asked because the Bible and Tradition have been a primary source of my oppression as a Queer Christian of color. They have been a tool the Church employs to continue its campaign of dehumanizing and demonizing the sexuality and even the very lives of Gay people. Furthermore, except in a few denominations, we are not welcome as whole human beings in Christian churches. For this reason, many of us see the Church, along with its Scriptures and Traditions, as a primary enemy and oppressor and have found spiritual support elsewhere.

For those who remain we must determine why. Many Gaymen have accepted the metaphor as real and reside in the metaphor. That is, they see, in some way, the biblical metaphor as the authoritative description of the "Truth." In many cases it was because they entered into the metaphor at an early age through the efforts of parents or caretakers and were taught to believe in the biblical story as the Truth through their formative years. This teaching was reinforced in every part of their socialization process, in one way or another, even by people who were themselves unchurched.

For these Gaymen, seeing themselves as the oppressed, identifying themselves with the oppressed of the Bible and with the "God" of the oppressed, has liberating possibilities. Christian Gaymen are engaged in writing liberating theologies and stretching the biblical metaphor to include us in the biblical story. Others of us, whose experiences and critical examination have placed us outside the biblical metaphor and do not see it as the "Truth" but still identify ourselves as Christian, must come to terms with why we remain Christians.

My resistance to authority and the Bible's property and purity codes prevent me from entering into the metaphor. I see its world and spiritual view as relative, not universal. The biblical metaphor has the proclivity to co-opt struggle, to pacify the oppressed. The biblical metaphor—Church, Scripture, and Tradition—does not see itself as participating in the social construction of oppression of gay people and, hence, is not self-critical or repentant. Its program of liberation is partial and not determinative because the metaphor calls for obedience to spiritual authority and the hierarchy of the nonrational, not for critical thinking and integration of the nonrational with the rest of the personality.

On the other hand, the biblical metaphor's value as a tool against the spiritual encroachment and exploitation by the ruling class has been historically proven. Its sacraments and rituals have the power to open us to sacred space, to the imagination. Even with its limitations, it provides hope, comfort, and healing for the oppressed. The task of uncovering and utilizing that value is a collective task that must be undertaken critically with a respect for the traditional and experiential background of the participant in this theological liberative process.

THE BLUES, JESUS, THE CROSS, RESURRECTION, AND CHRIST

Jesus was a man of color who loved men. The Jesus stories tell us that Jesus prayed, fasted, partied, and hung out with his friends, his men friends, and he loved them. This Asian-born, loving man, whose ancestors had a long, shared history with Africa, this loving man of color, loved men and showed it and talked about it and encouraged it. Jesus, like myself, and the community of my ministry, was a man of color, whose ministry, we are told by the stories, healed them. Jesus died on a cross.

The Blues are part of a continuum of African traditional religion. The story of Jesus and his Cross is a Blues story as well, a Legba story: Legba, Ellegua, the Orisha is the Spirit of the Crossroads. Legba, a God of the African Diaspora, is the Spirit behind the Blues. The Cross/Blues is told as a time of struggle, crises, and opportunity for transformation, for liberation; Blues Time, Cross Time, time for hope born of struggle; getting through the yesterday today time of Here, through the birth channel of hope into tomorrow, into the spirit of resurrection. Resurrection is the time of emergence from yesterday's struggle with renewed strength, vision, and hope for today's and tomorrow's. Gay/Queer affirmative ministry is a midwife to the birthing.

Christ, the early church's attempt to universalize the Jesus story, became the means by which Jesus' spiritual-political message for the poor and oppressed was co-opted by privileged classes and transformed into a spiritual system that excluded the egalitarian message taught by Jesus. To reclaim Christ we must see the Christ as the creative energy available to us through our passion for justice and mutual relation, another name for Immanuel.

LIBERATION, SALVATION, AND GRACE

My neighborhood childhood peers, in the process of raping me, called me into awareness of my sexual difference, called me into the beginnings of my awareness and questionings of my sexual identity. It was because I was other that I was raped. I did not know what that otherness meant. The fact of the rapings called me to question the why of this childhood exile.

It was my working at jobs from the age of five that gave me the awareness of my working-class status and its connection with my color and cultural background. I was not the boss. The boss paid for my time, and everything I created in the time I worked for him belonged to him. I was never to rest in the time I worked for him.

I have resisted external authority from early childhood. This resistance is a product of my early rebellion against the racism in public schools and at work. I was positively reinforced by my foster families in my efforts toward independence. From childhood, then, spiritual struggles reflected the material struggles for liberation. They were from the same piece of cloth. The most vital and important parts of me were to be suppressed in the name of some outside authority. These are the doors I have had to walk through first to understand "God," sin, salvation, Jesus, Christ, the Resurrection.

No!

I was not here when the mountains crested out of the oceans, nor when the sun sent the planets spinning in their orbits, nor when the first critters emerged from the muck. I was not present when the first horrors of creation occurred. I did not create this pattern of coming into being. However, my "being-ness" brings the consciousness of the feeling of pain and horror into the world. I am not able to withstand the "awe-some awe-full-ness" of the creation's face without struggling to change it. My innocence is shattered in the comprehension of the full face of reality.

How can I stand in acknowledgment of my birthright of freedom? First I must find my will to freedom, my volitional acknowledgment and learning of Here and how Here came to be. I must first accept the gift of courage born of the struggle to be Here in Freedom. In this acceptance, I must submit to the reality of my frailty/my incompleteness in my aloneness and admit to the need of community.

"Freedom's just another word for nothing left to lose." It is only when nothing works to keep the wolf from devouring your soul and you've tried everything else that you reach for the hem of the garment/ that you climb the tree/that you pay for the pearl of great price. That payment/that climb/that reach is the Confession of the recognized fragility, the realized limitation of our individuality, the recognition of the need for community in conscious critical struggle for transformation and liberation. The activity that comes out of this witness/testimony/ confession, this recognized need for community relationship is concrete living prayer, informed struggle for liberated space, time to hope, envision, to imagine the possibility of freedom, a time of meditation. This meditation is an invitation for Grace, the gift of the experience of resurrection.

The process of liberation is an historical one. It is inexorable. It is not an event of a few months, a few years. Oppression is a result of long-term historical forces, human responses to natural and social environmental conditions. Africans became slaves not out of some divine plan, but rather as a result of geographical location, planetary resource distribution, different technologies, and social organization. The African-American liberation from slavery was a 240-year process, a process of learning, critical awareness, and seizing historic opportunities. African-American womanists speak of the "everyday-ness" of the liberation struggle, the weaving of small gains into major actions. Rosa Parks's bus ride was such an event, made of centuries of learnings, decades of labor and church organizing, all coming together at an historic opportunity. The community was prepared for the opportunity.

Maintaining the spirit of the struggle over the time necessary to learn the skills and tools necessary for liberation is a theological task. The gospel story of Jesus suggests to me that he had an image of the historical process of liberation. He came from a culture that had a millennium of resistance practice.

The purpose of a Queer/Gay affirmative theology of healing is to participate fully and mutually in the process of struggle for liberation through the sharing of creation's gifts. But liberation itself is no tea party, not the end of struggle. For the oppressed, it is only through struggle for justice and liberation, through the development of ever-increasing critical awareness, that the gift of Grace and Hope occurs. It is this process of intentional critical action that reveals the permanent necessity for the liberative struggle against any organization, system, action, and behavior that might evolve into oppressive social and personal structures.

Jesus reminded us of the difficulty of the rich, the privileged, the self-righteous in finding Grace. His reminder was not a moralism but the accurate critical analysis of a Mediterranean peasant who knew the reality of struggle and created a liberative praxis. In doing so, he rigorously employed an awareness of the power of creative energy, the power of the Transcendence, on behalf of liberation and thereby demonstrated the truth of his observations. A theology that serves Queers/Gaymen of color, and especially those who live with AIDS/HIV, can benefit from the Blues Story of the Judean peasant on the Cross. Jesus did not do it once and for all or else the material conditions for oppression would no longer exist. Jesus did it for then. We have to do it now.

11

"DREAMS OF THE GOOD"

From the Analytics of Oppression to the Politics of Transformation*

Sharon D. Welch

I am not a Black Goddess,
I am not a Black Goddess,
Look at me
Look at me
I do what I can
That's about it
Sometimes I make it Sometimes I don't

I still get Night Terrors
And sometimes it takes me weeks to
Answer a letter or make a phone call
I am not a Black Goddess
I am not a Black Goddess
Once though, I was Harriet Tubman.
— Kate Rushin

*P*eople who work for social justice know full well the many barriers to effective, long-lasting, energizing social change. Buffeted by resistance from without and thrown off balance by distortions from within, they realize that it is a wonder—no, a miracle—that change occurs, that healing and transformation grace our lives.

Oppressive, exploitive political structures do not gracefully self-destruct when their deadly logic is exposed. Activists now have a rich tradition of social and political critique; we can readily become well versed in insightful, powerful critiques of the deadly logic of oppression. We can, for example, read Mary Daly's devastating, thorough indictment of phallocracy. For Daly, *sexism* and *patriarchy* are terms too mild to describe the reach and destructiveness of patriarchal oppression.[1] John Stoltenberg delineates the roots of male violence against women in homophobia and male violence against other men, and the torturous constrictions of an artificial two-gender cultural system.[2] Angela Davis recounts the volatile interaction of racism, sexism, and capitalist exploitation.[3]

These writers share a painfully accurate awareness of the devastating interaction of external oppression and internalized oppression. Daly, for example, throughout her work writes of the struggles of women against what she calls "patriarchal demons" and "potted and plastic passions." She depicts eloquently the ongoing, spiraling process of unearthing ways in which we have internalized beliefs, habits, and expectations that confine us and other women:

> The radical be-ing of women is very much an Otherworld Journey. It is both discovery and creation of a world other than patriarchy. Patriarchy appears to be "everywhere." . . . Nor does this colonization exist simply "outside" women's minds, securely fastened into institutions we can physically leave behind. Rather, it is also internalized, festering inside women's heads, even feminist heads.[4]

The existing analyses of oppression are weighty, exhaustive delineations of the networks of oppression. Read in isolation from active work for social transformation, their effect can be paralyzing and the transformative power overlooked. Read in the context of work for social justice, the effect of these analyses can be quite different, sustaining a self-critical, even a humorous sensibility.

The excerpt from Kate Rushin's poem, "The Black Goddess," above, captures a sensibility that accompanies much long-lasting, effective work for social change. In this essay I explore this sensibility as manifest in a particular strategy, in one aspect of work for justice. I explore the ways in which the dynamics of effective resistance escape the dualism and ordering of Enlightenment rationality. The logic and sensibility at work in effective resistance can neither be encapsulated in the certainties of Christian triumphalism nor accurately described as a tragic view of life.

In Rushin's poem, note her detailing of the vagaries of everyday life: here the barriers to social change are not cosmic, but almost comic in their familiarity and ordinariness. The limits mentioned are common, not tragic or grand in their sweep. Yet, in the midst of unreturned phone calls and unanswered mail, acts of courage, healing, and justice emerge with terrible power and clarity. Rushin's reference to Harriet

Tubman is startling. Tubman accomplished remarkable feats, leading over 300 slaves to freedom, in the face of extraordinary obstacles. Apart from other effects of slavery, Tubman could neither read nor write, and she was subject to unpredictable sleeping bouts resulting from an overseer's striking her when she defied his cruelty and stood up for another slave.[5] Kate Rushin's poetic invocation of Harriet Tubman is a gift of hope, a reminder of the potential coexistence of the ordinary and the audacious in all of our lives.

Harriet Tubman's work for freedom was resisted by white slaveholders. Many of us find our work for justice and freedom challenged by the slaveholder, the sexist, the racist within. Throughout history, people have been propelled into work for social change when they have come to recognize their dual identity as oppressor and oppressed. In his groundbreaking history of African-American women and men, John Hope Franklin describes the dual identity that shapes the lives of Euro-Americans. When this dual identity was recognized, the results were far-reaching, women and men finally seeing the injustice of owning slaves or tolerating slavery while petitioning for greater economic and political freedom for themselves. Franklin describes such a transition after 1763:

> As the colonists saw in England's new colonial policy a threat to the economic and political freedom that they had enjoyed for several generations, they also seemed to recognize a marked inconsistency in their position as oppressed colonists *and* slaveholders. . . . The resurrection of the hated Navigation Acts and the imposition of new regulations like the Sugar Act of 1764 brought forth eloquent defenses of the colonists. . . . They began to think of their dual role as oppressed and oppressor. Almost overnight the grave but quiet efforts of Benezet and Woolman bore fruit, as some colonial leaders began to denounce not only England's new imperial policy but slavery and the slave trade as well.[6]

The tension between competing and conflicting social roles and expectations continues. As a woman, I am simultaneously exploited, marginalized, and, by virtue of the collective political struggles of women, empowered. The movement for the full humanity and dignity of women is central to my life and work. Also, because of my race, I am an oppressor, moving from being an agent of racial oppression to an ally with people of color. Like most Americans, my class location is mixed: I stand in the complex intersection of putative social privilege and actual economic marginality that characterizes the American middle class.

While supposedly a privileged group, it has seen during the Reagan-Bush years a steady erosion of the job security and incomes of its factory workers, managers, and "white collar" professionals.[7]

I have long been an activist, but I have discovered a new depth of political analysis and strategies for social change in the last few years from women and men leading diversity-training workshops. In these workshops, people experience the complexity and tensions of their identities as oppressor and oppressed, as agent of oppression in the process of becoming an ally against injustice, as target of exploitation and member of an empowered, resisting group.[8] I will describe this work and what I am learning from it.

EQUITY INSTITUTE

When I moved to the University of Missouri, I joined a team of people who were conducting diversity workshops. Some of the members, including myself, were trained at Equity Institute, an organization based in the San Francisco Bay area. Others had come to this work by other means. What I have found in these workshops is a way of dismantling racism, sexism, heterosexism, anti-Semitism, class exploitation, and discrimination against people with disabilities that is seemingly simple yet profoundly complex in the dynamics that the workshops acknowledge and unleash. Similar work is being done by other groups, under other names. William Jones, for example, leads workshops on uncovering the "grid of oppression." I know only the Equity model well, however, and will focus on it in this essay.[9]

Equity Institute provides diversity training for a wide range of people and organizations. Since 1982 they have worked with over seventy thousand people from more than eight hundred institutions (schools, businesses, synagogues and churches, community service and social change organizations). The Equity staff leads workshops designed to reduce sexism, racism, classism, anti-Semitism, ageism, ableism, and heterosexism.

Equity workshops are based on the work of Erica Sherover-Marcuse. She poses a sharp challenge to activists: Why is it that the oppressed, even as we gain power, repeat patterns of oppression? Why do we treat each other in the way the oppressor has treated us? And, most importantly, how can we stop the cycle of oppression? In the past, I had heard questions of this kind as reactionary, as justifications for maintaining a known, albeit unjust status quo, rather than risking the chaos and likely oppressiveness of social disruption. Sherover-Marcuse raises the question with revolutionary intent. She argues that we must face the troubling dynamics within movements for social change, the destructive perpetuation of patterns of oppression even in the midst of work for justice. She cites Herbert Marcuse's formulation of this disturbing phenomenon:

> Are revolutions perhaps not only defeated, reversed and undone from outside; is there not perhaps in the individuals themselves already a dynamic at work which *internally* negates a possible liberation and gratification, and allows them to submit not only externally to the forces of denial?[10]

What accounts for, and more importantly, what can change, the "perpetuation of oppression by the oppressed" (S-M, 134)? Sherover-Marcuse builds on the analysis of internalized oppression by feminist and Third World theorists. She argues that "struggles for liberation are often eroded and defeated 'from within' by the effects of internalized oppression" (S-M, 122). Unless the "reproduction of domination" is challenged, social change does not succeed and alliances fail.

The costs of internalized oppression are high. Working against internalized oppression is not easy, and yet the tone of Sherover-Marcuse's work is one of hope and energy:

> In the last two decades Third World and feminist theorists and writers have dissected the phenomenon of internalized oppression. . . . Different as their points of departure may be, their concern with this issue parallels the concern articulated by Western Marxists. . . . If it is true that "the formulation of a question is its solution," at least on the plane of theory, and if it is true that "humanity sets for itself only those tasks which it can solve," then this convergence may have much more than a merely anecdotal significance. (S-M, 134–35)

Sherover-Marcuse, in conjunction with other activists, has developed practices that interrupt the perpetuation of oppression, practices that can elicit or support "emancipatory subjectivity." She defines emancipatory subjectivity as "those attitudes, character traits, beliefs, and dispositions that are both conducive to and supportive of the sort of radical social transformation that the young Marx characterizes as 'universal human emancipation'" (S-M, 1–2).

A key element in the development of emancipatory subjectivity is the recognition of the ways in which individuals and groups are shaped by internalized oppression. Internalized oppression takes many forms: it is women defining our worth in terms of our acceptance by men and legitimation by male institutions; it is progressive men regarding women's concerns as less important than the "real issues" of poverty, war, ecological destruction, all the while using women's energy for their own ends. Internalized oppression is being shaped by the values of the oppressor. It leads oppressed people to see themselves as they are seen by the oppressor—as less intelligent, less moral, less valuable. It leads oppressed people to act like oppressors even in our work for social change, instituting our own hierarchies, using power over each other:

> The heart of this perspective is the recognition of the phenomenon of internalized oppression. This recognition entails the understanding that an oppressive society recreates itself in its victims' hearts and minds in the form of behavior patterns and attitudinal habits which are installed and "nourished" by the normal functioning of social intercourse itself. . . . The effects of systematic mistreatment sediment themselves in the consciousness (and sub-consciousness) of the oppressed and . . . in the course of time these effects acquire both a "natural appearance" and a life of their own. As a result, oppression is recycled; mistreatment is passed along by the victims themselves. Having internalized the norms and values of the dominant group, members of an oppressed group often mistreat each other in an unconscious imitation of their own suffering. (S-M, 4)

How do we "unlearn" these destructive habits of thought and action? Sherover-Marcuse states that we can. The workshops of Equity Institute are designed to amplify the process of recognizing internalized oppression and learning new ways of relating to ourselves and others. She claims that this work does not "happen by itself" while we are involved in other forms of political work, directly challenging oppressive economic and political structures. "This 'unlearning' ought not to be regarded as a phenomenon which just 'happens' in the course of other 'more significant' transformative activity, but as a project in its own right, meriting both sustained and focused effort. The *deliberate undoing*, at the level of subjectivity, of the effects of an oppressive social order is actually a particular kind of 'doing' " (S-M, 5).

The practice of emancipatory subjectivity does not replace other forms of political work. It is one dimension, an essential dimension, of multifaceted work for social change. Recognizing and exorcising (Daly) the oppressor within makes us more effective in our transformation of oppressive structures without.

Sherover-Marcuse celebrates the transformation of external social structures *and* the transformation of subjectivity that are intrinsic to the civil rights movement, the New Left, the women's movement, the gay and lesbian movement, and the peace movement:

> In these movements attempts at the transformation of subjectivity have often taken the form of "self-help" groups, "consciousness-raising" groups or "affinity groups." Such groups have operated on the principle that the transformation of consciousness also requires "emotional work": bringing to awareness feelings, memories, experiences that may have appeared to have only a personal meaning but whose broader social significance can be discovered precisely through the sharing of "individual" life stories and experiences. (S-M, 140)

The workshops she initiated help us move from being agents of oppression to allies, from targets of oppression to empowered individuals and groups (S-M, 137). A practice of subjectivity uncovers "the awareness of being socialized into the roles of oppressor and oppressed" (S-M, 139). It is not accidental that such awareness is "buried": "part of the socialization process is the pervasive *mislabeling* of this process itself. . . . The *traumatic* nature of the experience is denied" (S-M, 139–40). These traumatic experiences are also privatized and their social and political locus and impact masked. Through workshop activities, we can remember, grieve, and rage over this traumatic socialization; we can celebrate a personal and collective history of resistance. We can resist oppression now because we have already, often as children, resisted our socialization into the roles of oppressor and oppressed (S-M, 140).

The creation of emancipatory subjectivity is ongoing. Sherover-Marcuse emphasizes that we cannot escape our conditioning; there is no "external vantage point" from which we can critique the present and develop strategies for social change free from any oppressive influences (S-M, 141). The solution to the "permanent risk of contamination by the toxins of domination" is an ongoing practice of accountability to those of us who are oppressed, along with ongoing practices of critique and revisioning strategies for social change (S-M, 141).

Turning from theory to practice, we must ask: what are the elements of a workshop that are designed to evoke and sustain emancipatory subjectivity? The constitutive elements are relatively straightforward, yet each assumes an understanding of the complex interaction of internalized oppression and emancipatory subjectivity. The workshop follows a simple structure, one familiar to people involved in group dynamics and team building. People are welcomed as individuals, introduce themselves to each other, and are then involved in exercises designed to ease communication. The warm-up activities and introductions, while often simple, have a complex purpose, highlighting and valuing something in each individual without directly referring to or highlighting such differences in social status as one finds in a professor, student, dean, or secretary.

The aim of warm-up activities and organized introductions is the evocation of a sense of community in which the individual is valued. From the beginning of the workshop, the diversity of experience is brought to the fore. It becomes clear that in this group we work together on the basis of a shared humanity, a common matrix that includes significant differences as well as similarities. The exercises embody a post-Enlightenment view of common humanity. Our humanity includes difference. Our humanity is also seen as both gift and task—a bond that may sustain us in work together if nurtured and cultivated or, possibly, even created.

Of course, the exercises and workshops are themselves artifacts of Western culture and reinscribe defining elements of that culture. For instance, most activities are more verbal than tactile. Yet these exercises reflect a culture in transition as codes of communication are variously acknowledged, challenged, and supplanted by other codes. In many warm-up activities, for example, people are encouraged to communicate nonverbally: the focus is on silent observation or on moving one's body.

The workshop does not begin with soul-searching questions or self-revealing activities, for it is assumed that at this time at least, people do not trust each other and the workshop facilitators. The momentum of the workshop acknowledges and challenges and hopefully supplants the rational, self-protective accretions of our culture's many systems of oppression. Growth requires vulnerability (a point I will defend later), and, in our society, it is rational to protect and guard that vulnerability in a room of strangers or even acquaintances and coworkers.

The spiraling movement of the workshop manifests the extent to which, at this time, trust is possible, vulnerability a plausible stance. The introductions and warm-up activities play a key role in clarifying who is here and what the dynamics of the groups will be. Further information is provided by two other workshop components: a survey of needs and a presentation of guiding assumptions. While a partial survey of the needs of the group is best done in advance (otherwise the whole workshop may miss the mark), an on-the-spot survey, especially if at least partially shared, helps people understand more about whom they are working with and where their concerns fit in the tapestry of the particular group and its task.

Another essential element of the Equity model is the acknowledgment of the context of our work: a world rife with injustice, a world in which we are searching for support, insight, and challenge in our work for justice. Talking about oppression is not easy. We are all shaped by it; we are all hurt by it. And those hurts do not disappear when we enter a workshop. In fact, they may be more acute, our sensitivity heightened by our need for allies, by our search for ways of working together to challenge injustice. During the course of the workshop, just as in the course of daily life, it is more likely than not that we will say or do something that offends someone else, say or do something that is not merely annoying but replicates patterns of oppression. When this happens, people are encouraged simply to say "ouch." No elaborate attacks on the offender or justifications of why the remark or action was oppressive are needed. Similarly, the offenders, if they understand what is being pointed out, may respond simply by saying "I'm sorry." No defense of good intentions or elaborate justifications of what was really meant are necessary.

The value of this open acknowledgment of conflict, and the encouragement to express it readily, is, once again, to invoke a modicum of trust and safety in an unsafe world. Its aim and the reality from which it derives mark a significant departure from the codes of Western speech. On the one hand is the recognition that trust is needed for self-disclosure to occur. And, like the therapist or pastor, the group is promised confidentiality—giving one the freedom to explore and try new reactions. The value of "safe space" is also affirmed, even as it is simultaneously challenged and redefined. In women's groups, safe space has meant the opportunity to talk without interruption and without censure. Even within the women's movement, however, the illusion of safety has run aground on the shoals of oppression-induced difference. The guideline of expressing "ouches" is, therefore, necessary. It is explicitly stated that we operate within a different kind of safety. We assume good intentions, and we assume that oppression is ubiquitous and that we will hurt and offend each other. To challenge the codes of Western communication again, hurt and offense do not have to be the last words. They do not have to be experienced as closure, as the end of trust, cooperation, and safety. Rather, the response to hurt by all involved can signal a spiraling process of discovery and growth.

With this foundation, the group moves to an exploration of some form of oppression. The aim here, while building on concepts and analysis, is not primarily analytical. Rather, the goal is to evoke or invoke a dynamic, a movement from being an agent of oppression to being an ally, from being members of a targeted group to being empowered. The successful evocation of movement requires several stances. First, the learning is experiential. There are no lectures, but rather a process of self- and group-discovery. The aim of these activities is to elicit the knowledge of the group and their own resources for compassion and action. Second, workshops conclude with time for reflection on further action and further commitments to oneself and to others.

Ann Berlak describes the power of a seemingly simple exercise, often used at Equity:

> All members of the class stand on one side of the room in silence. (The facilitator) makes it clear that students are free not to participate at any time. She begins by asking, "Will all of those who are African-Americans walk across the room. . . . Stand for a moment and see who is with you. . . . See who is left behind. Notice how you feel to have walked across. Notice how you feel to have stayed where you are." Silence for several moments. "You may return." This process is repeated for a dozen or more designations of groups that are oppressed in our society.[11]

Berlak names the "inexplicable power" of the exercise as it brings into dramatic relief the contours of oppression. Here, in this workshop, in this room, we see each other as individuals and as people who have been shaped by the forces of oppression. Our identities are not simple, either oppressor or oppressed, agent or victim. As Berlak states, the exercise is revelatory:

> Everyone has been both target and non-target. The power imbalances of the society have been presented and represented experientially, as well as the multiple places in which each of us stands. The mood is sombre. There are tears.[12]

To participate fully in the "power walk" is to see the face of oppression, defiance, survival, and hope. The emotions that accompany walking across the room, and standing, in pride, joy, and defiance as a resisting, empowered member of a targeted group, are intense and revelatory. The insight that comes from being left behind, looking at the others across the room, respecting their courage, looking at those who are left with you, in earnest expectation that we can be allies together, is, again, deeply moving and potentially revelatory. The exercise can reveal the tremendous resources we have to counter oppression: the beauty and dignity of those of us who endure, survive, and transform the cycles of injustice.

Effective action must come from within, from our collective well-spring of compassion, rage, grief, and imagination. These workshops assume that our experience is multivalent, both sustaining and challenging oppression. The activities elicit and bring into play the threads of creativity and resistance. When the workshop is successful, we glimpse the energy and power of being allies.

What is the significance of these simple yet profound exercises, these attempts to nurture and expand emancipatory subjectivity? In the following pages I explore the ramifications of these practices, moving from a consideration of the questions at the heart of ethical/theological inquiry to meditations on the criteria for conceptual and political adequacy, or, to put it more baldly, to a consideration of paradoxes of truth, order, and justice.

DREAMS OF THE GOOD AND
THE KILLERS OF DREAMS

Do our dreams die because we do not know whether to believe them? No. They die because we do not know how to live them.

In her profound meditation on the tragedy of racism in the United States, Lillian Smith describes the complex interaction of values, religious ideals, and the soul-twisting power of racist institutions, practices, and beliefs. Her analysis, written in the 1940s, remains timely and compelling, a disturbing account of the complicity of genuinely good people in the oppressive institutions of racism. Smith depicts a phenomenon that is all too common—people who firmly hold ideals of freedom, justice, and equality, yet find themselves acting against those ideals as individuals and as members of social groups and institutions.

Lillian Smith describes racism as a problem that is known but unthinkable, a system of values, laws, and power that could, and often did, erupt in the terrible violence of lynchings, cross burnings, and terrorizing of blacks by whites:

> Even its children know that the South is in trouble. No one has to tell them; no words said aloud. . . . Some learn to screen out all except the soft and the soothing. . . . But all know that under quiet words and warmth and laughter, under the slow ease and tender concern about

small matters, there is a heavy burden on all of us and as heavy a refusal to confess it. The children know this "trouble" is bigger than they, bigger than their family, bigger than their church, so big that people turn away from its size. They have seen it flash out . . . and shatter a town's peace, have felt it tear up all they believe in.[13]

Smith describes the strictures of racism, the inflexible separation of black and white, coexisting with hospitality and courtesy:

I knew by the time I was twelve that a member of my family would always shake hands with old Negro friends, would speak . . . graciously to members of the Negro race unless they forgot their place, in which event icy peremptory tones would draw lines beyond which only the desperate would dare take one step. . . . I learned to cheapen with tears and sentimental talk of "my old mammy" one of the profound relationships of my life. I learned the bitterest thing a child can learn: that the human relations I valued most were held cheap by the world I lived in. (Smith, 19)

Smith carefully delineates the threads of "color and race . . . and politics . . . and money and how it is made . . . and religion . . . and sex and the body image . . . and love . . . and dreams of the Good and the killers of dreams" (Smith, 16–17). She provides a detailed, poetic genealogy of racism, exploring the way in which a power structure which thoroughly violated the humanity of blacks was sustained in spite of the Christian and democratic ideals of the whites who implemented and were complicitous with racism. She gives the example of her father, "who rebuked me for an air of superiority toward schoolmates from the mill and rounded out his rebuke by gravely reminding me that 'all men are brothers,' " yet who also instructed her "in the steel-rigid decorums I must demand of every colored male" (Smith, 18).

Smith also describes the interlocking matrix of structural injustice and psychological terror, the means by which injustice is kept in place. She offers a phenomenology of the creation of the oppressor, the deformations and twists of consciousness and conscience that enable people who regard themselves (and are regarded by others) as compassionate, rational, people of principle and integrity to be at the same time the agents of oppression:

Something was wrong with a world that tells you that love is good and people are important and then forces you to deny love and to humiliate people. I knew, though I would not for years confess it aloud, that in trying to shut the Negro race away from us we have shut ourselves away

from so many good, creative, honest, deeply human things in life. I began
to understand slowly at first but more clearly as the years passed, that the
warped, distorted frame we have put around every Negro child from
birth is around every white child also. (Smith, 27–28)

How do we break the "warped, distorted frames" of oppression, the
habits of perception, of action that constitute the oppression of women,
of minorities, of lesbians and gays? Lillian Smith's work is a paradigm
for the sort of analysis that can be done for every form of oppression—an exploration of the means by which cruelty becomes common-
place, by which indifference to human suffering is enforced.

What causes the break between ideals and practice? Smith raises a
searing challenge for ethicists, activists, and theologians. How do we
account for the many times in human history when firmly held ideals
and principles are betrayed in practice? How do we explain, and most
importantly, effectively challenge this disjunction? Smith provides no
solace in a resigned acceptance of human finitude or sinfulness. I too
find it impossible to accept, as tragic but inevitable, the persistence of
racism, sexism, and other numerous forms of exploitation and oppression. The betrayal of ideals in practice is eminently deserving of critical
thought.

The thesis guiding this essay is quite simple. Do our dreams die because we do not know whether to believe them? No. They die because
we do not know how to live them.

By focusing on the challenge of how to live ideals I sidestep certain
philosophical and theological issues and find myself confronted with
others. One debate that I find irrelevant is that of either the necessity or
the danger of establishing firm foundations for our ideals. People or
groups whose ideas and critical principles were firmly grounded in
some form of absolutes—either the truths of reason, revelation, or the
dynamics of history—are as susceptible to their betrayal as those whose
ideals are justified more loosely. Being firmly grounded in the "revealed
Word of God" has not led the majority of Christian congregations to
take courageous stands against racism and for equality between women
and men. Those congregations and groups of believers who have been
in the forefront of work for social justice have long been in the minority.[14]

At this point, I consider the source of the "dreams of the good" to be
irrelevant. It does not matter so much if they stem from revelation,
reason, the authority of tradition, the gift of the imagination, or from a

wager on the possible abundance of life. What is needed, in any case, in every case, are practices of solidarity, practices of living out these firmly held or defiantly grasped dreams of transformation and justice. To know that they are grounded in some form of absolute says nothing about the challenge of how to live the dream, how to become aware of the barriers from without and tensions from within, the interplay of external oppression and internalized oppression that accompanies work for justice.

I focus on the challenges of practice because I have found myself profoundly challenged and have seen others equally challenged by specific patterns of resistance. The creation of emancipatory subjectivity is ongoing, continuously unfolding, and disruptive of deeply held patterns of acting. The practice of a powerful workshop provides training in habits of learning and responding that enhance long-term work for justice. These practices, learning how to live out our dreams, are essential. Without them, our ideals of justice and our analyses of oppression remain lifeless and abstract.

I described the practices of a diversity-training workshop. In the next section I explore further ramifications of these practices, and delineate ways in which they challenge common patterns of gauging the value and power of political strategies. Such an analysis is part of a genealogy of resistance. It is important to note the movement here: from resistance, from participation in alternative and transforming practices to a deeper critique of the culture of oppression. In my earlier work I developed Foucault's insight that we can only see a system of logic as a particular system of reasoning and not as Truth itself, when we already participate in another system of establishing the contours of rationality and irrationality, truth and error. I applied that insight to ethics, and argued that we can see the foundational flaws in a system of ethics only as we are shaped by alternative systems of value.[15] I am now extending the principle to the realm of strategy and practice: we can best see the correlation between habits of perception, judgment, and response and systems of oppression when we experience alternative structures of perceiving, judging, and responding. The exercises of a diversity-training workshop, while seemingly simple, have, in fact, a complex goal: allowing people the opportunity to experience alternative and transformative practices. Such moments of alterity unlock further processes of social critique, and most importantly, provide resources for envisioning strategies for social change and for surviving the chaos of social change.

DARKNESS ARRIVES

Darkness arrives
splitting the mind open.

Something again
is beginning to be born.
— Muriel Rukeyser[16]

The long and bitter history of racism among European and Euro-American people is paralleled by an even longer history of stigmatizing darkness. In using images of darkness positively, Muriel Rukeyser does so in awareness of the racist legacy of allusion and projection. Is it possible to loosen the bonds of this imagery by reversing it? It can be dangerous to reverse such imagery. Reversal could lead to the implication that there is some actual connection between the white Western fear of darkness and the actual lives and culture of peoples who have been defined as dark. When we speak of the "darkness that arrives," we refer to a construct, to the constellation of forces that have been defined as dangerous and symbolized as dark by Western culture. These forces — the events of chaos, ambiguity, failure, rage, pain, and grief — in themselves are no more connected to people of color than they are to peoples who have defined themselves as white. What happens to Europeans and Euro-Americans, however, when we find creative resources in these elements of human experience that have been grouped together and feared? I am not at all certain if this move is one that should be repeated. Yet I find, for now, impetus for thought and action by welcoming the once-feared darkness, by speaking, as Brigit McCallum does, of healing spiritual/political work as endarkenment, rather than enlightenment.

Feminist theologians, along with African-American, Asian, Latin American, and Asian-American theologians of liberation, ground our theologies in the challenges of revolutionary practice. The impetus for analysis is an encounter with harsh, inexplicable realities. The move from liberal theology and politics to liberation theology and politics comes from an encounter with a suffering too deep for words. For me, the break has come again and again. I first realized the limits of reform by allowing myself to see the massive damage of patriarchal oppression: the campaign of terror that continues against women, the continuous threat of rape, assault, and murder at the hands of fathers, lovers, friends, and husbands. Violent deaths of women are most likely to occur from assaults by men they know, frequently by an abusive husband when a wife tries to leave the relationship.

Our world is shaped by the violent oppression of women, African-Americans and other people of color, and gays and lesbians. To begin our thinking, our analyses, with these realities, is to follow an imperative more appropriately symbolized in Rukeyser's imagery than in the imagery of enlightenment. First, we experience the jolt of horror, of pain, grief, and rage that accompanies even momentary openness to the costs of oppression. Darkness arrives: clear typologies, categorizations, and linear progressions fly out the window and a weighty mix of complex reality remains. Yet, with this openness to darkness, the mind splits open: new insights, feelings, appreciations, thoughts, categories of juxtaposition, and patterns of active response flow out. Thought does not end. Chaos and disorder do not have the only word, just an essential one in evoking other fluid patterns. The dynamic is one of moving with apparent paradoxes, not resolving them.

Resistance begins with chaos, with the experience of suffering that shatters worlds of meaning, that destroys comfortable patterns of feeling and action. The action that follows such immersion in suffering is also intrinsically chaotic and ambiguous, a defiant creation of new strategies or a courageous attempt to keep alive patterns of action that embody trust, hope, and human dignity.

A typology of thought and action, deeply influenced by the Enlightenment, may be used to understand the dynamics of work for justice. The articulation of human nature and strategies for evoking and sustaining emancipatory subjectivity and revolutionary action may be described in terms of pragmatism. My approach is undoubtedly pragmatic, in one sense. I am concerned with what works to evoke and sustain justice, with what sustains habits of resistance to injustice, habits of creative experimentation with alternative social structures. In all of this I am concerned more with the type of human nature that may be created than with the elements of human nature that inevitably perdure. I am not interested in questions of essential human nature, or of firm foundations for norms, values, and ideals. My concern is how to implement ideals and visions of human community, irrespective of their basis in truths or Truth.

In this work I find in American pragmatism a philosophical and political tradition as misleading as it is illuminating. The logic of my work, while decidedly practical in the sense of liberation theology's focus on praxis, cannot readily be contained within the structures of American pragmatism. Despite all the denials, disavowals, and demurrals of philosophers, American pragmatism still manifests Enlightenment assumptions about "human nature," "foundations," progress, domination of nature, control, and success. These assumptions lead too often to cynicism and despair, to acquiescence in the status quo. The firm foundations I invoke are habits: embodiments of ideals and visions, patterns of perception and response. The logic here seems typically pragmatic in that the criterion of truth is the creation or enhancement of a just community.[17] But this superficial description misses the core: the darkness that splits the mind open. In work for justice, we succeed by failing. Failure, mistakes, conflicts, disruption, the chaos of human interaction, is a constitutive part of work for justice.

Myles Horton was an activist who knew full well the chance of success and failure. He was one of the founders of the Highlander Folk School, and for over fifty years he worked with people developing strategies for civil rights, labor reform, equitable working conditions, and economic justice. In his autobiography, he claims that "If you analyze them, you can learn more in some ways from failures than from successes." He continues:

> There's a lot to be learned from successful organization over a specific issue, from achieving a specific victory, like preventing a building from being torn down or getting a new sewer system. However, some equally valuable learning takes place when you escalate your demands to the place where you finally lose. Now if you don't push to the place where you might fail, you've missed a wonderful opportunity to learn to struggle, to think big and challenge the status quo, and also to learn how to deal with failure.[18]

The dynamic here could not be further from a glorification of suffering, or a romantic conviction in the merits of the suffering of the innocent. Failure is not good in itself. Yet there is a dynamic unleashed by being willing to fail and by being able to analyze failure. Much of the work at Highlander was and is directed toward freeing people's imaginations, helping us escape the internalized limits of only reaching for easily attained goals:

> I've always thought it was important to persuade people to be willing to fail because if you're not willing to fail, you'll always choose easy goals. Your sights are limited by what you do. The pursuit of an expanding, unrestricted goal that is always receding in front of you, as you get a clearer view of where you're going or would like to, is not an experience to shun. The opposite experience occurs when the goal is a limited reform, or some easily attained thing.[19]

There is a marked contrast between Horton's understanding of practice, which includes failure, and American pragmatism. Some theologians argue that feminist theology and other North American theologies of liberation are fundamentally pragmatic. Rebecca Chopp, for example, locates American feminist theology squarely within the pragmatic tradition, defining pragmatism as a philosophy that "arises out of problems and dysfunctions of a particular situation," and is driven by "the desire that things can and must be different."[20] I agree that feminist theology is shaped by pragmatism, yet I find that the influence of pragmatism on feminists is as dangerous as it is helpful, propelling us to focus on political action, while hampering our ability to cope with the forces unleashed by that action.

Central to the pragmatic tradition is its concern with "human progress, betterment, and moral development."[21] C. S. Peirce, for example, applied to critical thought what he calls "the sole principle of logic which was recommended by Jesus; 'Ye may know them by their fruits.' "[22] Peirce claims that in following this principle of logic, human beings are engaged in a collective process, working for an end that we may only glimpse.[23]

The problem with the pragmatic attitude and our focus on the effects of a concept, of our attention to the fruits of our actions, is the danger of defining effects in terms that are expedient, simplistic, or short-term. In working against deep-seated oppression, we quickly learn that there are no ready solutions, no plausible five-year plans to save the earth, dismantle racism, and stop male violence against women. This confrontation with the limitations of our political will and creative imagination is all too often paralyzing. In my work as an activist in Nashville, Memphis, and Cambridge, I often encountered this troubling dynamic. I would be involved in a campaign trying to get middle-class Euro-Americans to take a stand on some particular issue, for example, the nuclear arms race, divestment of funds in South Africa, or male violence against women. At first, people would be justifiably reluctant to sign a petition, write a letter, or participate in a demonstration because they did not know enough about the issue to make an informed decision. We would then provide the necessary education. The response that followed was often extremely disheartening. With education about apartheid or the nuclear arms race or male violence against women came the conviction that the problem was too big to do anything about! Many middle-class Euro-Americans were simply paralyzed by the incongruity between the obvious enormity of the problems and the uncertain efficacy of any strategies of resistance and prevention. I have been challenged by the work and writing of African-American women to realize that such paralysis can be overcome. Responsible action can begin where much middle-class thought stops. We begin by acknowledging that we cannot imagine how we will win. This is the beginning, not the end, of critical reflection and action.[24]

TRUTH AND FOLLY

It is difficult to discern the difference between the impossible and the unlikely, but our emphasis on practice as the criterion of truth can stay "true" as we leave room for "divine madness" or folly. To go only with the plausible is to censor ourselves. Yet to reach for the improbable requires embracing the very real likelihood of error, defeat, stumbling. We can learn to accept defeat as our pragmatism is expanded—as defeat is taken seriously as a sign, not a final verdict. Let me give an example. A white friend once said that he feared talking to blacks because "I'm afraid I'll say something wrong." Say something wrong? Don't worry. Of course you will. You will say something wrong. Men will say "something wrong" to women, whites will say "something wrong" to blacks, and we will all live through it. We may actually learn from it. We who say "something wrong" may learn about the extent of our complicity with oppression, just as we learn ways to resist that complicity, ways to avoid making that particular statement or doing that particular act again.

According to a West African proverb, "To stumble is not to fall but to move forward faster." To imagine stumbling as moving forward faster has required for me a radical shift in evaluating the success or failure of political action. It requires accepting, even anticipating failure and learning how to grow with the information gained and forces unleashed by errors and defeat. Myles Horton testifies to the power of working with defeat: "If I had to make a choice between achieving an objective and utilizing the struggle to develop and radicalize people, my choice would be to let the goal go and develop the people."[25]

To accept failure requires relinquishing an image of oneself and one's movement or organization as exceedingly rational, fair, and wise, relatively impervious to pressures to act defensively and reactively, in ways that reinforce the privilege of oneself and one's group. I advocate an ironic awareness of the capacity for error and self-deception in oneself and in others. Such awareness, as Kate Rushin reminds us, need not be paralyzing. It can be, rather, quite empowering: enabling us to learn from failures and go on, rather than being paralyzed by guilt, shame, shock, and despair.

Working on deep-seated problems with diverse groups leads most often to conflict, not harmony, to chaos and turmoil, not efficiency and efficacy. The fruits of our work for justice include pain, as well as healing, failure and loss as well as transformation. Berniece Johnson Reagon, activist and musician, in her dedication of a song to Harriet Tubman, reminds us of the costs of working for social change:

> And when there is a promise of a storm,
> if you want change in your life,
> walk into it.

> If you get on the other side,
> you will be different.

> And if you want change in your life,
> and you are avoiding the trouble,
> you can forget it.

> So Harriet Tubman would say,
> "Wade on in the water,
> it's going to really be troubled water."

Pragmatists can easily fall into the trap of narrowly defining success. Without the development of a critical understanding of the interaction of failure and success, we choose actions that are more likely to bring superficial harmony and efficiency, actions that are by definition supportive of the status quo. William Jones describes this tendency in his work on the grid of oppression. From work against racism and sexism in the United States and in South Africa, he finds a common pattern of response to demands for change. When demands for change are finally taken seriously, the initiative or policies proposed by those in power are, inevitably, policies that will have the least effect. From the pragmatic perspective, this response makes sense: one is making some changes in response to pressure without significant disruption or dislocation. Those of us working for deep-seated, fundamental change, however, realize that long-term effectiveness requires social dislocation.

The inability of American pragmatism to incorporate radical calls for justice is not accidental. Cornel West describes the ambiguities and promise of American pragmatism. He argues that the core of this movement of thought is "a future-oriented instrumentalism that tries to deploy thought as a weapon to enable more effective action."[26] He finds in it a fierce commitment to democracy and an antipatrician rebelliousness. Although there are elements that can be expanded into what West calls "prophetic pragmatism," he claims that the tradition of American pragmatism (from Ralph Waldo Emerson through William James to Richard Rorty, with quite a few stops on the way) is limited by fear of "the subversive demands" of excluded peoples:

> This rebelliousness, rooted in the anticolonial heritage of this country, is severely restricted by an ethnocentrism and a patriotism cognizant of the exclusion of peoples of color, certain immigrants, and women yet fearful of the subversive demands these excluded peoples might make and enact.[27]

Why were, and are, many pragmatists afraid of the "subversive demands of excluded peoples"? What is missing in their and our understandings of action and human community that subversion is resisted, rather than embraced? I find a portion of the answer in images of truth as enlightenment, rather than endarkenment, in concepts of human community that overemphasize order and devalue the creative, constitutive power of chaos, in images of success that elude both the power of some forms of defeat and the always-to-be-expected way in which success seeds, if not its own defeat, its critique and transformation.

One of the most valuable lessons I learned from the Equity Institute was the ability to face defeat and pain with compassion and equanimity. In the workshop that I attended, one session "failed." In trying to lead a workshop on heterosexism, we replicated the patterns of racial oppression. People were angry, hurt, frightened, and confused. In helping us learn from the failure, one of the trainers said that such breakdowns often occur. We have all been deeply wounded by systems of oppression, and the pain of each group cannot be fully honored simultaneously. There is not enough time and space, and groups are slighted. Even though we are committed to work for justice, we are shaped by the structures of injustice and our actions reflect that heritage. Men committed to justice for women do not automatically escape a life of sexist socialization. Good intentions do not immediately erase habits of domination and exclusion. The facilitator of our workshop, a midwife, likened the pain we were experiencing to the pain of childbirth. She drew on her work with women giving birth to understand the pain of error and "failure." She said that just as no child is born without intense pain, the birth of a new world is accompanied by struggle and agony. In Rukeyser's words, "Something again/is beginning to be born."[28]

Simple questions and exercises can unleash powerful emotions and bring deep-seated fear, animosity, grief, and despair to the surface. Harmonious, polite relationships are disrupted by the eruption of repressed conflicts. Such disruption can mark the beginning of healing. One facilitator explored the dynamics of doing workshops in fraternities on acquaintance rape. The purpose was to help men know, emotionally and intellectually, the cost of their actions. The reaction of the men during the workshop itself was often intensely negative, hostile, dismissive, or seemingly aloof and unaffected. While it may have seemed that the workshops were ineffective, the hostility itself was an accompaniment of real change. Changes were occurring—old patterns being broken, new ones being evoked. The facilitator confirms this in what happens afterward: the reports she receives of ongoing debates and discussion, the reports of changes in attitudes and behaviors, the requests her office receives for more workshops, for further confrontation and interaction.

We cannot heal the wounds of oppression until we forthrightly acknowledge the immensity and complexity of the wounds. Men can hear and be profoundly shaken by the rage of women. Euro-Americans can hear and be transformed by the rage of African-Americans. My hope for fundamental social change is grounded in the incredible resilience I see in the lives of people who continue to work for justice: the ability to accept the costs of change, accepting the fact that our strategies, our visions of what can heal us are partial, fluid, always growing and changing, a dance of failure and hope, growth, risk, and pain. In her poetry, Muriel Rukeyser expresses the paradox of our work for justice:

> A miracle has even deeper roots,
> Something like error, some profound defeat.
> Stumbled-over, the startle, the arousal,
> Something never perceived till now, the taproot.[29]

Part Four
Race, Integration, and Transformation

12

AMERICA'S ORIGINAL SIN

The Legacy of
White Racism

Jim Wallis

*T*he United States of America was established as a white society, founded upon the genocide of another race and then the enslavement of yet another. These founding events of our nation are not just historical. They also have theological meaning. The systematic violence, both physical and spiritual, done first to the indigenous people and then to black Africans was, indeed, the original sin. In other words, the United States was conceived in iniquity.

Whatever else is "right" about the United States cannot and does not cover over or erase that original sin. The good things about this country and the reasons many have come here need not be denied or dismissed, but the brutal founding facts of nationhood must be faced up to. Like any sin, this one must be dealt with, for the sake of our integrity but also because the legacy of that original history is still with us. An American future worthy of its best ideals depends on our honestly coming to terms with our origins and their continued influence.

Our history has affected us all in profound ways, still shapes our national experience, and obstructs the fulfillment of our professed values. Its face is dramatically revealed in the continued devastation of native, black, and other communities of color; in the legacy of benefit still enjoyed by most white people; and in the fear and anger of many whites facing shrinking economic realities and the temptation to scapegoat racial minorities.

The nation's original sin of racism must be faced in a way that we have never really done before. Only then can the United States be "rediscovered."

To talk this way today is to be immediately accused of being rhetorical or, worse yet, of being "reminiscent of the sixties." The reaction is instructive and revealing. The historical record of how white Europeans conquered North America by destroying the native population and how they then built their nation's economy on the backs of kidnapped Africans who had been turned into chattel are facts that can hardly be denied. Yet to speak honestly of such historical facts is to be charged with being polemical or out of date. Why?

THE CHANGING FACE OF RACISM IN THE UNITED STATES

Racism is no longer a hot topic. After the brief "racial crisis" of the sixties, white America, including many of those involved in the civil rights movement, has gone on to other concerns. Also, the legal victories of black Americans in that period, as far as most white Americans are concerned, have settled the issue and even left many asking, "What more do blacks want?" Federal courts have recently interpreted civil rights legislation—originally designed to redress discrimination against black people—as applying to the grievances of whites who believe affirmative action programs have "gone too far." In addition, popular racial attitudes have changed, as attested in opinion polls and in the increased number of black faces in the world of sports, entertainment, the mass media, and even politics.

Indeed, in the decades since the passage of momentous civil rights legislation, some things have changed and some things have not. What has changed is the personal racial attitudes of many white Americans and the opportunities for some black Americans to enter the middle levels of society. (The word *middle* is key here, insofar as blacks have yet to be allowed into the upper echelons and decision-making positions of business, the professions, the media, or even the fields of sports and entertainment where black "progress" has so often been celebrated.) Legal segregation has been lifted off the backs of black people, leading to an expansion of social interchange and voting rights, and that itself has led to changes in white attitudes. What have not changed, however, are the systematic and pervasive character of racism in the United States and the condition of life for the majority of blacks and other people of color. In fact, those conditions have worsened.

Racism originates in domination and provides the social rationale and philosophical justification for debasing, degrading, and doing violence to people on the basis of color. Many have observed how racism is sustained by both personal attitudes and structural forces. Racism can be brutally overt or invisibly institutional, or both. Its scope extends to every level and area of human psychology, society, and culture. Prejudice may be a universal human sin, but racism is more than an inevitable consequence of human nature or social accident. Rather, racism is a system of oppression for a social purpose.

In the United States, the original purpose of racism was to justify slavery and its enormous economic benefit. The particular form of racism, inherited from the English to justify their own slave trade, was especially venal, for it defined the slave not merely as an unfortunate victim of bad circumstances, war, or social dislocation but rather as less than human, as a thing, an animal, a piece of property to be bought and sold, used and abused. The slave did not have to be treated with any human consideration whatsoever. Even in the founding document of our nation, the famous constitutional compromise defined the slave as only three-fifths of a person. The professed high ideals of Anglo-Western society could exist side by side with the profitable institution of slavery only if the humanity of the slave was denied and disregarded.

The heart of racism was and is economic, though its roots and results are also deeply cultural, psychological, sexual, even religious, and, of course, political. Due to two hundred years of brutal slavery and one hundred more of legal segregation and discrimination, no area of the relationship between black and white people in the United States is free of the legacy of racism.

In spiritual and biblical terms, racism is a perverse sin that cuts to the core of the gospel message. Put simply, racism negates the reason for which Christ died—the reconciling work of the cross. It denies the purpose of the church: to bring together, in Christ, those who have been divided from one another, particularly in the early church's case, Jew and Gentile—a division based on race.

There is only one remedy for such a sin and that is repentance, which, if genuine, will always bear fruit in concrete forms of conversion, changed behavior, and reparation. While the United States may have changed in some of its racial attitudes and allowed some people of color into the middle class, white America has yet to recognize the extent of its racism—that we are and have always been a racist society—much less to repent of its racial sins. And because of that lack of repentance and, indeed, because of the economic, social, and political purposes still served by the oppression of people of color, systematic racism continues to be pervasive in American life. While constantly denied by white social commentators and the media, evidence of the persistent and endemic character of American racism abounds.

The most visible and painful sign of racism's continuation is the gross economic inequality between blacks and whites. All the major social indices and numerous statistics show the situation to be worsening, not improving. The gap between white and black median family income and employment actually widened in the two decades between 1970 and 1990. And the Reagan and Bush administrations were like an economic plague to the black community; black unemployment skyrocketed, and the major brunt of slashed and gutted social services was borne by black people, especially women and children.

It is the economy itself that now enforces the brutal oppression of racism, and it happens, of course, invisibly and impersonally. In the changing capitalistic order, manufacturing jobs are lost to cheaper labor markets in the Third World or to automation while farm labor becomes extinct; both historically have been important to black survival. In the new high-tech world and service economy, almost the only jobs available are at places like McDonalds. That blacks and Latinos are disproportionately consigned to the lowest economic tier is indisputable proof of racism. The existence of a vast black and Hispanic underclass, inhabiting the inner cities of our nation, is testimony to the versatility of white racism twenty years after segregation was officially outlawed.

The pain of economic marginalization is made worse by the growing class distinctions within the black community itself. Middle-class blacks, having taken advantage of the legal gains of the 1960s, have further distanced themselves from the poor black population. Never has the class and cultural split in the black community been so great. In Atlanta, Washington, D.C., and other cities, a black elite prospers and lives an entirely different social existence, not in proximity to but in full view of an increasingly resentful and angry black underclass.

The cold economic savagery of racism has led to further declines in every area of the quality of life in the black community—health, infant mortality, family breakdown, drug and alcohol abuse, and crime. The majority of black children are now born to single mothers; a primary cause of death for young black men today is homicide; and nearly half of all prison inmates in the United States now are black males.

Despite landmark court decisions and civil rights legislation, two-thirds of black Americans still suffer from education and housing that is both segregated and inferior. Such conditions, along with diminishing social services, lead to despair, massive substance abuse, and criminality, and the fact that this reality is still surprising or incomprehensible to many white Americans raises the question of how much racial attitudes have really changed.

In the face of such structural oppression, the deliberate rollback of civil rights programs during the Reagan and Bush administrations was even more callous. The resurgence of more overt forms of white racism and violence, as exemplified by the incidents in Howard Beach and Bensonhurst, New York; Forsyth County, Georgia; and other places, is quite foreboding, as further occasions when the discontented alienation of poor whites is displaced and expressed against blacks instead of against the system that oppresses them all and has always sought to turn them against each other.

The connection of racism to U.S. militarism should, by now, be painfully clear. First, increased military spending causes cuts in social services to the victims of the system, who are disproportionately people of color. Second, the military definition of national security puts a prior claim on vast material, scientific, and human resources that could otherwise be directed toward achieving justice, which then is proclaimed as not being a practical financial option. Third, lacking other educational and job opportunities, racial minorities are herded into dehumanizing military service in disproportionate numbers and then assigned to combat units. And finally, young black men from the ghetto face the defined enemies of the United States on the field of battle, usually other people of color from the Third World—in places such as Vietnam and Central America—where they kill and are killed.

The failure of the mostly white, middle-class peace movement in the United States to make such connections and enter into a vital political partnership with oppressed racial minorities is a primary reason for the ineffectiveness of the movement. Even in the peace movement, racism becomes a debilitating force that robs us of opportunities to work toward a more just and peaceful nation.

The strategies for how black people must confront and finally overcome the ever-changing face of white racism in America must always originate within the black community itself. White allies have and can continue to play a significant role in the struggle against racism when black autonomy and leadership are sufficiently present to make possible a genuine partnership. But an even more important task for white Americans is to examine ourselves, our relationships, our institutions, and our society for the ugly plague of racism. Whites in America must admit the reality and begin to operate on the assumption that theirs is a racist society. Positive individual attitudes are simply not enough, for, as we have seen, racism is more than just personal.

All white people in the United States have benefited from the structure of racism, whether or not they have ever committed a racist act, uttered a racist word, or had a racist thought (as unlikely as that is). Just as surely as blacks suffer in a white society because they are black, whites benefit because they are white. And if whites have profited from a racist structure, they must try to change it. To benefit from domination is to be responsible for it. Merely to keep personally free of the taint of racist attitudes is both illusory and inadequate. Just to go along with a racist social structure, to accept the economic order as it is, just to do one's job in impersonal institutions is to participate in racism in the nineties.

Racism has to do with the power to dominate and enforce oppression, and that power in America is in white hands. Therefore, while there are instances of black racial prejudice against whites in the United States today (often in reaction to white racism), there is no such thing as black racism. Black people in America do not have the power to enforce that prejudice.

White racism in white institutions must be eradicated by white people and not just black people. In fact, white racism is primarily a white responsibility. We must not give in to the popular temptation to believe that racism existed mostly in the Old South or before the 1960s or, today, in South Africa. Neither can any of our other struggles against the arms race, Third World wars, hunger, homelessness, or sexism be separated from the reality of racism.

The church must, of course, get its own house in order. It is still riddled with racism and segregation. The exemplary role of the black church in the struggle against racism offers a sharp indictment to white churches, which still mostly reflect the racial structures around them. The church still has the capacity to be the much-needed prophetic interrogator of a system that has always depended upon racial oppression. The gospel remains clear. The church still should and can be a spiritual and social community where the ugly barriers of race are finally torn down to reveal the possibilities of a different American future.

A TALE OF TWO CITIES

My neighborhood of Columbia Heights runs along Fourteenth Street, a scene of Washington, D.C.'s much-publicized, so-called riots following the assassination of Martin Luther King, Jr., in the bitter spring of 1968. The now infamous "riot corridor," as the area is still called, even today bears the scars of the frustrated and angry violence that erupted when black people's hopes were suddenly and brutally cut down. Burned-out buildings and vacant lots remain after more than twenty-five years.

Several years ago, my sister Barbara was walking through the neighborhood with her five-year-old son, Michael. Michael surveyed the scene on the block and, looking up at his mother with puzzlement, asked, "Mommy, was there a war here?"

Indeed, the empty shells of buildings, piles of rubble, and general devastation all around could easily give that impression. Perhaps the eyes of a child can see what jaded adult vision quickly passes over or too easily accepts—there was and is a war here. It goes on every day, and the casualties are everywhere. The people who inhabit this and similar neighborhoods are not only neglected and ignored by political decision makers, they are war victims. They are the dead and wounded of a system that has ravaged their lives and their communities. It is no wonder that those who make it through refer to themselves as "survivors." But many are not surviving. The forces that have declared war on them are global and impersonal, but the consequences for the people are very personal indeed.

For most of the nation, the inner-city neighborhoods of Washington, D.C., have been invisible. Everyone knows "official Washington" with its marble, monuments, and malls. But "the other Washington" has been off-limits to the blue-and-white tour buses and to the consciousness of the rest of the country. Here are substandard tenements instead of stately government offices. Here children play in back alleys with glass, trash, and syringes instead of running in beautiful parks. Here the only monuments are to neglect, indifference, and the stranglehold of entrenched racism on the city that proclaims itself a beacon of freedom to the world. Here the homeless huddle literally in the shadows of the great houses of state power, trying to keep warm by sleeping on the grates that expel hot air from the heating systems of the State Department, the Pentagon, and the halls of Congress.

Even the name, *Washington, D.C.*, tells the tale of two cities. The white residents and professionals who run the federal capital live in "Washington." The black residents who are the city's vast majority (70 percent) are from "D.C."—the District of Columbia. This capital of the "free world" is still virtually a segregated city, especially in housing, schools, and social interchange. A word often heard in D.C. is "colony." The District of Columbia did not obtain even partial home rule until 1974. But still, District residents (700,000 people) have no voting representation in Congress, and all actions taken by the elected city government are subject to congressional veto.

In Washington, D.C., subway routes follow class and racial lines, carrying middle-class commuters around downtown, through gentrified areas of the city, and out into the suburbs—avoiding black ghettos. The buses running along the affluent white and black "gold coast" of Sixteenth Street are new and air-conditioned, while just two blocks away, old, hot, and broken-down buses run along the infamous Fourteenth Street corridor through a major black ghetto. All this exists under a black city government.

To be fair, the increase in black political power over municipal governments has given black political leaders all the problems of modern urban life, including inadequate city budgets, without any power or leverage to change the national policies and priorities that create the problems in the first place. Nevertheless, transcending the growing barriers between the relatively affluent middle class and the impoverished underclass is one of the most important and problematic challenges facing the black community.

The forces of housing gentrification and real estate speculation are slowly pushing black residents into more overcrowded neighborhoods or out of the city altogether. Once-poor ghetto neighborhoods are being transformed into upscale yuppie enclaves with prices too high for any of their former inhabitants.

But neither Washington, D.C.'s extremes of wealth and poverty nor its racial polarization have been well known beyond the "beltway," the highway encircling the metropolitan area. For most Americans—at least white Americans—the nation's capital has been best known as the site for great high school trips, or for the Cherry Blossom Festival, or as the home of the Redskins. Mostly, Washington, D.C., is known as the most powerful city in the world, and it is no wonder that its powerless, predominantly black underside has been so easily and so long overlooked.

But suddenly Washington, D.C., began making national and international headlines—not as the center of power but as the "murder capital" of the nation. Quickly, the media cameras so used to turning away from "the other Washington" focused their attention on black neighborhoods overrun with drugs and guns. D.C. got famous. *Newsweek* did a cover story that spoke of the "two Washingtons," while nervous local officials rushed to assure anxious tourists that the killing was limited only to "certain parts of the city."[1]

In 1983 I traveled to the war zones of Nicaragua on the first team of a project known as Witness for Peace. In a refugee resettlement camp, I met a thirteen-year old boy named Agenor, who made a great impression on me. His baseball cap, tattered shirt, and beat-up tennis shoes reminded me of the kids who run up and down the streets of my own neighborhood. But this thin Nicaraguan boy carried a heavy automatic weapon on his back. He was a member of the citizens' militia, defending against contra attacks and a feared U.S. invasion. As I returned home, Agenor's face, with his searching brown eyes and shy smile, was etched in my memory.

I met Eddie on the street the day I got back. He was also thirteen. While telling Eddie about my trip, I had a terrible thought. If the U.S. government continued to escalate its war in Nicaragua and eventually sent troops, Eddie—a young black man from a poor family with few other options—would be the first to go. That had been the pattern in the Vietnam War. At that moment, I imagined the awful possibility of Eddie and Agenor meeting on some Nicaraguan battlefield, raising their guns to aim at each other, and one or both being killed. The great ideological confrontation between East and West would come down to Eddie and Agenor shooting each other—two young men, one black and one brown, dying in the name of a global conflict between two white superpowers. Instead of that horrible picture, I tried to imagine Eddie and Agenor playing baseball together.

Eddie never died on a Nicaraguan battlefield, as I had feared. But Eddie did die on the streets of his own neighborhood. He became, for a short while, the latest victim and the newest statistic in the city's epidemic of violence.

We are losing a whole generation of young people in our cities to poverty, drugs, and violence. Washington, D.C., is a city out of control, reeling from the brutal consequences and tremendous suffering of a global economic, social, and spiritual crisis that has yet to be named, understood, or addressed. The city stands now as a parable unto the world. The crisis in the capital of the wealthiest and most powerful nation tells the story of the crisis the whole world now faces. In Washington, D.C., today, we see a mirror of what the global system has become. Its brutal paradoxes have become a parable that can teach us what we must learn if we are to survive.

Washington, D.C., is literally the symbol of power. People stream to the official city to exercise power, to influence power, or just to be around power. The power holders and the power groupies alike are intoxicated with the smell of it. The key word here is access. Access to power—that is what everyone is always fighting for in this town. Power, like money, becomes its own justification. How you get it or what it is used for are beside the point; having power is what is important.

As power defines official Washington, powerlessness defines "the other Washington." Here are the people who clean the hotel rooms, cook the food, and drive the cabs for the powerful—if they have work at all. The work force has been reduced to an underemployed labor pool supplying the bottom rungs of the service economy. If Washington is the most powerful city in the nation, D.C. is the most powerless, without control even over its own affairs and destiny. As the "Last Colony," D.C. symbolizes the relationship many other parts of the world have with official Washington.

The revealing paradoxes exist on almost every level of life in Washington, D.C. Housing costs are among the highest in the country, as are the rates of homelessness. Infant mortality is at Third World levels in the same city with more lawyers and real estate developers than any other. Black youth unemployment is upwards of 60 percent, while white professional couples with two incomes search for investments. Scholastic Aptitude Test scores for D.C. public school students are 100 points below the national norm, while the city's private school students score 100 points above it. Nineteen million tourists spend $1.5 billion each year here, while the D.C. jail runs out of money for toilet paper. The downtown hotel business is booming, while more and more women and children move into the city's shelters or onto the streets. Washington's affluent suburbs are rated among the most desirable places to live in the nation, while the death rate in black D.C. increases due to a lack of good health care. Young white men pay some of the highest college tuition rates in the country at local universities, while their black counterparts are nine times more likely to be victims of homicides.

Washington, D.C., is a microcosm of the dynamics that now govern the world order. The current drug war brings all these contradictions into sharp relief. No one knows the exact numbers, but an extraordinary percentage of D.C. youth is involved in the drug traffic. As in source countries such as Colombia, drug trafficking has become a livelihood for the poor. In the high-stakes atmosphere of drugs and money, life becomes cheap indeed. In Colombia, now, it costs only $40 to have someone murdered. In both Colombia and Washington, D.C., poverty sets the stage for tragedy, and the drama of drugs simply carries out the executions.

In the current economic and cultural environment, it becomes very difficult to tell young black people, "Just say no to drugs." What we are in effect telling them is to be content working part-time at McDonald's (the eighth-largest employer in D.C.) and pursue the American dream as best they can. In a changing economy, the better jobs and brighter future are just not there.

Meanwhile, the dominant images that assault them daily—through television, movies, and popular music—tell young people that their very worth and status as human beings come from how much they can possess and consume. Fancy clothes, new cars, a nice house, and lots of gold around their necks become the aspirations of inner-city youth. In that, they are no different from most Americans. The crucial difference is that these inner-city, primarily black youth are virtually denied legal access to the alluring attractions of U.S. consumer culture. They are blocked out by an economy that has no room for them.

Washington, D.C., like the rest of the global system, is now run by a two-tiered economy. At the top is a highly lucrative and booming sector of managerial and professional elites, while at the bottom is an increasingly impoverished population that services the high-tech economy but whose labor and even consumption are less and less needed. Whole sectors of the global economy are now simply defined outside of the economic mainstream. And to be shut out of the global economy means to be consigned to death. Like Jesus' parable of the rich man and the beggar Lazarus, millions and millions of God's children are now shut outside the gate of the global economy.

More and more children live in poverty in America. One out of every five children and half of all black children are born poor. The gap between the rich and poor has steadily grown as a changing economy leaves more and more people behind. The swelling ranks of the hungry and homeless, now including many families, point to a highly visible moral contradiction in a nation that prides itself on its standard of living.

In the United States, public school education, health care, low-cost housing, the family farm, and the industrial workplace are all in a state of crisis. Crime is out of control, while the proposed solutions fail to deal adequately with either underlying causes or individual responsibility, neglecting both perpetrators and victims. The fight against racism has been halted at the highest levels of government, and its ugly resurgence is upon us. Hard-fought progress made by women for equal rights is now under attack from many quarters. The nation's foreign policy continues to violate its expressed values and causes untold human suffering principally to poor people of color. Our collective conscience has been numbed.

Things are especially hard on the black and brown minority youth who inhabit our inner cities. They are the ones whose dreams and hopes

for the future have been denied. There is no room for them in this society, and they know it. With no place, no stake, and no future available
to them, they are finding their own road to "success." And it is a very
dangerous road indeed, with many casualities strewn along the way.

In our neighborhood, children eight, nine, and ten years old wear
beepers on their belts. It is not because they are young lawyers and doc-
tors, but because drug dealers call the children at play when a drug run
has to be made. It is safer for dealers to use children for their drug runs,
with detection and punishment less likely. Young people can make
more money in a day than they ever dreamed possible. Thousands of
dollars are available to them in an economy that has never offered them
more than uncertain, part-time employment at minimum wage. And
many are taking the option.

In a series of articles called "At the Roots of the Violence," *The
Washington Post* described the unwritten code of conduct of the drug
dealers in their own words: "Never back down. . . . Be willing to kill or
die to defend your honor. . . . Protect your reputation and manhood at
all costs. . . . " The drug dealers who live by this code are known on the
street as "soldiers." A reporter asked one of them why they are always so
ready to shoot. "I guess it's greed for that money," was his answer. *The
Post* then commented on the code of the streets: "It is a way of behaving
that flies in the face of traditional American values."[2]

Is that really true? What values are reflected in U.S. foreign policy?
What code of ethics governs the wars of Wall Street? Does not the en-
shrinement of greed and glorification of violence every day on television sets and movie screens reinforce cultural values? What message
does their society give black youth every day about what is most important in life? Have they not been convinced, like most everyone else in
the United States, that status and success come by way of material acquisition? Does the way people get rich even matter in our country?
With great danger to themselves and others, are not these children of
the poor pursuing the same glittering materialistic dream of others, in
the quickest and perhaps the only way they see open to them?

Perhaps our dominant cultural values now reflect the emptiness of
our situation most of all. It is television that now rules the popular culture. Consumption has become our highest cultural value and social
purpose. In fact, material consumption is the only universal form of
social participation that Americans have left. Everything else has been
either marginalized or completely co-opted by the frenzied desire for
things.

Consumption is the thing that both the rich and poor, white and black, and everyone else in between seem to care most about. Not only does consumption define the culture, materialism has *become* the culture in the United States. There is no longer any doubt that things are more valued than people and that people have, themselves, become commodities. We are faced with an almost totally economic definition of life. The result is a culture that has lost its meaning.

Drugs are not the only narcotic here. The money that comes from drugs is the addiction that is leading to the violence. That addiction—the addiction to materialism—is fed every hour of every day in this society. It is not only legal to feed that addiction, it is the whole purpose of the system. It is our reason for being as a people—to possess and to consume.

The images dance before us every waking moment. The images attract, lure, create desire; they awaken the greed and covetousness of our worst selves. Our children are glued to the TV screen; the beat of incessant consumption pounds in their ears. Shopping malls have become the temples, shrines, and communal centers of modern U.S. life.

After creating such an overpowering, all-encompassing, all-defining addiction, we block its satisfaction to the poor. It is an unspeakable cruelty to create an addiction and then deny its satisfaction, the whole time feeding the desire. Materialism is literally killing the poor, while at the same time it is destroying the nation's soul. The violent underside of U.S. society is not a social aberration that we can safely and morally distance from "traditional U.S. values." Rather, the frightening carnage is a frustrated mirror image of the twisted values that now govern the wider society.

We should know by now that we cannot have an economic system that leaves masses of people behind without ensuring endless conflict. We should know by now that growth and progress that abuse, exploit, and destroy our natural environment will end up choking us to death. We should know by now that we cannot deny human dignity to our neighbor because of race or class or sex without destroying our own soul. The logic of the system is literally killing us.

FROM INTEGRATION TO TRANSFORMATION

Will not the problem of racism and the consequent economic marginalization of black America be solved by integration? No, says a rising tide of voices, especially in the black community. Integration, the ruling national concept of race relations in the decades since the civil rights movement, has not produced what was promised. Instead of equality, integration has meant selective assimilation for middle-class blacks while the urban underclass and rural poor are simply left behind.

In the critical areas of income and employment, education, housing, and health, life for most black Americans is still separate and very unequal. Despite increased visibility in the media and popular culture, black America has yet really to enter the social and economic mainstream and, most significantly, genuinely to share power in what is still a white society. Not only is justice yet to be achieved through integration, but the black sense of self and the community has been greatly diminished, say many critics. Indeed, what is most wrong with integration is simply this: it has always been and continues to be on white terms.

Rapidly changing demographics in the United States will only serve to further heighten the failures and contradictions of integration as growing populations of Hispanics, Asians, and other people of color combine with African Americans to transform America's racial "minorities" into the new national majority. Even *Time* magazine ran a cover story on "America's Changing Colors" and asked, "What will the U.S. be like when whites are no longer the majority?"—a reality it predicted by the year 2056.[3]

This is a cultural and psychic shift of enormous proportions as a country established by and for white Europeans becomes a nation where most people will trace their descent from Africa, Latin America, or Asia. White America, which has yet to come to terms with its "minorities," is totally unprepared for its own minority status. Yet that fundamental identity shift is now inevitable and, in many parts of the country, is already occurring. In light of this seismic disruption in American history, the present concept of integration will soon be even more outmoded.

It is vital to take an honest look at the failures of integration for blacks and whites in order to move toward a more genuinely democratic vision of race relations for America's multicultural future. Maybe the most important question to be asked is whether "integration" was really ever the goal of the black freedom movement of the 1950s and 1960s. Perhaps the concept of integration, as it developed in the years following the civil rights movement, can be better understood as the white society's attempt to contain, control, and reduce the potential impact of the most important social movement in recent American history.

Certainly, the motivations and aspirations of social movements and their participants are many, varied, and even often contradictory. And surely many involved in the civil rights movement were simply interested in an end to legal separation and the opportunity for black people to assimilate individually into the mainstream of white American society. However, as important commentators point out, at the heart of the black freedom struggle was a call for social transformation.

If the freedom movement was not simply aiming for integration into the dominant values and structures of the white society, but rather envisioning a fundamental transformation of that social order, the revisiting of these questions is indeed a dangerous discussion. The answers to the questions depend greatly on which streams and leaders of the movement we are referring to, both then and now. It is clear that Martin Luther King, Jr., especially in his later years, and Malcolm X were both calling for radical social transformation rather than assimilation. But with the assassinations of the movement's two greatest leaders, assimilation gradually took precedence over transformation. The result has been the selective and still partial integration of the black middle class, the social and economic abandonment of the black majority, the widespread white attitude that the "racial problem" has been solved, and a country whose basic structural realities remain unchanged.

In other words, integration has proceeded under mostly white terms and control. Integration has never been a two-way street and, indeed, was never meant to be. It has always been, in every way, white-directed.

One example is my own high school, which was all white when I attended it more than two decades ago. It is now more than one-third black. In a recent conversation with a teacher there, I asked how much the curriculum has changed over the years. Not at all. African-American history, culture, and perspectives were still absent, and when some students formed a black student union, the white perception was that integration wasn't working.

In another *Time* cover story on the black middle class, the magazine reported that "the passions and sufferings of the civil rights struggle have culminated, as they were meant to, in the mundane pleasures and pangs of middle-class life."[4] That is indeed what *Time* magazine wants and needs to be true. But the problem is not just that *Time* missed the spiritual center of the freedom movement. Rather, like all the governing institutions of American life, *Time* has a powerful vested interest in defining the movement's goals as assimilation instead of transformation. The threatening possibilities of the black freedom struggle can thus be checked, domesticated, and even co-opted while making Martin Luther King, Jr.'s birthday a national holiday sponsored by Coca-Cola.

It must also be said that integration has allowed white liberals to feel good about "racial progress" and what they have done to "help" blacks. By not challenging the structure of white power and privilege, integration has, in different ways, served the self-interests of both white conservatives and liberals.

Vincent Harding, an active participant in the civil rights movement and now one of its best historians, believes the freedom movement is not yet over:

> We didn't see the depth of what we had to do. To root out things that are centuries deep takes tremendous imagination and experience. We have been thinking much too superficially about what integration means. If we look seriously at our country today, we will discover that the changes we need cannot come about without great energy and sacrifice. We thought we had done our sacrificing in the '60's and wonder why it hasn't worked. But we are trying to redeem the soul of America and you don't do that in a decade. We must not settle for elitist solutions but open our eyes to the hurt and pain of the masses of the people.[5]

Integration begs the question—integration into what? What kind of a society prefers selective assimilation to transformation? The answer is one which still seeks to cover over the fundamental question of justice and compassion. Integration has served that cover-up.

The reign of insatiable materialism over human dignity in American society destroys the souls of rich and poor alike. And the acceptance of an economic system based on theft from the poor at home and around the world will continue to keep masses of people at the bottom. In a white-controlled society, a disproportionate number of those will be people of color.

When the Sojourners Community moved to the inner city of Washington, D.C., in 1975, we quickly discovered that the black residents of our Southern Columbia Heights neighborhood were not particularly interested in forming an integrated church. What our neighbors were interested in was working together on the issues of housing, food, and education. Out of a common agenda came the sharing of faith and struggle in Bible study and prayer groups, retreats, and celebrations of thanksgiving for the work we've been given to do together. Slowly, we are learning that equality will come from partnership in a shared struggle more than integration for its own sake.

The movement we must make is from integration to transformation. Integration of white and black elites in an unjust society leaves too many people out and the fundamental questions of justice unanswered. The spiritual heritage of the freedom movement is one of personal and social transformation, and that spirit must be reclaimed now. White society has preferred integration to equality. The integration of paternalism and dependence must come to an end. In its place will be a multicultural partnership of equals—a partnership for the democratic transformation of the United States.

Any new vision will have to challenge fundamentally the system at its roots and offer genuine alternatives based on the critical moral values that we still possess. Since such a challenge and such an alternative are unlikely to come from the top of U.S. society, the vision will have to originate from the bottom, the margins, and those middle sectors of society where dislocation and/or more independent social values offer the possibility of new imagination.

Two crucial constituencies for such a task are the poor themselves and places within the religious community where fresh thinking and renewal are now taking place. The future will not be constructed from the mere shuffling of elite personnel at the top, but rather will be a response to a transformation of values and action at the grassroots.

Despite the lack of recognition, we are indeed in a social crisis. It is a crisis that confronts us with choices—critical choices of national values and direction. Honest truth telling and bold moral vision for the future are urgently needed. The combination of the two is in fact the essence of what political leadership must be in the days ahead. A discernible hunger exists in the nation for just such leadership. The U.S. people deserve to be offered such a choice. And, even more important, we have a religious responsibility to offer it. That has always been the prophetic vocation.

The biblical prophets challenged the way things were, while at the same time helping people to imagine new possibilities. They were not afraid to confront the king, to defend the poor, or to say that what God had in mind was far different from what most people had settled for. Rankled by injustice, sickened by violence, and outraged by oppression, the prophets defined true religion as "doing justice, loving mercy, and walking humbly with your God."

Our political convictions must grow out of that kind of faith—a faith that does justice. We should be less interested in the ideologies of Left and Right than whether justice is really done—especially to the marginalized and downtrodden for whom the God of the Bible seems to have such a special concern. That same biblical perspective sees the accumulation of wealth and weapons as the wrong road to national security and instead offers the possibility of an economy that has room for everyone, an environment treated as a sacred trust, and a commitment to resolving our conflicts in ways that do not threaten the very survival of the planet.

That political vision directly confronts the barriers of race, class, and sex which so violate God's creative purpose and still wreak such violence among us. To enjoy a culture in which human values and creativity can truly flourish will mean being set free from our captivity to consumption and its totally economic definition of life. What is most human rather than what is most profitable must become the crucial question.

The most pressing issue today is that we really have no sense of solidarity with one another—no communion, community, or common bond. A very telling example indeed is what is happening in my neighborhood.

A whole generation of black youth is being destroyed. But for most people in our nation, this is just an inner-city problem, a crime problem, a drug crisis, or a violence issue. What is really happening is that a whole generation of *us* is being destroyed; but white America does not see it that way. It isn't *us*. It's *them*. How can we call people who are desperately poor and struggling to survive a "permanent underclass?"

But they are us, and we are them. And we are deeply connected. If we fail to see these connections, we are simply not going to make it. All of our other problems stem from this one. At the heart of these issues is one single issue—that we have lost our sense of being brothers and sisters, daughters and sons of God. We are the children of God, who are inextricably bound to one another. And we will either live together or die as those who forgot that they were part of a common destiny.

It is time to hear the words of the prophet Amos: "Let justice roll" into the streets of oppression and drugs and hopelessness, and also into the avenues of luxury and fear. "Let justice roll" into the ghettos and barrios and squatter camps, but also into the affluent suburbs of comfort and indifference. "Let justice roll" into the boardrooms of corporate wealth and the corridors of political power.

"Let justice roll" into a church made lukewarm by its conformity and isolated by its lack of compassion. "Let justice roll" and set free all the captives—those under bondage to poverty's chains and those under bondage to money's desires. "Let justice roll"—and let faith come alive again to all those whose eyes long to see a new day.

13

BLACK THEOLOGY AND LATIN AMERICAN LIBERATION THEOLOGY

A Framework for Race and Class Analysis

George C. L. Cummings

*R*elationships between the economic order, culture, and theology are part of the terrain of the dialogue between black theologians of liberation, who take as their point of departure the struggle against white racism, and Latin American liberation theologians, who take as their point of departure political and economic exploitation. In this essay I intend to discuss the evolution of a conceptual framework for comprehending the relationship between racist oppression and economic and political structures, as well as to suggest some programmatic strategies for establishing a future which will be more humane.

In the Ecumenical Association of Third World Theologians (EATWOT), for example, theologians of liberation have been engaged in a dialogical encounter designed to develop a theology of liberation which accounts for a wide variety of oppressive experiences. It is their stated commitment to develop an analytical framework for integrating the sociopolitical, economic, and cultural dimensions of exploitation. This essay emerges out of my intensive study of the history of that encounter and is intended as a contribution to it.

My participation in constructing a theoretical framework to assist their continued dialogue and partnership is grounded in a number of commitments. The first is based on the biblical understanding of liberation as integral to the whole of humanity. K. C. Abraham contends that the biblical notion of *shalom*, normally crudely translated as meaning *peace*, is more profoundly understood as a reference to a social real-

ity that brings all of life to fruition.[1] Abraham's interpretation is that
shalom "visualizes a life which encompasses the prosperity of (all) the
earth and (all) people and their happiness. . . ."[2] Liberation, then, is an
all-encompassing, liberative vision that addresses itself to the diverse,
yet interrelated, forms of oppression in the world.

The second commitment grows out of the first. It is to meet the need
expressed at the 1981 EATWOT meeting in New Delhi. There African
and African-Diaspora theologians as well as Asians and Latin Americans affirmed that "a relevant theology for the Third World should include both the cultural and the socio-economic aspects of people's lives.
In most theological efforts today, stress is on one to the near exclusion
of the other."[3]

A Third World theology of liberation is one that grows out of the
particular experiences of all of those who are oppressed and is articulated and negotiated by those who represent diverse traditions. This is
the commitment that EATWOT, internationally, has been engaged in
for almost two decades.

The third commitment is grounded in recognition of the common
role that blacks in North America and the oppressed throughout the
world play within the dominant economic world order. The existence
of dependent colonies, external or internal, as sources of cheap resources and labor and as overseas markets that enhance the profit margins of multinational corporations has been well documented. This
common "Third Worldness" as exploited peoples has been decisive in
helping Third World people to recognize that their common enemy is
an economic world order that presumes their marginalization.

A fourth commitment springs from acknowledgment of the need for
strategic coalitions in a common struggle against a civilization whose
idols are white supremacy and profit maximization for its own sake.

A fundamental presupposition undergirding this synthesizing
project, then, is that black theologians from North America and other
Third World liberation theologians are copartners in the task of developing a coherent vision of liberation, as well as in developing specific
strategies to enable the attainment of liberation. Liberation theology
has claimed to be revolutionary theology—that is, a theology aimed at
social transformation. If it is true that a revolutionary theology must set
forth a coherent and comprehensive analysis of the structures of domination, provide a specific vision of that which is hoped for, and establish the strategy for attaining liberation, then a theology of liberation
which emphasizes the common experiences of "Third-Worldness" must
take seriously the need to materialize its commitments in concrete his-

torical movements organized around the struggle for liberation. This is especially so if liberation theology is not to become just another academic theology that locates its raison d'être not with the struggle for world transformation but with seminary faculties and libraries.

CONTRIBUTIONS AND SHORTCOMINGS OF BLACK THEOLOGY AND LATIN AMERICAN LIBERATION THEOLOGY

The dialogical engagement of black theology and Latin American liberation theology has highlighted their conflict over the primacy of race or class. It has also accented their respective foci: racial oppression for black theologians and class oppression for Latin Americans.

Black theologians declare that racial oppression is the central contradiction of black life in North America. Black theology of liberation has therefore set forth a critique of the racist values, structures, and attitudes that have decisively shaped the lives of African-American people. Their profound criticism of racism has identified white supremacy as a decisive force in the formation and evolution of liberal-capitalist America. Black theology, in an attempt to erect a sustained antiracist theological tradition, has focused attention on those historical, cultural, and religious sources within the African-American tradition that have enhanced and sustained black life.

Black theologians have considerable support for their central theme that race is the determinative factor in the definition of social status in North America and, further, that white supremacist values pervade American society. The central enemy for black theologians is "the radical sin of Western Christianity—the ideology of white supremacy."[4] In that vein, Cornel West has made a significant contribution by tracing the evolution of the idea of racism within modern discourse. According to West, "the structures of modern discourse," defined as

the controlling metaphors, notions, categories, and norms that shape the predominant conceptions of truth and knowledge in the modern West . . . are circumscribed and determined by three major historical processes: the scientific revolution, the Cartesian transformation of philosophy, and the classical revival.[5]

West traces the appropriation of "classical aesthetic and cultural norms" and their intellectual legitimation by primarily marginal disciplines within the natural sciences in order to demonstrate that "the

emergence of the idea of white supremacy" was an inevitable consequence of that "creative fusion."[6] West's central thesis is that

> the idea of supremacy in the modern West [cannot] . . . be fully ac-
> counted for in terms of the psychological needs of white individuals and
> groups or the political and economic interests of the ruling class, [but
> rather] . . . the idea of white supremacy emerges partly because of the
> powers within the structure of modern discourse—powers to produce
> and prohibit, develop and delimit, forms of rationality, scientificity, and
> objectivity which set perimeters and draw boundaries for the intelligibil-
> ity, availability and legitimacy of certain ideas.[7]

This thesis becomes even more important for our current project
when West's distinction between "discursive" and "non-discursive"
structures emerges. According to West, "discursive structures, such as
theoretical formations (or, in Marxist terms, an ideological superstructure) do not have a necessary direct correspondence with . . . nondis-
cursive structures, such as a system of production (or, in Marxist terms,
an economic base)."[8] On that basis, West criticizes orthodox, traditional, revisionist, and vulgar Marxists whose historical studies

> focus primarily on powers within non-discursive structures—e.g.,
> powers of kings, presidents, elites, or classes—and reduce the powers
> within discursive structures to mere means for achieving the intentions,
> aims, needs, interests, and objectives of subjects in non-discursive struc-
> tures.[9]

This "reductionism," he continues,

> is not wrong: it is simply inadequate. It rightly acknowledges notewor-
> thy concrete effects generated by the relationship between powers in dis-
> cursive structures and those in non-discursive structures, but it wrongly
> denies the relative autonomy of the powers in discursive structures and
> hence reduces the complexity of cultural phenomena.[10]

In this respect, West is in agreement with other progressive Marxists
such as Lucius Outlaw and Maulana Karenga in North America, José
Carlos Marietegui, the father of Latin American Marxism, and Antonio
Gramsci, who all accentuate the relative autonomy of the ideological superstructure (discursive structure) from the economic base.

Black theology, then, has emerged as a critique of white supremacy
embodied in the structures of American society in general, and white

theology in particular, while establishing an independent theological tradition that has supported and enhanced the movement for black liberation. Black theology has been criticized, however, by Latin Americans for its lack of a critical posture toward capitalism. This is in part due to the ambiguous attitude of black theologians toward the liberal vision of capitalist America and their inclusion within it. In that regard, West also astutely observes that

> Black theologians do not utilize a social theory that relates the oppression of Black people in the overall makeup of America's system of production, foreign policy, political arrangement, and cultural practices. . . . Black theologians hardly mention the wealth, power, and influence of multinational corporations that monopolize production in the marketplace and prosper, partially because of their dependence on public support in the form of government subsidies, free technological equipment, lucrative contracts, and sometimes even direct transfer payments. . . . Black theologians do not emphasize sufficiently the way in which the racist interpretation of the Gospel they reject encourages and supports the capitalist system of production, its grossly unequal distribution of wealth, and its closely connected political arrangement.[11]

This major shortcoming in black theology has been exacerbated by the inability of its theologians to be precise concerning the specific content of the liberated society for which they hope. The foregoing critique notwithstanding, black theology's positive contribution has been its determined attitude concerning the significance of racial identity as a definitive factor in determining social status.

Latin American liberation theologians have made a positive contribution by affirming the importance of the economic base for determining the contours of Latin American societies. For them, the affirmation that class struggle lies at the core of their economic system and that, as such, Latin America could be better understood according to the standards of Marxist class analysis, is critical. Even as black theologians urge an affirmation of the significance of race, Latin American liberation theologians urge an affirmation of the significance of class. However, while black theologians have emphasized the importance of black culture and religion—thus focusing on cultural liberation and bypassing economic relationships of power—Latin American theologians all too often have emphasized economic analysis while paying little attention to the popular religions and cultures of Latin America.

Latin American liberation theologians, I contend, have been the victims of dependency on Europe in at least two significant ways. First, their appropriation of Marxist class analysis has been so thoroughly bound by European norms that they have insisted on the primacy of the economic base over the ideological superstructure. This manner of appropriation goes back to the core of the Marxist problematic of the relationship between the economic base and the superstructure.

Second, and this is an example of the relative autonomy of racism as an aspect of the ideological superstructure of Latin American civilization, the Latin Americans' inability to address the problem of racist domination substantively suggests that their analysis of Latin American society was considerably determined by their perhaps unconscious concession to the sin of white superiority. Thus, in that situation, the ideological superstructure (racism) conditioned the appropriation of an analytic mode that would describe the structure of domination in Latin America. Their focus on what West has called "non-discursive structures" has reduced their capacity to view the "discursive structures" as relatively autonomous and has significantly shaped their approach to the problem of domination on the Latin American continent.

The glaring absence of references to blacks in their writings only demonstrates the insignificant role to which the "discursive structures" has been relegated. Unlike black theologians, who recognize the power and life of cultural and religious values and attitudes in shaping people's lives, Latin American theologians have tended to assume the orthodox Marxist position, which perceives "discursive structures" as having only subordinate significance. This criticism is supported by their persistent insistence that the revolutionary transformation of society will include the resolution of the problems of the "minority" races of Latin America. The foregoing criticism is not to suggest that social analysis focused on class is incorrect for Latin America; it is intended as a challenge to broaden their conception of social analysis in order to be more inclusive as well as more true to their own situation.

The challenge for Latin American liberation theologians and black theologians, then, is to find a social theory which will account for both race and class domination, and to define their specific relationship to each other in their two different contexts.

CLASS AND RACE: A HIGHER ANALYSIS

Marx set forth his notion of ideology in a now well-known dictum, "the ruling ideas of any particular epoch are the ideas of the ruling class." He thereby posed ideology as the structural legitimation of the rule of the oppressor class. According to West, however:

Gramsci deepens Marx's understanding of the legitimation process by replacing the notions of ideology with his central concept of hegemony. For Marx, ideology is the set of formal ideas and beliefs promoted by the ruling class for the purpose of preserving its privileged position in society; for Gramsci, hegemony is the set of formal ideas and beliefs and informal modes of behavior, habits, manners, sensibilities, and outlooks that support and sanction the existing order.[12]

Antonio Gramsci, in fact, appropriated the term *hegemony* from Lenin, who, along with other Russian Marxists, had used the term to describe the role of the proletariat in the revolutionary movement. Gramsci considered the notion of hegemony to be Lenin's greatest theoretical contribution. Gramsci used the term to refer to the process by which the proletariat gained leadership over all the forces opposed to capitalism and welded them into a new homogeneous politico-economic historical bloc. Concerning hegemony Gramsci wrote: "the realization of hegemonic apparatus, insofar as it creates a new ideological terrain, determines forms of consciousness and of methods of knowledge."[13]

Michael Omi and Howard Winant, Marxist writers who concur with West that Gramsci's concept of hegemony is valuable in relating race and class, provide a helpful definition of the concept:

Hegemony is the thoroughgoing organization of society on behalf of a class which has gained the adherence of subordinate as well as dominant sectors and groups. Often summarized as rule by means of a combination of coercion and consent, hegemony is better understood as the creation of a collective popular will by what Gramsci calls "intellectual and moral leadership." The exercise of hegemony extends beyond the mere dissemination of "ruling class" ideas and values. It includes the capacity to define, through a vast array of channels (including the basic structures of economic, political and cultural life), the terms and meanings by which people understand themselves and their world.[14]

Within this framework, Omi and Winant conclude that it is possible to reinterpret the process of class formation as not simply economically determined. Classes can be viewed as "(1) multiply determined, (2) historical actors [which] themselves are (3) effects of the social struggles in which they were formed."[15] Hegemonic culture, then, is comprised of the traditions and current practices that "subtly and effectively encourage people to identify themselves with the habits, sensibilities, and worldviews supportive of the status quo and the class interests that dominate it."[16] In other words, they argue, it is a culture which is successful in persuading people to "consent" to their oppression and exploitation.[17]

According to Gramsci, hegemonic culture could be manifest in support of whatever class is in the dominant position. The critical link for Gramsci is the role that intellectuals play in obtaining the consent of the subordinate group to their own domination:

> The intellectuals of the historically progressive class, in the given conditions, exercise such a power of attraction that, in the last analysis, they end up by subjugating the intellectuals of the other social groups; they thereby create a system of solidarity between all the intellectuals, with bonds of a psychological nature and often of a cast character.[18]

Thus, the worldview of the ruling class is so diffused by its intellectuals that it becomes the "common sense" of the whole society. And as long as capitalist hegemony continues, the proletariat remains unaware of the contradictory nature of capitalist society and of the possibility of transforming it. A necessary part of the ideological hegemony of the capitalists is their ability to represent their own interests as those of society as a whole.

Gramsci, then, was the first Marxist theorist to analyze seriously the way in which the bourgeoisie perpetuate their domination through consent, rather than coercion, based on the manipulation of the "so-called organs of public opinion—newspapers and associations."[19] To establish its own hegemony the working class must be able to present itself as the guarantor of the interests of society as a whole. Here again, the intellectuals of the working class become the critical link, since in Gramsci's framework it is their contribution to establish the contours of a counterhegemonic culture, grounded in the oppositional forces, which may be disseminated throughout the society. Thus, each social class "creates together with itself, organically, one or more strata of intellectuals which give homogeneity and an awareness of its own function not only in economic but also in the social and political fields."[20]

Organic intellectuals articulate the collective consciousness of their class in the political, social, and economic spheres, mediate the relationship between the "world of production" (economic base) and "the complex of superstructures," and secure the consent of the masses for the policies of the society. Thus, the development of a group of intellectuals organically connected to the oppressed class is a necessary precondition for revolutionary transformation, since they are able to articulate a counterhegemonic culture that may "represent genuine opposition to hegemonic culture of habits, sensibilities, and world views that cannot be realized within the perimeters of the established order."[21]

West elaborates on Gramsci's notion of hegemonic culture by defining four categories for understanding cultural processes: "hegemonic, pre-hegemonic, neo-hegemonic, and counter-hegemonic."[22] According to West:

> Hegemonic culture is to be viewed as the effectively operative dominant world views, sensibilities, and habits that sanction the established order. Pre-hegemonic culture consists of those residual elements of the past which continue to shape and mold thought and behavior in the present. . . . Neo-hegemonic culture constitutes a new phase of hegemonic culture; it postures as an oppositional force, but, in substance, is a new manifestation of people's allegiance and loyalty to the status quo. Counter-hegemonic culture represents genuine opposition to hegemonic culture.[23]

Appropriation of Gramsci's notion of hegemonic culture and West's elaboration of it contributes to the thesis of this essay in several very important ways. First, the notion of hegemonic culture—when culture is defined in the holistic sense—acknowledges the significance of the cultural superstructure as a significant determining factor in defining social relationships. This is precisely the intention of Lucius Outlaw, who proposes a reworking of Marxist anthropology. Outlaw acknowledges that while

> it is the case that the economic order plays a principal role in the structural determination of a social formation, hence in the determination of social classes, it is also the case that (1) political and ideological relations are co-constitutive of social classes; (2) these latter relations have their base in other (non-economic) spheres of the social formation (in political and civil/cultural realms); (3) these other realms have their own relatively autonomous structural and dynamic principles which constitute them; (4) there they may, at a specific historical conjuncture, function as more or less (relatively) autonomous dimensions.[24]

Acknowledgment of the relative autonomy of the cultural dimension and of the superstructure, as well as other dimensions that compose it, allows us to have a more dynamic understanding of the relationship between an economically based and a culturally based definition of the ideological superstructure of human society.

Second, the appropriation of Gramsci's notion of hegemony restrains the tendency to view culture as simply a negative influence and as the creation of the ruling class for purposes of self-legitimation. Counterhegemonic culture presumes the significance of culture from the "underside of history" as expressing the oppositional aspirations and hopes of the oppressed class. Within this framework it is possible to perceive the value of popular culture, insofar as it is counterhegemonic. This is the reason for the insistence of black theologians on the valued contribution of black culture.

Black culture and black religion have often served as counterhegemonic expressions against the hegemonic culture of white racists, and therein lies their importance as a struggle-sustaining worldview for black people. West is correct in asserting that the "present challenge confronting black theologians is to discover and discern what aspect of Afro-American culture and religion can contribute to a counterhegemonic culture in American society," and to connect these discoveries with a special analysis of the economic conditions which also define black lives.[25] This is also true of Latin American liberation theologians, who have tended to downplay the importance of popular religion and culture for the liberation struggle. Acknowledgment of the power of racism in their context would enhance the possibility of an intentional quest for the counterhegemonic culture that exists in Latin America among the indigenous and black oppressed.

Third, the notion of hegemony allows for the dialectical interplay of the economic base and the superstructure. Understanding the relationship between an economic base and the superstructure avoids mistaking the economic factor as the absolute determining influence on the evolution of human society. Concurring with Cabral, Outlaw, West, Omi, Winant, and Karenga, I affirm that

> Central to our conception of race *and* class as evolving sets of social relationships is the notion that non-economic, non-accumulation-based factors such as ideology, organization and strategy are crucial to the formation of both races and classes. Such political and ideological factors are not the mere reflections of objectively determined "material" (i.e., economic) interests, but are themselves forces shaping the very definition of interests. In other words, as opposed to viewing these factors as being determined by the economic location of a race or class, we assert that such factors may be crucial to establishing the economic location itself.[26]

This recognition enhances the possibility of analyzing political and economic factors in relationship to culture and viewing them as relatively autonomous factors in the social formation of racist societies.

The acknowledgment by black theologians and Latin American theologians of their deficiencies, as well as their willingness to apply the concept of hegemony in their respective situations, would have at least four consequences: (1) a renewed focus on their respective social contexts in order to analyze the structures of domination in a new light; (2) the development of a cadre of intellectuals for the purposes of creating a counterhegemonic culture; (3) the evolution of a more global vision of liberation; and (4) the cultivation of a specific, concrete plan for envisioning and attaining liberation by both black and Latin American liberation theologies. The underlying conception of truth here affirms praxis as the forum through which the validity of truth claims can be evaluated. Thus, practical activity in history becomes meaningful as the context in which values, interpretations, and descriptions can be tested and conflicts resolved. It is an important component of any theology that claims to be liberating and revolutionary.

THE CHALLENGE FOR THE NEXT GENERATION OF BLACK THEOLOGIANS

A second generation of black theologians has begun the task of constructing a theology of liberation that comprehends this project.[27] While the first generation developed the broad outlines of a contemporary black theology that probed the linkage between religiocultural values and racial oppression, it has been those in the second generation who have sought to evolve an explicit analysis of the religiocultural traditions, values, and symbols that define African-American life, their autonomous activity and status, and their crucial link to power in the United States. At the same time, these new voices seek to develop specific modes of analysis for understanding how these traditions, values, and symbols have functioned both as a means of sustaining racist domination and as a context for sustaining an oppositional worldview of resistance, hope, and struggle.

It has been demonstrated above that the pioneers of black theology articulated a critique of white theology and the racist practices of white Christians; it was also explored above how black churches have been influenced by the dominant culture. It is now necessary to evolve a theoretical framework within which to evaluate the explicit functions of religion, culture, and language as structures of domination or, alternatively, as structures that sustain hope and resistance.

An example of the contributions being made by those black theologians who constitute this second generation may be found in *Cut Loose Your Stammering Tongue: Black Theology in the Slave Narratives*.[28] In this work, Will E. Coleman issues a specific challenge to contemporary black theologians when he suggests that it must concentrate "on the Hermeneutical, Linguistic-poetical front as well as in the political, social and economic struggle for a full humanity. . . . "[29] Coleman here echoes my own threefold challenge: contemporary black theologians should (1) incorporate the thematic universe of the black poor into their discourse; (2) develop a specific mode of analysis that will provide a comprehensive understanding of the diverse structures of domination within U.S. society; and (3) create specific criteria for scrutinizing the emancipatory or oppressive intent of values, symbols, and metaphors within a context of racist oppression.[30]

The efforts of this second generation, then, bring together several divergent strands. First, the texts of the African-American story provide them with counterhegemonic images, metaphors, symbols, and values that sustained an oppositional perspective of resistance and hope in the past, and provide raw material for the creation of emancipatory modalities in the present. This task, however, also depends on the capacity of contemporary black theologians to discover those counterhegemonic traditions and images that actually enable the oppressed to struggle for their emancipation. As has already been suggested, Gramsci's notion of hegemony, as well as West's helpful elaboration and critique of Gramsci's foundational work, will be useful in that task.

More specifically, counterhegemonic religion and culture represent genuine opposition to the sensibilities, habits, and worldviews of the dominant society and represent possibilities that cannot be realized within the parameters of the established order. Starting with that theoretical basis enables contemporary black theologians critically and self-consciously to develop criteria for evaluating African-American religions and cultures and to determine whether particular practices, images, symbols, and values have been emancipatory. Romanticizing the liberative content of every aspect of those religions and cultures is thereby avoided. This becomes especially significant in light of the current emphasis on Afrocentric ideas.

Another focal point that has emerged in the second generation is the desire to shift discussion away from definitions of black theology as a theological enterprise based on the African-American story, and toward one which investigates African-American discourses as signifying processes, political rhetorics of emancipation from oppressive situations. In other words, by treating theologies as "rhetorical," they may be construed as discourses of persuasion. By treating them as "political," all discourses may be understood as arising out of, and creating postures toward, the social order. In fact, they are assumed to be so, even when they include no specific references to such matters. Utilizing this approach, black theologians have been able to explore not only the ways in which African-Americans, who are constrained by a racist society, employ the Christian tradition, but also the role of these discourses as both emancipatory and failed practices in transforming the social order.[31]

Poststructuralist theories expose the complex way in which language is a process of signifying, in distinction to a merely representational medium through which the directly oppressive forces can be identified merely with semantic forms. For that reason, second-generation black theologians are probing black writers, slave narratives, black folk culture, black intellectual traditions, black music, and other expressions of African-American religions and culture in order to examine each genre as a text. But since discourse is a construction of a particular social world not always of its author's intent, such texts hide as much as they tell. Therefore they cannot be grasped merely by their "obvious" semantic intent. By extending a reading of texts to include their rhetorical construction—the tropes of problem and resolution, the rhetoric of rationality and evidence, implied audience, posture toward reality invoked, the polyphonic character of the text, the way the African-American is a subject matter, and other such questions of how the text persuades—it is possible to treat each text as a set of complex effects. These must be respected as strategies of a particular, local social world, one which excludes and creates meanings about what is emancipating and oppressive for African-Americans.

Furthermore, a second-level reading of each text is made possible by the use of Marxist cultural theory, a tool of analysis that views religious and cultural discourses as realities of the social formation of contemporary capitalism. In the United States, capitalism's ideological partner has been white supremacy, which may be defined as a system wherein the modes of production are so related to economy, state, religion, and culture that discourses which order social desire toward consumption, white dominance, and male dominance become the persuasive language of the society. With the assistance of such writers as Raymond Williams, Amilbar Cabral, Manning Marable, and other Marxist theoreticians of culture, it has been possible for the second generation of black theologians to understand discourse as more than a locally con-

structed rhetoric, for it is also the result of cultural practices shaped by
a social formation which creates a variety of positions of subordination,
as well as options for resistance.

From an analysis of the posture toward the world created by each
text, it is possible to inquire about the reach of the strategies of emancipation, along with an assessment of the linkages within each text to
the larger social processes constructed for them. The link between work
that engages in analysis of the social order and analysis of its language is
obvious; it constitutes an important element of the challenge taken up
by the second generation of scholars. This project is necessary due to a
number of factors: the complex diversity of views within the African-
American community, the increasing class stratification within that
community, and the widespread growth of the black underclass since
the civil rights movement.

In the context of these emerging analytical possibilities, the major
challenge of black theologians is to show how theology can be a resource for assessing what counts as emancipatory in the texts of the
African-American story. While earlier black theologians broadly described the possibilities of utilizing African-American history, culture,
and religion as a context for black theological discourse, the second generation must advance upon that earlier work by elaborating and recon-
ceptualizing traditional theological categories in light of the insights
evolved from the use of instruments of social analysis and a Marxist
theory of culture. For example, the traditional concept of *pneumatos*, as
in pneumatological Christology, has been one attempt to reconceive the
criterion of assessment in regard to a commitment to history.

Finally, contemporary black theologians need to evaluate and recon-
ceptualize the nature, identity, and mission of the black church. What,
for example, does it mean to be the church in light of the insights de-
rived from social analysis or in relation to the images, practices, symbols, values, and institutions that purport to embody a commitment to
the gospel in the modern world? The political commitments of the
black church, despite its immense contribution to the struggle for black
liberation, require considerable scrutiny to discern whether its institutional self-interests are hegemonic, neohegemonic, prehegemonic, or
counterhegemonic.

Black theologians can contribute to the black church by assisting this
institution to engage in a critical self-evaluation of its *identity* and *mission*. Black theological discourse has been defined as distinctively Christian and liberative, or emancipatory, practice because its resistance to
oppression is ordered by rules of a Christian grammar that are consis-

tent with the liberating work of the Christ of God. Nevertheless, as Coleman suggests, there is a continuing need to probe the nature of the intersection of Christian and so-called non-Christian images, values, and practices within the texts of the African-American story.

The task awaits those scholars in all generations who seek to devote themselves to the continued African-American project of human liberation on all levels. The vocabulary, values, images, metaphors, sensibilities, and institutions in the African-American community must be challenged to fulfill the humanizing mission of the gospel in the world. In the final analysis, the transformation of racist structures will be achieved in the practical organization of concrete historical movements that facilitate the achievement of the common goal of holistic liberation. It is in historical movements of the oppressed that diverse perspectives, ideologies, and analyses are forced to engage together in the intentional process of securing each individual's rights to self-determination, in community, in such a manner as to resolve significant differences. Oppressive structures will finally be changed as the struggling oppressed are empowered to eradicate their oppression.

It is within this context that Christians everywhere can celebrate the reality of a God who is both future, as the liberator of the oppressed, and present, as the actualization of liberation. Christians have often been content to interpret the meaning of the faith. Now the faith of the oppressed, however, works to change the conditions of their lives for the betterment of all humanity.

14

LIFE ON THE BACK OF THE BUS

The Continuing Saga of Race Relations in the United States

David Batstone

> *If a house burns down,*
> *it's gone,*
> *but the place —*
> *the picture of it —*
> *stays, and not just*
> *in my rememory,*
> *but out there,*
> *in the world.*
> —Toni Morrison,
> *Beloved*[1]

*I*t was just another bus ride through the "flatlands" of Oakland on into Berkeley. Three of us — all white, two male, one female — were accustomed to representing the racial minority on this urban jaunt. But the ensuing course of events was anything but typical.

While Oakland, California, takes pride in calling itself "the most integrated city in the United States," its neighborhoods can be identified largely along racial and socioeconomic lines. The Oakland hills that border the city are a virtual white suburbia (with some exceptions) comprised of beautiful homes situated on wooded lots and enjoying exceptional parks and city services. Those who cannot find an affordable home in the hills typically move farther out, to the lily-white "bedroom communities" that lie over the other side of the hills.

The flatlands, on the other hand, are a zone of color—skin color, that is. Its residents are mostly African-Americans, though now also Hispanic- and Asian Americans. They live in considerably smaller homes, crowded apartment buildings, and teeming tenements situated in a distinctively urban sprawl. In Oakland, socioeconomic status is determined by the slope of your street.

It was with an acute awareness of that racial and class divide that I, along with a small group of middle-class whites motivated by religious commitment and social conscience (and an unidentified dose of guilt?), moved into the heart of the Oakland flatlands in the early 1980s. Our group's original goal was, if not naive, quite simple: to build bridges where racism and socioeconomic marginalization had forged a wedge. Our method was equally unsophisticated: to listen, watch, and learn while establishing relationships within the neighborhood.

Before completing even our first six months in the flatlands, we were approached by Greg Martin, an African-American male who, having grown up in the neighborhood, was concerned about the lack of basic life opportunities for black youth beyond those offered by the burgeoning drug trade. Though he had developed relationships with many of the local youth through sports programs, he dreamed of establishing a recreation center. The major obstacle he consistently encountered, however, was the lack of adequate facilities in the flatlands. The large downtown churches, on the other hand, held magnificent facilities but, due to the effects of "white flight" from the urban areas in the 1950s and 1960s, few members who might utilize them. Astutely Greg surmised that we might stand a better chance than he of persuading one of those churches to make its building available for a youth center. The plan worked to perfection, and shortly thereafter together with Greg we inaugurated "The Neighborhood Recreation Center" in a downtown Baptist church. Within a decade the center matured into a place where urban youth could not only hang out after school, but also avail themselves of programs in homework tutoring, computer training, food assistance, self-esteem formation, spiritual development, and wilderness camping treks.

It was nearly seven years after we had moved into the Oakland flatlands that the bus incident occurred. It began normally. Since all of the seats were already occupied when we boarded, we slowly wound our way down the aisle toward the back of the bus, where we could stand in relative comfort. Once at the back, having grabbed the rail protruding from the ceiling for stability and balance, we each moved into our private thought worlds in subconscious obedience to the laws of urban anonymity.

Several moments later we were jerked out of our trance by a loud scream: "Hey, this white motherfucker just stepped on my foot." Looking casually over at who was being identified as a clumsy oaf, I was stunned to realize that the owner of that voice, seated nearly four feet away from me, was a black male in his early twenties looking in a fit of rage directly at me.

While I continued looking at him in a silence born of confusion, he rattled off another series of insulting expletives that grew angrier by the second. Though I was convinced that I could not have possibly been near his foot, I sensed that humility was in this case the wisest action: "I am really sorry that I stepped. . . . " Before the apology could be completed, my words were cut short by another sizzling barrage, and this time he was peppering his insults with threats: "Don't you talk to me, white boy; I don't want to hear a word come out of your mouth or I'll break your jaw. Don't you even look at me or I'll cut you up."

It was then that the embers of hatred ignited throughout the back of the bus as other males joined in with their own taunting shouts, now degrading all three of us, each contributing his own idea how we might be taught a lesson. In reaction to the fact that two of us were wearing berets that had been acquired during work in Latin America, the remarks took on a surprising cast:

"Look at them, they look like terrorists or something!"

"I bet they're anti-American, trying to overthrow our government!"

"Man, they look like communists!"

Tension quickly engulfed the entire bus, a wave of black faces from front to back irresistibly swept toward us like water toward the shore. But the response was varied: while some eyes joined in the laughter, some unmistakably expressed pity for our situation, others betrayed a fear that violence might ensue and leave no one untouched, and still others—who were surely mirroring our own thoughts—communicated their wonder at how we had ever allowed ourselves to be put into this situation.

Then, just as the atmosphere was ready to explode, the drama turned: A middle-aged black woman seated next to the young man who had started the melee boldly turned to him and said, "Why don't you just shut up? He hasn't done anything to you." All attention immediately shifted away from the three of us, the back of the bus turned silent, and all eyes fixed on the new protagonist.

"Oh, so look here, we have with us an Oreo who has come to help the white folks!" the young man jeered.

"It's not about color, young man; it has to do with respect for other people, something you obviously never learned in your home," she reacted acidly.

"Who do you think you are, my mother? Listen, bitch, no one was ever at home for me so don't you come off trying to tell me how to act," he said bitterly, then quickly added, "Besides, I never learned to lick white folks shoes clean!"

The words spilled out quickly for both: "It's people like you who make white folks think we're nothing but failures," she said evenly.

From there the conversation degenerated into more name-calling and threats, the young man threatening to slap her if she kept talking, she retorting that he would be in for a real fight if he did. The other passengers in the back of the bus, many of whom were once gleeful participants, now said nothing, absorbed by the painful rhetoric. The standoff came to an abrupt halt when the woman, realizing that the bus had reached her destination, rose quickly and scampered off the bus. Even though it was another five minutes or so to Berkeley, neither the young man nor anyone else on the bus redirected their attention toward the three of us. To the contrary, the young man spent the entire time verbally abusing the woman who had dared to intervene.

WINDOWS INTO OUR SOCIAL WORLD

Why focus on this particular incident, especially when the roles of "innocent victim" and "oppressor" are made murky? After all, there is no shortage of examples that clearly and unequivocally indicate the extent and force of racial oppression presently suffered by the African-American community and other people of color within the present social system of the United States. It seems ironic, even cynical, to reflect on this kind of event given the potent symbolism of Rosa Parks and a bus seat at the historical genesis of the civil rights movement in this country.

Highlighting this bus incident, then, could be interpreted as an attempt to relativize the specifics of those racist social, political, and economic structures that characterize our society. In other words, one might expect to hear the following proposition: Since all people are susceptible to racism and prejudice as manifestations of the larger reality of evil—the universal human condition—the situation calls for individual conversion and self-transformation toward an ideal that transcends the particularities of skin color, sexual and gender orientation, or class location. The bus incident, it might be argued, is merely one more example of the necessity of such "moral imperatives."

Though this logic is not completely void of truth, the present essay will contend that once rational propositions become the primary or sole consideration of ethical analysis, "moral imperatives" themselves become riddled with historical contradictions. For, as Jürgen Habermas has argued, meaningful rational conversation regarding ethics necessitates first establishing social conditions that allow for a more inclusive process of defining moral action itself:

> The cognitive capacity to justify moral action norms has to be supplemented if it is to become effective in the context of ethical life. . . . Without the capacity for judgment and motivation, the psychological conditions for translating morality into ethical life are missing; . . . without "fitting" forms of life to embodied moral principles, the social conditions for their concrete existence are missing.[2]

Indeed, my choice of event has been consciously made for effect. My experience on the Oakland bus embodies certain social representations that the dominant cultural consciousness, that is, U.S. "popular opinion" or "conventional wisdom," will read as a validation of its own relative innocence and, therefore, as a justification to maintain effective social control. As Søren Kierkegaard expressed in so many different ways, however, "innocence is ignorance," a quite deliberate "unknowing" that is sustained for power via the guise of moral superiority. In this essay it will be proposed that all such pretensions to and presumptions of innocence must be demystified by the memory and story of those who have suffered the barbs of injustice and exclusion in their very flesh.

Yet the complexity of the bus incident also precludes utopian generalizations and acritical idealizations of the "privileged position" of the victim. Though it may appear antithetical to the foregoing comments, it must be underscored how vital it is that every action in the social drama be brought into the ethical arena and engaged through critical reflection, else the patterns of established domination will not be truly transformed, merely mirrored and repeated.

It is at this place—where tension, high emotion, ambiguity, and contradiction muddy the waters of clear vision—that true dialogue and confrontation must transpire. Though rhetorical diatribe and moralistic withdrawal perhaps enable one to feel more secure in one's own convictions, they rarely open possibilities for new behavior nor enrich understanding of the concrete other, however limited those openings.

The bus incident, therefore, will be used as a window through which to view the larger conversation of race, class, and gender. On the one hand, it is ludicrous to suppose that, given the enormous complexities of the relationships which these categories encompass, one limited example might illuminate much of anything. Nevertheless, by sinking roots deep into the particularities of this incident, some understanding might be reached to guide conversation and behavior regarding other diverse, equally complex experiences.

MEMORY AND THE END OF INNOCENCE

The dominant culture in the United States suffers from a severe case of historical amnesia. The meaning of events, as well as their relative social value, are largely determined by reference to momentary relevance and immediate consequence and cause. Since it is widely assumed that in each passing moment the individual is granted one's own new present, memory is regarded more as a matter of warm reminiscence (yearbooks and sock hops) than it is recognized as a dynamic creative force in the formation of personal and collective identity.

In many respects, this ahistorical consciousness is an inevitable fruit of the Enlightenment goal of setting reason free from the conditions imposed by tradition and authority. Critical thinkers realized that history (in the form of tradition) was being utilized as a weapon in the hands of those who wielded social power within their feudal society, justifying both their "historical right" to rule and their determination of the boundaries and character of public "truth." Consequently, Immanuel Kant and others celebrated the growing awareness of a universal reason that promised to transcend the manipulation of historical interests. What they did not perceive, however, was the inescapably limited horizon inherent in their own Olympian view. Not that they should be thereby judged too harshly, for centuries later we who are the heirs of this rational consciousness also commonly fail to recognize—despite having passed through the "second Enlightenment" of Karl Marx—the blinders engendered by our own sociocultural location.

For instance, take the bus incident. The young males lashed out against us solely based on the color of our skin. My moral axioms, among which I include that "all people are created equal," lead me to conclude that my human dignity and rights were unjustly abused. Hence, viewing the incident as an isolated moment of my own personal existence suggests, on the one hand, my own *innocence* and, on the other hand, the immoral *racist behavior* of a specific group of black males.

But by recourse to historical memory "universal reason" itself may be critiqued (critical consciousness thereby comes full circle), placing the foregoing interpretation of a specific event within a wider perspective. For no event is an island unto itself. It forms part of a deeper stream of meaning, however much the capacity to examine particular events as if by "freeze frame" creates the illusion of their autonomy. In other words, though individuals and communities may be removed in terms of time or cultural space from the genesis of any given social dynamic, every event has a "career" to which it is bound.[3] Directed to the present case, then, one must investigate whether there is more to the anger of the black males on the bus than at first may meet the eye.

Nearly three decades have passed since Martin Luther King, Jr., wrote from a jail cell in Birmingham an impassioned letter to eight white Alabama clergymen in an effort to convey the deep pain of racism that motivated the black freedom movement and to rebut their calls for "patience":

> We have waited for more than 340 years for our constitutional and God-given rights. . . . When you have seen hate-filled policemen curse, kick and even kill your black brothers and sisters with impunity; when you see the vast majority of twenty million Negro brothers [and sisters] smothering in an airtight cage of poverty in the midst of an affluent society; . . . when you are harried by day and haunted by night by the fact that you are a Negro; . . . plagued with inner fears and outer resentments; when you are forever fighting a degenerating sense of "nobodiness"; then you will understand why we find it difficult to wait. There comes a time when the cup of endurance runs over, and men [and women] are no longer willing to be plunged into the abyss of injustice where they experience the blackness of corroding despair.[4]

If the "cup of endurance" was running over for blacks in the early 1960s, imagine the present levels of disillusionment, despair, and frustration within the African-American community, especially given the dearth of meaningful social transformation during the last thirty years. Every injustice listed by King is at least as prevalent today as it was at the time of the writing of his letter: the travesty of the police beating of

Rodney King in Los Angeles in 1992 was no new revelation, at least to the black community, that a predominantly white police force and court system view justice with glasses tinted by racial color. The income gap between whites and blacks has actually widened in the last three decades, making the disparity of affluence and poverty that much more obscene. Over 43 percent of all African-American children live in poverty. While many young blacks go to early graves and jail cells, the ones who survive are faced with the debilitating prospect of up to 50 percent unemployment. Finally, the infant-mortality rate for blacks in this country, 17.7 deaths per 1,000 births, stands at more than double the average for whites and is higher than the rate suffered by many Two-Thirds World countries, such as Malaysia.[5] By and large, African-Americans are still treated like "nobodies" in U.S. society, a double jeopardy of class and race (not to mention the triple jeopardy faced by black women) that leads to permanent conditions of poverty.

In Oakland, not even a natural disaster could hide the glaring inequities of structural racism which are patently evident in our "integrated" city. In October 1989, the Loma Prieta earthquake destroyed numerous poorly constructed apartment buildings and low-income hotels in the flatlands region. Many families, predominantly black, were forced to leave their condemned apartment buildings and seek accommodation either with relatives, in motels, or, in some instances, in their cars. Additionally, more than two thousand rooms at hotels used for the homeless were boarded up after the earthquake, leaving many of the residents, again predominantly black, with no money and few options for shelter.

Assistance from the Federal Emergency Management Fund (FEMA) was slow and ineffective. Those fortunate enough to receive aid were forced to wait for months. Even then, in order to qualify for FEMA's housing assistance victims had to show proof that they had lived at their address for at least 30 days, a requirement that eliminated scores of otherwise eligible tenants. Due to the instability of their income, many people cannot afford to pay an entire month's rent at a hotel and, therefore, spend the last week of the month on the streets until their welfare check arrives. At the time, the callousness of FEMA was chalked up to the insensitivities of a bureaucracy.

In October 1991, Oakland was again struck by tragedy when a large firestorm swept through its wooded highlands, destroying over three thousand homes. FEMA assistance began rolling in to the predominantly white victims of the fire within six days. While only one-third of the earthquake victims received assistance from FEMA two years earlier, more than two-thirds of the fire victims were granted help. Though FEMA claimed that it simply was not as prepared after the earthquake as it was in the aftermath of the firestorm, the simple fact remains that while many residents of the Oakland hills, aided by federal grants, were beginning reconstruction of their homes, many black victims of the earthquake were still without any secure shelter.[6]

This is the face of racism in the post–civil rights era. As Dr. Julianne Malveaux, a San Francisco-based economist and writer notes,

> You don't need five people in a room saying we're going to jam black people. But if you decide cities are last on your list, and 60 percent of African-Americans live in cities, you have targeted African-Americans. . . . I'm not willing to call it a conspiracy, [but] this is neglect that is not benign.[7]

The dream of integration has turned into the nightmare of segregated social opportunity and curtailed economic advancement. The following anecdote reflects yet another side to this more subtle, though nonetheless quite insidious, form of cultural racism. While carrying out research for his work, *Two Nations, Black and White: Separate, Hostile, Unequal*, political scientist Andrew Hacker discovered that dental hygiene was a field with one of the smallest percentages of black participation. He was quite surprised by that statistic because it seemed to him that dental hygiene would be a profession easily accessible to lower-income groups through educational programs offered at community colleges and technical schools. Once he called instructors in the field, however, the reason became clear: though in the past they had enrolled numerous black students, upon graduation the vast majority of them could not get jobs because "white people don't like black fingers in their mouths."[8]

Despite these harsh realities, many white people still assume that racism was destroyed with the abolition of separate drinking fountains and the general societal disapproval of racial slurs like *nigger* and *boy*. Bolstering such a positive appraisal of integration are such undeniable advances as a larger black middle class, the legal desegregation of the public schools, the weighted opportunities offered by entitlement and affirmative action programs, and, of course, the unparalleled success of the Michael Jordans and the Spike Lees of the entertainment world. The tenor of their conviction is quite familiar: "Although we may not have reached the ideal of racial integration and equality, we are making real progress."

"Progress" is typically the moral refuge of those who feel in control of the course of history. Though the term does imply an admission that the present is far from complete, its nuance rejects any connotation that such a situation is to be deemed intolerable. At root, it calls for an unbending faith in the future as the redeemer of the past and the present.

In his reflections on the philosophy of history, Walter Benjamin emphasized that faith in progress is, in most instances, seriously misplaced. Writing at a time when fascism robed its authoritarian reign in the gown of progress, Benjamin proposed a provocative analogy of history by reference to the Klee painting *Angelus Novus*:

> [Klee's figure] is how one pictures the angel of history. His face is turned toward the past. Where we perceive a chain of events, he sees one single catastrophe which keeps piling wreckage upon wreckage and hurls it in front of his feet. The angel would like to stay, awaken the dead, and make whole what has been smashed. But a storm is blowing from Paradise; it has got caught in his wings with such violence that the angel can no longer close them. This storm irresistibly propels him into the future to which his back is turned, while the pile of debris before him grows skyward. This storm is what we call progress.[9]

The wreckage of the black community in the United States has continued to pile up now for over 370 years, giving lie to the evolutionary myth of an ever-better future. Stories of the suffering ones, told in anger and in pain, expose the massive contradictions that undercut the assumed innocence of the dominant culture's story. The voices of the victims reveal the bestial irrationality lurking even within an "enlightened reason" and signal the regressive human costs of those values triumphantly praised as progressive freedoms. While the winners of history celebrate, or at least tolerate, the social order of the present, it is the conquered ones who never allow us to forget that *we all have both a past and a future*. Their stories engender a historical consciousness that names those "invisible forces" once thought to rule tyrannically over culture.[10]

A philosophy of history may also be fruitfully augmented by sociology. Until recently, the paradigm guiding the social sciences was that of classical physics, namely, "isolating a cause, determining a variable, measuring a force, defining a function."[11] Since every society was presumed to be constructed by the same "bricks and mortar," the primary task of the objective observer was to uncover and explain those social laws that produce the actual configuration, or "floor plan," of any given society, independent of time, space, or culture. In a modernist culture that practically worshipped technology and efficiency, the potential of increased engineering over both nature and society was certainly enticing.

Within the last two decades, however, that dominant paradigm has been shaken by a profound revolution in both approach and understanding. As Clifford Geertz indicates, analogies based on technology and rigid functionalism have given way to models that view the social system as a serious (though at times playful) game, a ritual theater, a network of inclusive/exclusive boundaries or "grids," or a behavioral text.[12] Without entering into the details of these overlapping yet quite distinctive interpretive approaches, it may be said that they signal growing recognition that any given social world is a willful arrangement. Hence, the rules, attitudes, representations, roles, and intentions practiced by the people who comprise any particular human society are neither ordained from heaven nor ruled by anonymous historical force. In simple terms, the formation of culture is now linked to the material conditions, the learned behavior (ritual), the perceived interest, the social power, and the moral imagination (or lack thereof) of its members.

Of course, not every individual or community comes to the social drama with *equal* power. Many members of a social system are forced to play roles that do not correspond to their interests or make possible the fulfillment of their moral vision. As a result, they become marginal characters who are shut out from the performative conversation that shapes a culture's social scripts.

"Racial integration has produced the symbols of progress and the rhetoric of racial harmony," Manning Marable eloquently notes, "without the substance of empowerment for the oppressed."[13] The "substance" to which Marable here alludes was at issue in the unequal treatment of disaster victims in Oakland: as a community, African-Americans have marginal access to the ownership of material resources, to marketable skills and education, to political leverage, and thus to real economic power. This intersection of race and class is often glaringly absent from discussions of racial relations in the United States, reflecting a widely held resistance to thinking in terms of class. Since opportunity in a capitalistic society will always be largely defined economically, however, those links must inevitably be made. Although the economic factors in the social marginality of the African-American community over the last three centuries have shifted—from human

commodity to legalized discrimination to structural marginalization—
the forces of oppression have nevertheless remained constant.
Those who hold social and economic power are not willing to surrender their claims of innocence so easily. In fact, the dominant culture
nearly always seeks to legitimate existing social arrangements by weaving a complex quilt of defining myths, ideals, values, practical knowledge, and anticipations. These themes not only function to bolster the
culture's own perception of innocence, but also aim to establish for one
and all that the social world could not be otherwise. It is this kind of
cultural storytelling that is represented by Arnold Toynbee's shocking
assessment of pan-African culture in his work, A Study of History:
"When we classify [hu]mankind by color, the only one of the primary
races . . . which has not made a single creative contribution to any of
our 21 civilizations is the black race."[14]

Tragically cut off from their own memories, the marginal, those
without meaningful social power, regularly have their identities fashioned by a cultural story not their own. That paradoxical twist became
painfully evident on the Oakland bus when several black men, seeking a
language and cause by which to express their "free-floating rage,"[15] lev-
eled accusations at the three of us about our own supposed "anti-
American" position. Invoking the national myth that addresses the
danger to freedom and order posed by enemies foreign and domestic,
they inexplicably perceived us as a threat to a social world that had, in
reality, produced their own social marginality. While their own memories informed them that white people were often an enemy to be hated
and feared, having designated us as such elicited a host of associations
of the "enemy" more characteristic of a ruling class, for example, over-
throwing the government, damage to public property, etc. Although
they themselves could likely only imagine participating in the "American dream," their identity was nonetheless intimately linked to its survival.

So complex are the links that bound all of us on the bus that day.
Though complete strangers, we each carried the fragmented memory of
our ancestral roots, the pain and shame of a horrific past. At some deep
level of our soul we each knew that we still bore the respective benefits
and curses of that legacy, in which access to privilege and power is reg-
ulated largely by birth. The bitterness of those contorted pasts was sufficient to burst the seams of social convention, producing a tense
conflict within which roles transpired that had not been consciously
scripted. In tragic irony, the dispossessed modeled the social power
which they had been taught by the cruel lessons of experience, while we

of "blessed race" were astounded by the injustice, despair, and power-lessness wrought by its exercise. The event had all the makings of a Faulkner novel:

> We see dimly people, the people in whose living blood and seed we our-selves lay dormant and waiting, . . . performing their acts of simple pas-sion and simple violence, impervious to time and inexplicable. . . . They are there, yet something is missing, they are like a chemical formula ex-humed along with the letters from that forgotten chest, carefully, the paper old and faded and falling to pieces, the writing faded, almost inde-cipherable, yet meaningful . . . just the words, the symbols, the shapes themselves, shadowy, inscrutable and serene, against that turgid back-ground of a horrible and bloody mischancing of human affairs.[16]

HUMAN IDENTITY IN COMMUNITY: MOURNING, GUILT, AND THE PURSUIT OF JUSTICE

I anticipate that many readers, particularly from the white community, will deem my reflections on the bus incident thus far as ludicrous since some moral responsibility has been laid on those whom social conven-tion and "common sense" identify as wholly innocent. Is this not yet another case of collective white guilt gone too far?

Yet mourning should not be uncritically equated with guilt. As German psychoanalyst Alice Miller notes, "mourning is the opposite of feeling guilt; it is an expression of pain that things happened as they did and that there is no way to change the past."[17] Although it may be dif-ficult to hear in our therapeutic culture, authentic sorrow is an appro-priate response to injustice. From cradle to grave, of course, we often receive a quite different message: feel good, expunge negative thoughts, liberate your shame, love yourself, and build a high self-esteem, all ac-tions of the will that promise to help us to reach our full potential as human beings.

Certainly these means to a healthy self-concept are, in and of them-selves, to be highly valued, pursued, and affirmed within our commu-nities. But they must never come at the price of denial. We must not simply wish away and ignore tragic historical realities because they do not make us feel good about ourselves or our world. In fact, the denial of pain, be it personal or collective, is one of the root sources of guilt; repressed feelings of shared responsibility are another. Anxiety, neuro-ses, and even more serious psychological dysfunctions do not derive from the experience of mourning but, to the contrary, grow from the desire to cohabit with historical wounds and the willingness to allow oneself to be fed by their destructive power. In essence, guilt is the debilitating force of repressed memories.

For that reason, actions born solely out of the motivation to rid oneself of guilt—the "activist" solution, which in its own way still places the self and its will to control at the center of the world—rarely address the actual situation of injustice. Victims of oppression are thereby once again treated merely as objects and manipulated for one's own redemption. They are not recognized as human beings to whom one relates in quite *unequal* ways. In short, patterns of control are maintained to stave off real sacrifices for mutuality and justice. It was these false expressions of "repentance" that Malcolm X so powerfully exposed.

> Is white America really sorry for her crimes against the black people? Does white America have the capacity to repent—and to atone? . . . Most American white people seem not to have it in them to make any serious atonement—to do justice to the black [community]. . . . What atonement would the God of Justice demand for the robbery of the black people's labor, their lives, their true dignities, their culture, their history—and even their human dignity? A desegregated cup of coffee, a theater, public toilets—the whole range of hypocritical "integration"—these are not atonement.[18]

No authentic racial dialogue will occur in U.S. society until the white community becomes deeply mournful that a majority of people of color in this country live in intolerable conditions of poverty, suffer from staggering unemployment, and are faced with limited social opportunities. In mourning we must acknowledge that these conditions are due not to sloth or genetically inferior capacities, but simply to a structural racism that bolsters the probability of a marginal cultural existence. Mourning has the potential to move a community toward an authentic repentance, beyond superficial solutions that, metaphorically speaking, install new carpets and drapes but allow the house's structure to rot. Until that day, the white community will continue to be wracked by guilt and fear, and many people of color will continue to be trapped in poverty, anger, and despair. Racism is a poison that stilts the growth, disfigures the identity, and curtails the freedom of all who get caught in its web.

SOCIAL JUSTICE AND IDENTITY POLITICS

Exposing the deep pathologies of U.S. culture relies on a critical awareness of the present informed by the recuperating power of memory. But these resources are not sufficient to set our communities free from the web of racial injustice. Profound liberation also requires nurturing and sustaining a spiritual and moral vision. It arises from the practical values and concrete engagements fashioned for a more just future. "Without a vision," the ancient Hebrew prophet said so well, "the people will perish."

In that respect, it must be questioned whether many poststructuralists have not surrendered too much of the quest for universals. At least since the 1970s, activist circles (working for social transformation) and academic circles (seeking to deconstruct the dominant umbrella of ideologies) may perhaps be best described as dominated by "identity politics." Defined oversimply, identity politics is a self-referential basis for political vision, one that stems from one's own essential identity as a member of an ethnic group, a community based on gender or sexual preference, a religious tradition, a narrowly defined political agenda, etc.

On one level, it can legitimately be asked whether politics, broadly understood, can ever be rooted in anything but identity, for how else might one conceivably arrive at a political consciousness? Yet, a moral vision limited to self-reference falls into its own cycle of absorption and chokes itself. The fragmentation and marginality of the progressive political movement in the United States for most of the last three decades is at least partial evidence for that judgment.

The present state of mutually exclusive advocacy positions might be a necessary stage in uncovering the contradictions within the universal-objectivist position, which has long dominated social and political theory in North Atlantic culture. Indeed, by too hastily generalizing the oppression of all peoples, particular oppressed groups regularly are subsumed into a larger "consensus agenda" of one brand or another that does not represent their own specific analyses and strategic goals. That, for instance, has often been the experience of women, who have not always found their concerns fully addressed by movements which raise the banner of race and class oppression alone. For that reason, Elisabeth Schüssler Fiorenza proposes a dialectic of particularity and intersubjectivity that is relevant for every public discourse concerned with social justice:

> On the one hand, too generalized an understanding of oppression and liberation serves the interests of the oppressive system, which cannot tolerate a critical analysis of their dehumanizing mechanisms and structures. . . . On the other hand, too particularized an understanding of oppres-

sion and liberation prevents an active solidarity among oppressed groups, who can be played against each other by the established systems.[19]

There is a point of identity isolation beyond which solidarity and mutual respect are no longer possible, a restricted space wherein potential allies are rejected out of hand. That happened at a religion and society conference held in Chicago. Well into the proceedings, a white female theologian stood up in the middle of the congress and announced, "I want you to know that everything that has been discussed here over the last few days has no validity because most of you were sons in the court of Pharaoh." She had returned to her seat for no more than a few seconds when a black theologian stood up in another part of the hall and shouted, "And I want you to know that what you have just said also lacks validity because you were a daughter in the court of Pharaoh." Those present still were reflecting on this explosive series of volleys when an Asian American theologian yelled out, "And I want you to know that what you have just said lacks validity because you were once a slave in the court of Pharaoh." The litany can go until no one would have a "valid" voice.

Affirmation of one's own identity as a member of a community, constituted by a past and a present, is a vital element in any liberation struggle. Yet, the parable of the theological conference suggests that identity politics and, in more general terms, an identity ethos lose their transformative power once their goal becomes the elimination of the voice of the other solely because it has an outsider status relative to one's own experience. An authentic struggle toward liberation, in distinction, is a pluralist collaboration that intentionally strives to include those voices that have never had the opportunity to participate fully in economic, social, political, and spiritual discourses, be they verbal or performative, and to do so on equal terms and with an appreciation for difference. The goal is not necessarily consensus but an environment of creative tension which potentially leads to mutual transformation.

Few theologians during the last century have formulated a vision binding human identity to a larger community as insightfully as Howard Thurman, who turned to the metaphor of *imago Dei* to express the affective-emotional sacredness and inherent worth of each and every concrete human being. Thurman was convinced that "community relatedness" must inexorably flow from an appreciation of our common universal ground, for each person then has the capacity to treat the other as if one is in the place where one ought to be, as a particular expression of the many faces of God.[20] Moral responsibility, Thurman therefore concluded, is circumscribed within the practice of love as grounded in justice and the interrelatedness of identity:

> It is in the moment of (mystical) vision there is a sense of community—a unity not only with God but a unity with all life, particularly human life. It is in the moment of vision that the mystic discovers that "private values are undergirded and determined by a structure which far transcends the limits of one's individual self." . . . Personality is something more than mere individuality—it is a fulfillment of the logic of individuality in community.[21]

On that basis, it is essential to search for a language and practice of rights and virtues that move beyond self-referential definitions and fixed boundaries around my or our rights and my or our virtues. Despite the complexities and contradictions inherent in the affirmation of meta-values, it is on that basis that duties and obligations also may be given their due consideration within the ethical arena, along with the identification of rights. Not that a full comprehension or interpretation of the character of meta-values and inalienable rights is ever self-disclosing; for that reason, to no identity group should be given the sole legitimacy to define their meaning for "the majority." Nor should it thereby be assumed that the answer lies in the uncovering of the "one true story" that undergirds the slippery notion monolithically denoted as "culture." In other words, there is no meta-story that defines for us the complete character of our meta-values. In actual fact, hermeneutical priority in the definition of values must be given to those who have been victims of the social system, for their redemption is the essential gateway to social reconciliation. The marginal reveal to us the roots of our shared fragmentation and dehumanization. The "other" uncovers a profound truth about ourselves and our culture.

Social discourse always takes place in an arena of power imbalance. Whenever conversants do not share even a minimum of vulnerability within concrete relations of power, it is not really conversation that unfolds but a subtle form of dictation. That is the message of this circus parable: An unexpected crisis arose at the circus one day. The mice refused to perform with the elephants. They were tired of merely serving as props for the elephant show, which had them running around to avoid the feet of the more powerful beasts. The mice demanded a show that would highlight their own skills. The circus master called the animals together for a meeting in an attempt to resolve the crisis. The elephants spoke first, saying to the mice, "We were shocked by your comments. Why not give our show another chance; we can learn to dance together." The mice did not hesitate to respond, "We already know how to dance with you; we jump whenever you move your feet. The problem is that you will never know what it means to dance with us."

What is required, therefore, is a constant dialogue broadly inclusive of a plethora of concrete commitments, specific engagements, and personal and communal passions. That process self-consciously struggles both to sharpen and to broaden the character and meaning of meta-values for any given society. Of course, that process of mutual critique needs always to expose and deconstruct the pretensions of the dominant group that its system is the actual embodiment of those values.

This defining process ought not to be confused with the notion of "play," the "reflective deconstruction and practical non-attachment" developed by those who have forfeited the notion of the subject and the possibility of weaving any coherent meaning and value for human existence.[22] In effect, those who have struggled for so long to become subjects of their own history are now cynically told by "pure" post-structuralists that their attempts to define the world are as meaningless as any other narrative. Despite its potential contribution to the critique of authority and the nonhierarchical ordering of community life, "play" as a category of political critique does not consider seriously enough the powers that maintain structures of injustice.[23] In fact, its own methodological possibility assumes the stability of the present social order, however contradictory to its own deconstructing method. For that reason Langdon Gilkey argues that "play" as a category for moral vision is "toothless in the face of oppression."[24]

Liberating action demands a vision of the world which, though it is not yet a reality, is in the process of becoming one because it is alive in the social consciousness of a people. The pursuit of inalienable rights, for instance, is an affirmation of the dignity of all human beings regardless of the heterogeneous identities existent within a global reality. It must be ruthlessly exposed that U.S. history reflects a monumental contradiction between the affirmation of that principle and its actual practice, both domestically and in foreign policy. That fact has already been well established in this essay. But it is also true that the duties implicit in a commitment to the principle of inalienable rights provide a signpost—the contours of which are ever clarified and adjusted through communal interaction—by which to clarify and discern the injustices of every present moment: "From something present something still more present has arisen, from a reality a higher reality."[25]

Returning to the bus incident, the black males repeated the same acts of hatred based on racial identity that had undoubtedly been utilized time and time again to dehumanize them. Every personal and social transgression must be named, regardless of its source. Racial hatred must be rejected directly and openly wherever it manifest itself, lest moral responsibility itself become a casualty of yet another form of self-proclaimed innocence.

In that respect, the words of Malcolm X to a Harlem street audience bring clarity to the cauldron of the struggle for human identity, burdened by guilt, sorrow, and anger, as it boils deep within our racist society:

> To approach the black man's struggle against the white man's racism as a human problem, I said we had to forget hypocritical politics and propaganda. I said that both races, as human beings, had the obligation, the responsibility, of helping to correct America's problem. The well-meaning white people . . . had to combat, actively and directly, the racism in other white people. And the black people had to build within themselves much greater awareness that along with equal rights there had to be the bearing of equal responsibilities.[26]

THE INTERVENTION OF "RACE-TRANSCENDING PROPHETS"

Cornel West challenges the leadership of grassroots communities to demonstrate the transformative moral power of the "race-transcending prophet," men and women who model the capacity to "get beyond the confines of race without ever forgetting the impact of racism on Black people in this society."[27] Though West is uncompromising in his critique of the racial and economic marginalization of the black community in the United States, he at the same time maintains that "we must always be explicitly moral in an all-inclusive manner so we resist all forms of hatred of the other, be it a hatred of individuals different from one's self, be it a Black, White, Jewish, or Korean person."[28]

The courage which that moral commitment demands is exemplified by the woman on the Oakland bus who challenged a raucous, threatening group of young males regarding the responsibility and truth of their actions, and did so on behalf of three people whose racial identity perhaps would not compel her naturally toward solidarity. She made herself vulnerable to the accusation of being a traitor (an "Oreo") to her own racial identity and suffered the painful humiliation which that treatment bears.

Of course, the hardened cynic might question her motivations for intervening, and perhaps even suggest that she was merely acting out of a dominated consciousness linked historically to the subjugation of black people to white culture. But the simple fact is that her intervention struck a blow against the pillars of accommodation that bolster the structural edifice of racism in U.S. society.

If asked, most white people in the United States would not identify themselves as racist. Perhaps some would not even be able to recall having direct interaction with a person of color (a statement in and of itself), while those who have established some form of relationship could point to the cordial nature of their personal exchanges, despite the covert tension and lack of understanding that likely lay beneath the surface. Confronted with the reality of structural racism, one would also expect a widespread plea of innocence since, by and large, most individuals feel quite powerless to establish or change social or economic policy and do not feel personally responsible for its presently ordered existence. But in response to each of these sincere positions, the challenge must be sounded that unless a white person living within the United States makes a deliberate choice actively to intervene to stop the oppression against the black community (and other communities of color) and fashion a life-style in active support of that commitment, then that person must continue to live with the burden and responsibility of his or her racism.

What is being referred to here as racial solidarity is not simply the selective appropriation of elements of black culture, such as grooving to rap music or enjoying the blues. This issue must be addressed because popular culture in the United States has the capacity to co-opt a wide diversity of historically specific cultural creations while stripping them of the sweat and tears that have brought them into existence. Surely that is largely due to the commercialization process that transmits popular culture to us; a cultural phenomenon in the United States is usually a sales phenomenon. And the most unlikely images have become sales phenomena within the pop culture of the nineties. Is there not something anachronistic in seeing (Malcolm) "X" baseball caps for sale in K-Mart together with the Walt Disney gear? King nostalgia takes on similar superficiality: while the film footage of King's "I have a dream" speech is now virtually a pop icon, film clips where he more directly talks about materialism, racism, and greed are more rarely seen.[29]

In a poem entitled "Why Madonna & All White People with Dread Locks Should Burn in Hell," an African-American woman expresses her rage at this simultaneous appropriation and denial of her culture:

My problem with these wannabes is that I don't think they want it all.
They want to pick and choose. . . . Their goal is to own, to claim, to
white-wash.

I say, if you really wannabe, claim the whole picture. Go ahead, you certainly helped to create it. Assume responsibility for the general malaise
that grips our black society. This is the environment which breeds the
creativity you so envy. The same society which binds us to the past and
blinds us to the future. Don't covet it, take it. But you better take it all.

Take the crack addicted babies & their strung out mamas and daddies
too. Own the fact that black men between 18 and 25 are an endangered
species. Embrace the hopelessness that infects the current generation, my
generation of black Americans.

Nah, you probably don't want all that. It is easier to steal the creative
product if you don't have to examine the source from which it emanates.[30]

The goal of racial politics is not the progressive integration of the
black culture into a majority, white culture; the transformation of racial
relations must go much deeper than that. True racial solidarity is only
manifest in specific acts of justice that address the root causes of social
and economic marginalization and identify the brutal consequences of
their destructive power. It demands democraticization of economic
structures and the social order, an opening of those spaces wherein
communities of color may participate in the society on the basis of their
own identity.

The primary challenge for the white community, therefore, is to *intervene* where racism actually exists, namely, in those social institutions
and economic structures in which they participate, to end their own accommodation and acquiescence to that system. Perhaps to many within
the white community it will not be readily apparent how the mecha-
nisms of exclusion and dehumanization covertly function within their
own institutions. For that reason, it is essential for whites to enter into
a real dialogue of praxis with the black community so that whites may
hear and appreciate the memories and stories of those who experience
racism in their own flesh. Entering an interdependency with our sisters
and brothers of color will surely challenge our attitudes, opinions, life-
styles, ideas, and viewpoints.

The white community must also stop feigning ignorance to cover up
its moral reticence. Often it is patently obvious what steps are required

to bring about meaningful social transformation, but they involve sacrifices deemed too costly. In that respect, Jonathan Kozol's indictment
of the "savage inequalities" of the educational system applies more
broadly:

> We propel ourselves through these endless cycles as if, after two hundred
> years of American education, we don't know what works and we are sud-
> denly about to find out. Once we find out, of course, we'll share it with
> the poor. Baloney. We know what works. We're just not willing to pay
> the bill. Even President Bush knows Head Start works, but he says we
> don't have $5 billion to provide it for every child who needs it. But some-
> how we found $50 billion to restore the emirate of Kuwait to his throne.
> Which is more important to [North] America?[31]

In conclusion, in active "discourse" the particulars of our experience
intersect with the meta-values of life and justice, infusing present praxis
with deep spiritual sensitivities yet also exposing the contradictions of
basic material realities. It is possible to move beyond the seemingly
ubiquitous "eschatological reservation" which plagues North Atlantic
theological ethics. "What to reflection is a contradiction," Gilkey deftly
proposes, "is to praxis a workable dialectic, a momentary but creative
paradox."[32] Action in response to present needs may be justified as
much by the potential it creates for envisioning future praxis as by its
immediate consequences. The ritual of praxis may give testimony to the
universal, healing power of love, beauty, and human dignity, which
move us across the limitations and ambiguities of the present.

On the other hand, where love, beauty, and human dignity are not
embodied in social structures or, as a result, in personal relatedness, that
society will decay. Nearly three decades ago Malcolm X prophetically
underscored the alternatives which would shape our social destiny:

> In our mutual sincerity we might be able to show a road to the salvation
> of America's soul. It can only be salvaged if human rights and dignity, in
> full, are extended to black men [and women]. Only such real, meaningful
> actions as those which are sincerely motivated from a deep sense of hu-
> manism and moral responsibility can get at the basic causes that produce
> the racial explosions in America today. Otherwise, the racial explosions
> are only going to grow worse.[33]

As I was dramatically reminded on an Oakland bus, we have not yet
heeded his warning.

NOTES

INTRODUCTION
David Batstone

1. Gustavo Gutiérrez, *A Theology of Liberation: History, Politics and Salvation*, Sister Caridad Inda and John Eagleson, trans. (Maryknoll, N.Y.: Orbis Books, 1973), 15.

2. I here cite, in a paraphrased version, an insightful remark made by my former colleague at New College Berkeley, Dr. Francis Andersen.

3. Henri J. M. Nouwen, *Reaching Out: The Three Movements of the Spiritual Life* (Garden City, N.Y.: Doubleday, 1975), 92.

4. Todd Gitlin, "Uncivil Society," *Image Magazine, San Francisco Examiner*, April 19, 1992; 13–17.

5. Clifford Geertz, *Local Knowledge: Further Essays in Interpretive Anthropology* (New York: Basic Books, 1983), 34–35.

CHAPTER 1. RETHINKING OUR HISTORIES
Robert McAfee Brown

1. Gustavo Gutiérrez, *Dios o el oro de las Indias* (Lima: CEP, 1989).

2. Both documents may be found in Robert McAfee Brown, ed., *Kairos: Three Prophetic Challenges to the Church* (Grand Rapids: Wm. B. Eerdmans, 1990).

3. Cf. Gustavo Gutiérrez, *The God of Life* (Maryknoll, N.Y.: Orbis Books, 1991), 84ff.

4. Karl Barth, *Church Dogmatics*, vol. 4/3, 2 (Edinburgh: T. & T. Clark, 1961), 780.

CHAPTER 2. RECLAIMING OUR HISTORIES
William Baldridge

1. Cotton Mather, *On Witchcraft, Being the Wonders of the Invisible World* (1693, reprint, Mount Vernon, N.Y.: Peter Pauper Press, 1950), 22. See also C. Mather, *Another tongue brought in to confess the great Saviour of the world or, some communication of Christianity, put into a tongue among the Iroquois Indians, in America. And put into the hands of the English and the Dutch traders: to accommodate the great intention of communicating the Christian religion, unto the savages among whom they may find anything of this language to be intelligible* (Boston: Printed by B. Green, 1907).

CHAPTER 3. RELIVING OUR HISTORIES
Elsa Tamez
Chapter translated from Spanish by David Batstone

1. "Aportes de los pueblos indígenas de América Latina a la teología cristiana," unpublished report from the II Consulta Ecuménica de pastoral indígena, held in Quito, Ecuador, June 30–July 6, 1986, 78.

2. Ibid., chap. 4a.

3. Leonardo Boff, *Nova evangelizacão: Perspectiva dos oprimidos* (Petrópolis: Vozes, 1990), 37.

4. According to Pierre Bonnard, *nous* in Romans 7 is an autonomous power of the discernment and knowledge of good, but it is only a theoretical understanding; in practice it has no effect because "it has come to sin," *Anamnesis: Recherches sur le Nouveau Testament* (Geneva: Revue de Théologie et de Philosophie, 1980), 138.

5. Cf. Elsa Tamez, *Contra toda conden: La justificación por la fe desde los excluidos* (San José: DEI, 1991), 114–26.

6. Klauspeter Blaser, *Esquisse de la dogmatique* (Lausanne: UNIL, 1987), 18.

7. The discussion is not new; for instance, Asian Christian theologians, who live in the midst of other religions, constantly attempt to respond to these challenges. Cf. *Christologies in Encounter*, in the series *Voices from the Third World*, no. 2 (EATWOT, 1988). Several Western theologians have also treated these themes; cf. Harvey Cox, *Many Mansions: A Christian's Encounter with Other Faiths* (Boston: Beacon Press, 1988).

8. In view of the five-hundredth anniversary of the Conquest, the indigenous religions pose a great challenge to the christological question within Latin American theology. The implications suggest that a reconstruction may be necessary.

9. Texts from the documents of Sahagún, *Códice matritense de la real academia*, no. 176ff., cited in Miguel León-Portilla, *Los antiguos mexicanos a través de sus crónicas y cantares* (Mexico: Fondo de Cultura Económica, 1961).

10. Ibid., 29.

11. For our Mexican ancestors there were five ages: five suns and five earths, the fifth age or the Fifth Sun was considered the present epoch, the creator and promoter of which was Quetzalcóatl. In the fifth age, or "Sun of movement," the movement of the earth and human beings was announced. In the previous four ages appeared the primordial elements of water, earth, fire, wind. The creation stories speak of the Sun of water (when those humans created with ashes were carried away by water and turned into fish), the Sun of the tiger, or earth (when the sun did not continue its path after midday, and at that hour it would become dark, and the tigers ate humans who, though giants, were fragile), the Sun of firestorm (when it rained fire and the earth's inhabitants burned), and the Sun of wind (when everything was carried away by the wind and humans became monkeys and were scattered in the mountains). See Primo F. Velázquez, trans., *Anales de Cuauhtitlán*, in *Códice Chimalpopoca* (Mexico: Imprenta Universitaria, 1845), 2:77.

12. M. León-Portilla, *Los antiguos mexicanos*, 17–20.

13. Cf. Román Piña Chan, *Quetzalcóatl, serpiente emplumada* (Mexico: Fondo de Cultura Económico, 1985), 38.

14. From the documents of Sahagún, *Códice matritense*, no. 180, cited in M. León-Portilla, *Los antiguos mexicanos*, 25.

15. R. Piña Chan, *Quetzalcóatl*, 39.

16. The stories of these Gods represent two distinct historic levels: one pertains to the origin of Venus and the Fifth Sun (related to Quetzalcóatl) and the other with the birth of the solar God Huitzilopochtli, from the time of the Aztecs.

17. R. Piña Chan, *Quetzalcóatl*, 65.

18. Fernando Alvarado Tezozomoc, *Crónica mexicana*, José M. Vigil, ed. (Mexico: José M. Vigil, 1878), 10, 13.

19. Laurette Séjourné, *Pensamiento y religión en el México antiguo* (Mexico: FCE/SEP, 1984).

20. Texts from Sahagún, *Historia general de las cosas de Nueva España* (1946) 3:47, cited in L. Séjourné, *Pensamiento y religión*, 16.

21. Texts from Sahagún, *Historia . . . de Nueva España*, 2:151–52.

22. L. Séjourné, *Pensamiento y religión*, 36. Further supporting this author's viewpoint, it may be said that Huitzilopochtli is the only deity which is properly of the Aztecs' own culture, and for their teaching they turn to Quetzalcóatl. In fact, Séjourné notes, "one is hard-pressed to illustrate the principle of reintegration in the great All in All by a solar identity that is fed by the blood of mortals." In that sense, there were no changes except in the cultic practices (ibid.).

23. Ibid., 35.

24. Cf. M. León-Portilla, *Los antiguos mexicanos*, 26.

25. Text from Sahagún, *Códice matritense*, no. 180, cited in M. León-Portilla, *Los antiguos mexicanos*, 36.

26. Cf. *La lucha de los dioses. Los ídolos de la opresión y la domesticacion de los dioses* (San José/Managua: DEI/CAV, 1980).

27. Cf. Franz Hinkelammert's rereading of Abraham's refusal to sacrifice Isaac in Genesis 22, *La fe de Abraham y el Egipto Occidental* (San José: DEI, 1988), 15–61.

28. Hernán Cortés, "Cartas de Relacion de Hernán Cortés," in *Crónicas de la Conquista* (Mexico: UNAM, 1987), 99.

29. Texts from Sahagún narrate the massacre with a singular emotivity, *Códice florentino*, vol. 12, chap. 20, cited in Miguel León-Portilla, *El reverso de la conquista* (Mexico: Joaquin Mortiz, 1987), 40–43.

30. Cited by G. Gutiérrez, *Dios o el oro de las Indias* (Lima: CEP, 1989), 144.

31. Ibid.

32. M. León-Portilla, *El reverso de la conquista*, 95.

33. Cf. Fernando Mires, *En nombre de la cruz* (San José: DEI, 1989), 48–75.

34. Antonio Mediz Bolio, trans., "Libro de Chilam-Balam de Chumayel", unpublished translation from Mayan dialect into Spanish (San José, 1930), 29–30.

35. It would seem that the qualification of "true" was seen by the indigenous people as a proper name, since for them there was no such thing as "false" Gods in distinction from "true" Gods.

36. "Libro de Chilam-Balam de Chumayel", 30.

37. This theory is applicable today as well. Julio de Santa Ana writes about actual human sacrifices which are generated by an economic system that can sustain itself only by producing victims. See Julio de Santa Ana, "Costo social y sacrificio a los ídolos," in *Divida externa e igrejas. Una visão ecumenica* (Rio de Janeiro: CEDI, 1989).

38. *Anales de Cuauhtitlán*, in *Códice Chimalpopoca*, 2:87

39. Cf. R. Piña Chan, *Quetzalcóatl*, 56.

40. The story descends from a *mestizo* descendent of Neztahualcóyotl, Don Fernando de Alva Ixtliloxóchitl. M. León-Portilla, *Los antiguos mexicanos*, 116–17.

41. Séjourné, *Pensamiento y religión*, 52.

42. Ibid., 18.

43. Eric S. Thompson, *Historia y religión maya* (Mexico: Siglo XXI, 1987), 227.

44. Cited in G. Gutiérrez, *Dios o oro*, 42.

45. Silvio Zavala, *Filosofía de la conquista*, 3rd ed. (Mexico: Fondo de Cultura Económica, 1984), 73.

46. Bartolomé de las Casas, *Tratados*, vol. 2 (Mexico: Fondo de Cultura Económica), 673.

47. R. Piña Chan, *Quetzalcóatl*, 78–80.

48. Alfredo Barrera and Silvia Rendón, trans., *El libro de los libros del Chilam Balam* (Mexico: Fondo de Cultura/SEP, 1984), 68–71.

49. This document deals with twelve missioners who were sent out to evangelize by Adrian the Sixth. In distinction from others who utilized or legitimated violent methods of evangelization, these twelve decided to concentrate on the key rulers and priests of Tenochtitlán, and explain to them their mission of evangelization. The manuscript was found at the beginning of the twentieth century in the Secret Archive of the Vatican Library. The fragments cited here are found in *A quinientos años*, no. 8 (Ajusco, D. F.: CENAMI, 1989).

50. Ibid.

51. Ibid.

52. Laurette Séjourné, *América Latina, Antiguas culturas precolombinas* (Mexico: Siglo XXI, 1987), 112.

53. Cf. ibid., 242–300; Miguel León-Portilla, *La filosofía náhuatl* (Mexico: UNAM, 1959).

54. *A quinientos años*, no. 8.

55. Ibid., 18.

56. Cited in M. León-Portilla, *El reverso de la conquista*, 79.

57. Clodomiro Siller, "Para una teología del Nican Mopóua," *Servir* 62 (1976): 167–68.

58. Clodomiro Siller, "El método teológico Guadalupano," unpublished essay.

CHAPTER 5. UNCOVERING A CIVILIZATION OF CAPITAL, DISCOVERING A CIVILIZATION OF WORK
Ignacio Ellacuría
Chapter translated from Spanish by David Batstone

1. Cited in Jon Sobrino, *Archbishop Romero: Memories and Reflections* (Maryknoll, N.Y.: Orbis Books, 1990), 38.

CHAPTER 6. THE ECONOMICS OF ECCLESIA
Jon Sobrino
Chapter translated from Spanish by David Batstone

1. To justify this thesis it is enough to recall that the mission of Jesus was that of announcing and making real the reign of God for men and women who were victims of the powers of this world. [Ed. note: Throughout the course of this chapter the Spanish word *misericordia* will be translated as "compassion." Though it may also be rendered as "mercy," it is believed that the nuance intended by Sobrino is best captured in English by reference to the former term.]

2. St. Ignatius, *Ejercicios Espirituales* (Barcelona: Editorial Balmes, 1964), numbers 136–148. The structure of St. Ignatius's treatment of wealth and poverty continues to have a tremendous force in the world today, that is, if one properly historicizes it. I hope this meditation, which touches on the most crucial problem in our world, is included in the celebration of the Ignatian anniversaries.

3. Especially after the events that have transpired in Eastern Europe, there exists a euphoria in the First World which leads it to ignore poverty in the Third World. But in Latin America things not only are not improving, they are actually going to get worse. Pointing to only one piece of data, the Latin American documentation center CEPAL contends that by 1995 Latin America will need $90 billion simply in order to equal the per capita income achieved in 1980.

4. The Eighth Commandment, which treats the world of deception and structural concealment, is a theme which is quite absent in the social doctrine of the church. That is very strange, given the fact that the church is an institution substantially grounded in the word, and the word may be a vehicle of both truth and deception, of unmasking and of concealment.

5. Cited in Jon Sobrino, *Archbishop Romero: Memories and Reflections* (Maryknoll, N.Y.: Orbis Press, 1990), 38.

6. With tremendous discernment St. Ignatius formulates the antithetical character of these two principles: poverty *against* wealth, being disgraced and scorned *against* worldly honor, humility *against* pride.

7. The treatment of compassion in this section has substantially appeared elsewhere, in Jon Sobrino, "La Iglesia samaritana y el principio-misericordia," *Sal Terrae* (October 1990).

8. Juan Luis Segundo, in his book *Theology and the Church: A Response to Cardinal Ratzinger and a Warning to the Whole Church* (San Francisco: Harper & Row, 1985), 44ff., demonstrates in detail that the goal of the Exodus was quite simply the liberation of a suffering people. He puts this forward in response to the first Vatican instruction regarding liberation theology, which contends that the goal of the Exodus was the creation of the people of God and the establishment of their religion in the covenant made at Mt. Sinai.

9. Compassion should also make one feel moved for those who suffer from "natural" causes. Nevertheless, its most ultimate essence is expressed in reaching out to those who suffer because they are "victims." Victims may be the result of both natural and historical evils, but in Scripture considerably more attention is given to victims of historical causes than those of natural ones.

10. Cited in Sobrino, *Archbishop Romero*, 43.

11. It is quite obvious that Ignacio Ellacuría, for example, allowed himself to be guided by the principle of compassion in all of his activities, but more specifically in his intellectual activities: theological, philosophical, and political analysis. It is important to mention that fact in order to underline that compassion is much more than feelings alone or solely a compassionate activism. It is as well a principle shaped by the exercise of the intellect.

CHAPTER 7. TRANSNATIONAL CORPORATIONS AND INSTITUTIONALIZED VIOLENCE
Mark Lewis Taylor

1. Dinesh D'Souza, *Illiberal Education: The Politics of Race and Sex on Campus* (New York: The Free Press, 1991), 71.

2. Rigoberta Menchú, *I, Rigoberta Menchú: An Indian Woman in Gutate-mala*, ed. Elisabeth Burgos-Debray, trans. Ann Wright (London: Verso, 1984), 49–50. For analysis of the much-disputed data concerning the unfolding of the attack, see Philip Berryman, *Christians in Guatemala's Struggle* (London: Catholic Institute for International Relations, 1984), 44–48.

3. Menchú, *I, Rigoberta*, 200.

4. Allan Nairn, "To Defend Our Way of Life: An Interview with a U.S. Businessman," in *Guatemala in Rebellion: Unfinished History*, Jonathan L. Fried, Marvin Gettleman, Deborah T. Levenson, and Nancy Peckenham, eds. (New York: Grove Press, 1983), 89.

5. Ibid., 90–91.

6. On "imperialism" as an analytic category in international relations, see Robert Gilpin, *The Political Economy of International Relations* (Princeton: Princeton University Press, 1987), 34–41. Granting the importance of some of the critiques of theories of imperialism, notably Lenin's, I here preserve use of the term to name complex structural relations of domination that function to systemically strengthen some nations at the expense of others.

7. The most well-documented study of this is Piero Gleijeses, *Shattered Hope: The Guatemalan Revolution and the United States, 1944–1954* (Princeton: Princeton University Press, 1991). Behind this work stands Richard Immerman, *The CIA in Guatemala: The Foreign Policy of Intervention* (Austin: University of Texas Press, 1982); idem, "Eisenhower and Dulles: Who Made the Decisions?" *Political Psychology* 1 (Autumn 1979): 21–38; and Stephen Kinzer and Stephen Schlesinger, *Bitter Fruit* (Garden City, N.Y.: Doubleday and Co., 1981).

8. Nairn, "To Defend Our Way of Life," 100.

9. Susanne Jonas, *The Battle for Guatemala* (Boulder, Colo.: Westview Press, 1991), 1–3, 178.

10. Ibid., 178.

11. Susanne Jonas and David Tobis, eds., *Guatemala* (New York: North American Congress on Latin America, 1974), 143–50. On other ways that TNCs co-opt local elites, see Kwamena Acquaah, *International Regulation of Transnational Corporations: The New Reality* (New York and London: Praeger, 1986), 66–67.

12. Nairn, "To Defend Our Way of Life," 102.

13. Jonas, *The Battle*, 77–78.

14. Ibid., 83. On the negative impact of IMF and World Bank "strucutural adjustment" policies, see Ross Hammond, Michael McCoy et al., eds., *An NGO Guide to Trade and Finance in the Multiluteral System* (New York: Non-Governmental Liaison Service, 1989), 18–20.

15. Hammond et al., *An NGO Guide*, 8–9.

16. Ibid., 9.

17. For one especially valuable summary of this critique of "structural adjustment" policies, see economist Carmen Diana Deere et al., *In the Shadows of*

the Sun: Caribbean Development and U.S. Policy (Boulder, Colo.: Westview Press, 1990), 87–120. Neither my own critique nor those summarized by Deere entail a wholesale rejection of "structural adjustment" policies. But fundamental reform is needed so that "adjustment programs . . . [are] designed to spur growth in a manner complementary with improving the distribution of income," so as to "not adversely effect the standard of living of the majority of the population—the rural and urban poor," 210). The ongoing North-South dialogue for reforming the IMF has laid out many of the reforms needed. See "The Group of 24 Deputies Report," *IMF Survey*, (August 10, 1987), 2–3.

18. Why I intentionally use here the masculine reference will become clearer below when considering the posture of the corporate community toward women.

19. Allan Nairn, "Guatemala: Central America's Blue Chip Investment," in Fried et al., *Guatemala*, 103.

20. Ibid., 102.

21. Nairn, "To Defend Our Way of Life," 89. This businessman requested anonymity.

22. Jonas, *The Battle*, 209.

23. Ibid., 124; Hank Frundt, "To Buy the World a Coke," in *Latin American Perspectives* (Summer 1987), 381–416.

24. For examples of this, see Tom Barry, Beth Wood, and Deb Preusch, *Dollars and Dictators* (New York: Grove Press, 1983), 128; and Susanne Jonas, "Overview" and "Contradictions of Revolution and Intervention in Central America in the Transnational National Era: The Case of Guatemala," in Marlene Dixon and Susanne Jonas, eds., *Revolution and Intervention in Central America* (San Francisco: Synthesis Publications, 1983), 303.

25. Jonas, *The Battle*, 198.

26. Nairn, "Guatemala: Central America's Blue Chip Investment," 103.

27. Ibid.

28. Jonas, *The Battle*, 105.

29. Ibid. Emphasis added.

30. Carol A. Smith, "Class Position and Class Consciousness in an Indian Community: Totonicapan in the 1970s," in Linda A. Smith, ed., *Guatemalan Indians and the State, 1540–1988* (Austin: University of Texas Press, 1990), 205–29.

31. Sheldon Annis, *God and Production in a Guatemalan Town* (Austin: University of Texas Press, 1987), especially chaps. 3 and 4.

32. For examples, see June Nash and Helen Safa, eds., *Women and Change in Latin America* (South Hedley, Mass.: Bergin and Garvey, 1986); and Chandra Talpade Mohanty, Ann Russo, and Lourdes Torres, eds., *Third World Women and the Politics of Feminism* (Bloomington: Indiana University Press, 1991).

33. Jonas, *The Battle*, 108.

34. Norma Stoltz Chinchilla, "Industrialization, Monopoly Capitalism, and Women's Work in Guatemala," *Signs* 3, no. 1 (February 1977): 38–56.

35. Lourdes Beneria and Martha Roldan, *The Crossroads of Class and Gender* (Chicago: University of Chicago Press, 1987); and Nash, *Women and Change*, 9.

36. Jonas, *The Battle*, 109; also see the comments on this as global problem in David Harvey, *The Condition of Postmodernity* (New York: Basil Blackwell, 1988), 153.

37. Jonas, *The Battle*, 109–10.

38. Laurel Bossen, *The Redivision of Labor* (New York: State University of New York, 1984), 320.

39. Hammond, *An NGO Guide*, 19; and Jonas, *The Battle*, 111.

40. For a key example, from Bolivia, of Third World women using their pain for organizing resistance and lament, see the film *Hell to Pay* (New York: Women Make Movies, Inc., 1988).

41. Jonas, *The Battle*, 149. The sources substantiating Jonas's summary are *Inforpress Centroamericana, Centroamerica 1988* (Guatemala: Inforpress, 1988), 107–10; and Americas Watch and British Parliamentary Human Rights Group, *Human Rights in Guatemala during President Cerezo's First Year* (New York: Americas Watch, 1987), 73ff.

42. Guatemalan Church in Exile (IGE), *Guatemala: Security and Development* (Mexico City: IGE, 1989); and Jonas, *The Battle*, 149.

43. Victor Perera, "A Forest Dies in Guatemala," in *Nation*, November 6, 1989.

44. Joel Kovel, *White Racism: A Psycho-history* (New York: Columbia University Press, 1970), 116.

45. Ibid., 116.

46. Harvey, *Condition of Postmodernity*, 292.

47. Ibid., 163.

48. Kovel, *White Racism*, 117.

49. Richard Barnet and Robert Muller, *Global Reach: The Power of Multinational Corporations* (New York: Simon and Schuster, 1974), 13–71.

50. This is acknowledged by even some of the most critical analysts. See, for example, Acquaah, *International Regulation*, 189–90.

51. Ibid., 82–83.

52. Holtmann, *An NGO Guide*, 31–35.

53. Kovel, *White Racism*, 117.

54. Joel Kovel uses the notion of "abstraction" to study not only Western class distortions, but also white racism in the United States. Kovel, *White Racism*, passim.

55. Jonas, *The Battle*, 179.

56. I have elsewhere explored the notion of the matricidal and matriphobic as operative not only in systemic gender injustice (sexism), but also in classism, racism, heterosexism, and homophobia. See Mark Kline Taylor, *Remembering*

Esperanza: A Cultural-Political Theology for North American Praxis (Maryknoll, N.Y.: Orbis Books, 1990), chaps. 3 and 4.

57. Kovel, *White Racism*, 117.

58. For a summary of the positive effects by a strong critic, see Kwamena Acquaah, *International Regulation*, 82–83.

59. As an example of a scholar who summarizes the debates on TNCs and who himself takes a "moderate" position between outright support or rejection of them, see Gilpin, "Multinational Corporations and International Production," again in *The Political Economy of International Relations* 231–62. For a similar summary, but with conclusions quite contrasting to Gilpin's, see Alexander's and Swinth's discussion of a "modernization school" that sees the social impacts of TNCs to be largely favorable, and a "dependency school," which stresses the predominantly unfavorable consequences. Archibald S. Alexander and Robert L. Swinth, *Essays in International Business* 7 (November 1987), 2–5.

60. See Alexander and Swinth, *Essays*, 25–72.

61. The fact of the presence and persistence of such dynamics may be the starting point for a theology of grace in contemporary contexts, especially a theology of grace that thinks it has a requisite gift for resisting political oppression and not simply, as so often in the history of Western theology, an unmerited favor given to relieve individuals' guilt-consciences.

62. Richard A. Falk, "Normative Initiatives and Demilitarization: A Third System Approach," in *World Order Models Project*, Working Paper No. 13 (New York: Institute for World Order, 1992), 6.

63. Ibid., 8.

64. Ibid., 7–8. Falk also discusses various limitations of the third system: its frequent fragmentation, its lack of autonomy, the lack of coordination among its different participants, its failures to achieve structural expression beyond utopian projection, etc.

65. See the commentary and challenge concerning right-wing Christians in the seven nations of Namibia, South Africa, Guatemala, Nicaragua, South Korea, the Philippines, and El Salvador in *The Road to Damascus: Kairos and Conversion* (Washington, D.C.: Center of Concern, 1989).

66. John DeGruchy and Charles Villa-Vicencio, eds., *Apartheid Is a Heresy* (Grand Rapids, Mich.: Eerdmans, 1983).

67. Richard Horsley, *Jesus and the Spiral of Violence* (Minneapolis: Fortress Press, 1993), 114.

68. Richard Horsley, *Sociology and the Jesus Movement* (New York: Crossroad, 1989), 106, 111, 113, 130. Compare Elisabeth Schüssler Fiorenza, *In Memory of Her: A Feminist Reconstruction of Christian Origins* (New York: Crossroad, 1983), 118–54.

69. Gustavo Gutiérrez, *A Theology of Liberation: History, Politics and Salvation*, Sister Caridad Inda and John Eagleson, trans. and eds., 15th anniversary ed. (Maryknoll, N.Y.: Orbis Books, 1988), 160.

70. Edward Farley, *Good and Evil: Interpreting a Human Condition* (Minneapolis: Fortress Press, 1991), 291.

71. Ibid., 39.

72. On this notion, see Robert Jay Lifton and Eric Markusen, *The Genocidal Mentality: Nazi Holocaust and Nuclear Threat* (New York: Basic Books, 1990), 258–77.

73. Friedrich Schleiermacher, *The Christian Faith*, H. R. Mackintosh and J. S. Stewart, eds. (Philadelphia: Fortress Press, 1976), 282–304.

74. For example, see the fruit of ongoing negotiations among theologians participating in the Ecumenical Association of Third World Theologians, in K. C. Abraham, *Third World Theologies: Commonalities and Divergences* (Maryknoll, N.Y.: Orbis Books, 1990).

75. Acquaah, *International Regulation*, 191.

76. Ibid., 162–73.

77. Ulrich Duchrow, *The Global Economy: A Confessional Issue for the Churches?* (Geneva: WCC, 1987), 77–78.

78. Holtmann, *An NGO Guide*, 33.

79. Richard Falk, *World Order Models*.

80. On the issue, see Nicholas Wolterstorff, *Until Justice and Peace Embrace* (Grand Rapids, Mich.: Eerdmans, 1983), especially chap. 5.

81. Jefferson Morley and Nathaniel Wice, "Fear of Music," *SPIN* (November 1991), 53–54, 56–59.

82. Audre Lorde, *Sister Outsider: Essays and Speeches* (Trumansburg, N.Y.: Crossing Press, 1984), 36–39.

83. See John Beverley and Marc Zimmerman, *Literature and Politics in the Central American Revolutions* (Austin: University of Texas Press, 1990), 154–60.

84. In Jonas, *The Battle*, ix.

CHAPTER 8. KEEPING A CLEAN HOUSE WILL NOT KEEP A MAN AT HOME
Emilie M. Townes

1. Mrs. N. F. Mossell, *The Work of the Afro-American Woman*, 2nd ed. (Philadelphia: Geo. S. Ferguson Company, 1908; reprint, New York: Oxford University Press, 1988), 22–24 [page references are to the reprint edition].

2. Ibid., 28.

3. Ibid., 115.

4. Ibid., 120.

5. Ibid.

6. Ibid.

7. Ibid.

8. Ibid., 47.

9. Ibid., 131.

10. Among those whom she quotes are the Reverend J. C. Price, president of Livingstone College; the Reverend D. Baker; the Reverend W. P. Breed; Frederick Douglass; Dr. N. F. Mossell; the Reverend Dr. B. F. Lee; Professor E. A. Bouchett; and Professor S. M. Coles.

11. Mossell, *Afro-American Woman*, 148.

12. Katie G. Cannon, *Black Womanist Ethics* (Atlanta: Scholars Press, 1988), 105. Cannon uses the term "unctuous moral agent" to describe Zora Neale Hurston. Yet the function of this moral agent to "look at the world with her own eyes, form her own judgments and demythologize whole bodies of so-called social legitimacy" should be applied in a womanist ethical framework.

13. William L. Andrews, ed., *Sisters of the Spirit: Three Black Women's Autobiographies of the Nineteenth Century* (Bloomington: University of Indiana Press, 1986), 35.

14. Alice Walker, *In Search of Our Mother's Gardens: Womanist Prose* (New York: Harcourt, Brace Jovanovich, 1984), 241–42.

15. Gerda Lerner, ed., *Black Women in White America: A Documentary History* (New York: Pantheon Books, 1972), 569.

16. Marian Wright Edelman, *Families in Peril: An Agenda for Social Change* (Cambridge: Harvard University Press, 1987), 106.

17. Mossell and Walker's understanding of the importance of mother-daughter dialogue cannot be underestimated. Such dialogues provoke and challenge. They are also instructional and awash with mother wit and plain common sense.

18. Although there were free blacks in the North, a recognizable black middle class did not emerge until the 1870s, until the United States had moved far enough away from its agrarian base to an industrial one. Blacks lagged behind whites in this regard in the 1800s.

CHAPTER 9. RESISTANCE AND THE TRANSFORMATION OF HUMAN EXPERIENCE
Ellen K. Wondra

1. See, for example, the critiques by bell hooks in *Ain't I a Woman? Black Women and Feminism* (Boston: South End Press, 1982) and *Feminist Theory: From Margin to Center* (Boston: South End Press, 1984); Angela Y. Davis, *Women, Race and Class* (New York: Vintage Books, 1983); Barbara Hilkert Andolsen, *Daughters of Jefferson, Daughters of Bootblacks: Racism and American Feminism* (Macon, Ga.: Mercer University Press, 1986); Rosemary Radford Ruether, *New Woman/New Earth: Sexist Ideologies and Human Liberation* (New York: Seabury, 1975); and Susan Brooks Thistlethwaite, *Sex, Race, and God: Christian Feminism in Black and White* (New York: Crossroad, 1989).

2. Elisabeth Schüssler Fiorenza, *Bread Not Stone: The Challenge of Feminist Biblical Interpretation* (Boston: Beacon Press, 1984), 5.

3. See, for example, Audre Lorde, "The Master's Tools Will Never Dismantle the Master's House," in *Sister Outsider: Essays and Speeches* (Freedom,

Calif.: The Crossing Press, 1984), 110–13; Kelly D. Brown, " 'Who Do They Say that I Am?': A Critical Examination of the Black Christ" (Ph.D. diss., Union Theological Seminary, 1988); Jacqueline Grant, *White Women's Christ and Black Women's Jesus: Feminist Christology and Womanist Response* (Atlanta: Scholars Press, 1989); and Thistlethwaite, *Sex, Race, and God*.

4. Schüssler Fiorenza, *Bread Not Stone*, 5.

5. Nannerl O. Keohane, Michelle Z. Rosaldo, and Barbara C. Gelfin, eds., *Feminist Theory: A Critique of Ideology* (Chicago: University of Chicago Press, 1982), vii.

6. Teresa de Lauretis, *Alice Doesn't: Feminism, Semiotics, Cinema* (Bloomington: Indiana University Press, 1984), 159, 182.

7. Teresa de Lauretis, ed., *Feminist Studies/Critical Studies* (Bloomington: Indiana University Press, 1984), 8.

8. T. de Lauretis, *Alice Doesn't*, 186.

9. Rosemary Radford Ruether, "The Future of Feminist Theology in the Academy," *Journal of American Academy of Religion* 53 (1985): 710–11.

10. See Thistlethwaite, *Sex, Race, and God*, passim.

11. See, for example, Emil Fackenheim, *To Mend the World: Foundations of Future Jewish Thought* (New York: Schocken Books, 1981); Albert J. Raboteau, *Slave Religion* (New York: Oxford University Press, 1978); Gerda Lerner, *The Creation of Patriarchy* (New York and Oxford: Oxford University Press, 1986); Virginia Fabella and Mercy Amba Oduyoye, eds., *With Passion and Compassion: Third World Women Doing Theology* (Maryknoll, N.Y.: Orbis Books, 1989); and Sharon D. Welch, *A Feminist Ethic of Risk* (Minneapolis: Fortress, 1990).

12. On the reasons for such reconstruction, see particularly Carter Heyward, *Our Passion for Justice: Images of Power, Sexuality, and Liberation* (New York: Pilgrim Press, 1984); and "Heterosexist Theology: Being Above It All," *Journal of Feminist Studies in Religion* 3 (Spring 1987): 29–38. See also E. Fackenheim, *To Mend the World*, 147–66.

13. See Fackenheim, *To Mend the World*, 201–15.

14. See Welch, *Feminist Ethic*, throughout.

15. Fackenheim, *To Mend the World*, 201–25.

16. Ibid., 239.

17. See Fackenheim on the *Muselmänner*, *To Mend the World*, 217; cf. Welch, *Feminist Ethic*.

18. Welch, *Feminist Ethic*, 77.

19. In distinction to pain, Dorothee Soelle defines affliction as involving physical, psychological, *and* social suffering. With Simone Weil, Soelle contends that " 'There is not really affliction unless there is social degradation or the fear of it in some form or another.' The degradation shows itself in the isolation that accompanies affliction," Dorothee Soelle, *Suffering*, trans. Everett R. Kalin (Philadelphia: Fortress, 1975), 13–14, quoting Simone Weil, "The Love of God and Affliction."

20. Fackenheim, *To Mend the World*, 217 and passim.

21. Gustavo Gutiérrez's translation of Job 19:25. See *On Job: God-Talk and the Suffering of the Innocent*, trans. Matthew J. O'Connell (Maryknoll, N.Y.: Orbis Books, 1988), 64, 121.

22. Ruether, "The Future of Feminist Theology," 710–11.

23. Margaret Walker, "We Have Been Believers," quoted as the epigraph of James H. Evans, Jr., *We Have Been Believers: An African-American Systematic Theology* (Minneapolis: Fortress, 1992).

24. Cf. Fackenheim, *To Mend the World*, passim; and the notion of the Lord of history as fellow sufferer and liberator found in African-American theology, Latin American liberation theologies, and elsewhere.

25. See Mary Daly, *Beyond God the Father: Toward a Philosophy of Women's Liberation* (Boston: Beacon Press, 1973); Carter Heyward, *The Redemption of God: A Theology of Mutual Relation* (Washington, D.C.: University Press of America, 1982); Rosemary Radford Ruether, *To Change the World: Christology and Cultural Criticism* (New York: Crossroad, 1983) and *Sexism and God-Talk: Toward a Feminist Theology* (Boston: Beacon Press, 1983), and various essays; and Patricia Wilson-Kastner, *Faith, Feminism, and the Christ* (Philadelphia: Fortress, 1983).

26. See the cogent critiques of white feminist Christologies by Brown, "Who Do They Say"; Grant, *White Women's Christ and Black Women's Jesus*; Rita Nakashima Brock, *Journeys by Heart: A Christology of Erotic Power* (New York: Crossroad, 1988); and Thistlethwaite, *Sex, Race, and God*.

27. Rosemary Radford Ruether, *Faith and Fratricide: The Theological Roots of Anti-Semitism*, intro. Gregory Baum (New York: Seabury, 1974), 248.

28. Ruether, *To Change the World*, 14–15. See also her *Sexism and God-Talk*. Cf. Heyward, *Redemption of God*, 42, 54–57, and passim. See also Luke 4:18-19.

29. Ruether, *To Change the World*, 15; idem, *New Woman/New Earth*, 64–65. Cf. Matt. 20:25-27.

30. Heyward, *Redemption of God*, 39, and passim.

31. Heyward, *Our Passion for Justice*, 17.

32. Ibid., 178.

33. Ruether, *Sexism and God-Talk*, 131, and passim.

CHAPTER 10. LOCATING MY THEOLOGY IN SACRED PLACES
Bill Smith

1. See Beverly Wildung Harrison, *Making the Connections: Essays in Feminist Social Ethics*, ed. Carol S. Robb (Boston: Beacon Press, 1985).

2. See Carter Heyward, *The Redemption of God: A Theology of Mutual Relation* (Washington, D.C.: University Press of America, 1982).

CHAPTER 11. "DREAMS OF THE GOOD"

Sharon D. Welch

*The title of this essay is taken from Lillian Smith, *Killers of the Dream* (New York: W. W. Norton, 1949).

1. Mary Daly, *Gyn/Ecology: The Metaethics of Radical Feminism* (Boston: Beacon Press, 1978).

2. John Stoltenberg, *Refusing to Be a Man: Essays on Sex and Justice* (New York: NAL/Dutton, 1990).

3. Angela Davis, *Women, Race and Class* (New York: Vintage Books, 1981).

4. Daly, *Gyn/Ecology*, 1.

5. Ann Petry, *Harriet Tubman: Conductor on the Underground Railroad* (New York: Pocket Books, 1959).

6. John Hope Franklin, *From Slavery to Freedom: A History of Negro Americans* (New York: Alfred A. Knopf, 1980), 81–82.

7. Barbara Ehrenreich, *Fear of Falling: The Inner Life of the Middle Class* (New York: Harper Perennial, 1990).

8. The summary and analysis here are based on my own experience, the writings of Erica Sherover-Marcuse, materials from the Equity Institute, and interviews with people who have conducted diversity workshops over the past five to ten years.

9. Further information about Equity Institute and its programs may be obtained by writing Equity Institute, 6400 Hollis Street, Suite 15, Emeryville, CA 94608.

10. Herbert Marcuse, cited by Erica Sherover-Marcuse, *Emancipation and Consciousness: Dogmatic and Dialectical Perspectives in the Early Marx* (New York: Basil Blackwell, 1986), 134. All references to Sherover-Marcuse are from this source unless otherwise specified. Hereafter referred to as (S-M) in text. For extensive discussions of the phenomenon of internalized oppression see Paulo Freire, *Pedagogy of the Oppressed* (New York: Herder and Heider, 1972); Frantz Fanon, *The Wretched of the Earth* (New York: Grove Press, 1963); Jean Baker Miller, *Toward a New Psychology of Women* (Boston: Beacon Press, 1976); Daly, *Gyn/Ecology;* bell hooks, *Feminist Theory: From Margin to Center* (Boston: South End Press, 1984); Cherrie Moraga and Gloria Anzaldua, *This Bridge Called My Back: Writings by Radical Women of Color* (Watertown, Mass.: Persephone Press, 1981).

11. Ann Berlak, professor and theorist of critical pedagogy, describes the use of experiential exercises in a college class (Humanities I), designed to challenge various forms of oppression. Ann Berlak, "Anti-Racist Pedagogy in a College Classroom: Mutual Recognition and a Logic of Paradox" (unpublished, 1991), 7. See also Ann Berlak, "Teaching for Outrage and Empathy in the Liberal Arts." *Educational Foundations* (Summer 1989).

12. Berlak, "Teaching for Outrage," 7–8.

13. Lillian Smith, *Killers of the Dream* (New York: W. W. Norton, 1949), 15. Hereafter cited as (Smith) in text.

14. Paul Johnson, *A History of Christianity* (New York: Atheneum, 1979).

15. Sharon Welch, *A Feminist Ethic of Risk* (Minneapolis: Fortress Press, 1990).

16. Muriel Rukeyser, "Recovering," from *Out of Silence* (Evanston, Ill.: TriQuarterly Books, 1992).

17. Sharon Welch, *Communities of Resistance and Liberation: A Feminist Theology of Liberation* (Maryknoll, N.Y.: Orbis Books, 1985).

18. Myles Horton, with Judith Kohl and Herbert Kohl, *The Long Haul: An Autobiography* (New York: Anchor Books, 1990), 176.

19. Ibid.

20. Rebecca S. Chopp, *The Power to Speak: Feminism, Language, God* (New York: Crossroad, 1989), 7.

21. Cornel West, *The American Evasion of Philosophy: A Genealogy of Pragmatism* (Madison: Univ. of Wisconsin Press, 1989), 49.

22. Peirce, cited in West, *American Evasion*, 50.

23. Ibid.

24. Welch, *Feminist Ethic*.

25. Horton, *Long Haul*, 180.

26. West, *American Evasion*, 5.

27. Ibid.

28. Rukeyser, "Recovering."

29. Muriel Rukeyser, "Fable," from *Collected Poems* (New York: McGraw-Hill, 1978).

CHAPTER 12. AMERICA'S ORIGINAL SIN
Jim Wallis

1. T. Morganthau, "Murder Wave in the Capital," *Newsweek* 133, March 13, 1989, 16–19.

2. Debbie M. Price, "At the Roots of Violence," *The Washington Post*, a 3-part series, April 2–4, 1989.

3. "America's Changing Colors: Beyond the Melting Pot," *Time* 135, no. 15, April 9, 1990, 28–35.

4. R. Lacayo, "Between Two Worlds," *Time* 133, no. 11, March 13, 1989, 58–62.

5. Vincent Harding, quoted in *Sojourners* (Aug./Sept., 1990), 5.

CHAPTER 13. BLACK THEOLOGY AND LATIN AMERICAN LIBERATION THEOLOGY
George C. L. Cummings

1. K. C. Abraham, "Freedom and Economic Life: A Christian Perspective," *Religion and Society* 26, no. 3 (September 1979): 44.

2. Ibid.

3. Final statement of the Fifth EATWOT Conference, August 17–29, 1981, reprinted in *The Irruption of the Third World: Challenge to Theology*, Virginia Fabella and Sergio Torres, eds. (Maryknoll, N.Y.: Orbis Books, 1983), 199.

4. Gayraud S. Wilmore, "Afro-American and Third World Theology," in *African Theology en Route*, Kofi Appiah-Kubi and Sergio Torres, eds. (Maryknoll, N.Y.: Orbis Books, 1979).

5. Cornel West, *Prophesy Deliverance! An Afro-American Revolutionary Christianity* (Philadelphia: Westminster Press, 1983), 50.

6. Ibid., 65.

7. Ibid., 49.

8. Ibid.

9. Ibid.

10. Ibid.

11. Ibid., 113.

12. Ibid., 119.

13. Antonio Gramsci, *Selections from the Prison Notebooks*, Quintin Hoare and Geoffrey Nowell Smith, eds. and trans. (New York: International Publishers, 1971), 365.

14. Michael Omi and Howard Winant, "By the Rivers of Babylon: Race in the United States," *Socialist Review* 13, no. 5 (September-October 1983): 43.

15. Ibid.

16. West, *Prophesy Deliverance*, 119.

17. Ibid.

18. Gramsci, *Prison Notebooks*, 60.

19. Ibid., 80.

20. Ibid., 3.

21. West, *Prophesy Deliverance*, 120

22. Ibid.

23. Ibid.

24. Lucius T. Outlaw, "Race and Class in the Theory and Practice of Emancipatory Social Transformation," in *Philosophy of Struggle: Anthology of Afro-American Philosophy from 1917*, Leonard Harris, ed. (Dubuque, Iowa: Kendall/Hunt Publishing Company, 1983), 123.

25. West, *Prophesy Deliverance*, 121.

26. Omi and Winant, "By the Rivers of Babylon," 59.

27. The distinction between the first generation of black theologians and the second generation is between the pioneers of black theology and the ones who followed them. The first generation includes James H. Cone, J. Deotis Roberts, Gayraud S. Wilmore, Major D. Jones, and Albert Cleage. The second generation includes such people as Dwight N. Hopkins, Josiah Young, Kelly D. Brown-Douglas, Emilie Townes, Will E. Coleman, and myself.

28. Dwight N. Hopkins and George C. L. Cummings, eds., *Cut Loose Your*

Stammering Tongues: Black Theology in the Slave Narratives (Maryknoll, N.Y.: Orbis Books, 1991).

29. Will E. Coleman, "Coming through Legion: Metaphor in Non-Christian Experiences with The Spirit(s) in African-American Slave Narratives," in *Stammering Tongues*, 102.

30. George C. L. Cummings, *A Common Pilgrimage: Black Theology (USA) and Latin American Liberation Theology: Towards a Theology of Religio-cultural, Socio-economic and Political Liberation*. Ph.D. diss., Union Theological Seminary, 1990; forthcoming, Maryknoll, N.Y.: Orbis Books, 1993.)

31. In choosing to utilize this approach I am indebted to many womanist and feminist theologians who utilize poststructuralist discourse theories and Marxist theories of cultural discourse in the development of their own projects. See, for example, Rebecca Chopp, *The Power to Speak: Feminism, Language, God* (New York: Crossroad, 1989). In addition, I am indebted to the work of the black literary scholar Henry Louis Gates.

CHAPTER 14. LIFE ON THE BACK OF THE BUS
David Batstone

1. Toni Morrison, *Beloved* (New York: Knopf, 1988).

2. Jürgen Habermas, "Questions and Counterquestions," in *Habermas and Modernity*, ed. Richard J. Bernstein (Cambridge: MIT Press, 1985), 214.

3. Clifford Geertz, *Local Knowledge: Further Essays in Interpretive Anthropology* (New York: Basic Books, 1983), 44.

4. Martin Luther King, Jr., "Letter from a Birmingham Jail," in *A Testament of Hope: The Essential Writings and Speeches of Martin Luther King, Jr.*, ed. James M. Washington (San Francisco: HarperCollins, 1986), 292–93.

5. Tom Morganthau et al., "Losing Ground: New Fears and Suspicions as Black America's Outlook Grows Bleaker," *Newsweek* 114, no. 14, April 6, 1992, 20.

6. Details of the inequities of disaster relief were provided by Marsha Ginsburg, "Fire Victims Benefited from FEMA's Quake Ordeal: Federal Officials Able to Bring Relief Fast This Time, But in '89 They Were Too Late for the Poor," *San Francisco Examiner*, February 16, 1992, B-1, 6.

7. Quoted in T. Morganthau, et al., "Losing Ground," 21.

8. Andrew Hacker interviewed on "Fresh Air," National Public Radio, March 31, 1992. See also Andrew Hacker, *Two Nations, Black and White: Separate, Hostile, Unequal* (New York: Simon and Schuster, 1991).

9. Walter Benjamin, "Theses on the Philosophy of History," in *Illuminations*, ed. Hannah Arendt (New York: Harcourt, Brace & World, 1968), 259–60.

10. For an excellent treatment of the "dialectics of progress" and the memory of suffering, see Johann Baptist Metz, *Faith in History and Society: Toward a Practical Fundamental Theology* (New York: Seabury, 1980).

11. C. Geertz, *Local Knowledge*, 23.

12. Ibid., 19–35. For a few of the pioneer works in this field, see Victor Turner, *Dramas, Fields and Metaphors* (Ithaca: Cornell University Press, 1974) and *The Ritual Process: Structure and Anti-Structure* (Ithaca: Cornell University Press, 1977); L. Wittgenstein, *Philosophical Investigations*, trans. G. E. M. Anscombe (New York: Macmillan, 1953); Peter Berger and Thomas Luckman, *The Social Construction of Reality* (Garden City, N.Y.: Doubleday, 1967); James T. Borhek and Richard F. Curtis, *The Sociology of Belief* (New York: Kreiger, 1983); Erving Goffman, *The Presentation of Self in Everyday Life* (New York: Garden City, N.Y.: Doubleday, 1959); idem, *Behavior in Public Places: Notes on the Social Organization of Gatherings* (New York: Free Press of Glencoe, 1963); Paul Ricoeur, *Time and Narrative*, 3 vols., trans. Kathleen McLaughlin and David Pellauer (Chicago: University of Chicago Press, 1984); Paulo Freire, *The Pedagogy of the Oppressed* (New York: Seabury, 1970); Hans-Georg Gadamer, *Truth and Method*, ed. Garrett Barden and John Cumming (New York: Seabury, 1975).

13. Manning Marable, "The Rhetoric of Racial Harmony: Finding Substance in Culture and Ethnicity," *Sojourners* (Aug./Sept., 1990): 17.

14. Arnold J. Toynbee, *A Study of History* (London: Oxford University Press, 1935), 221.

15. "Free-floating rage" is a term coined by Dr. Alvin Poussaint, a psychiatrist who teaches at Harvard Medical School, to identify the deep anger felt by many black youth. Poussaint suggests that much of it arises in response to the perception that white people are intentionally seeking to systematically eliminate them: "It is probably inevitable, given the long and bitter history of race relations in the United States, that some African-Americans now see conditions in the inner city in paranoid terms." Quoted in Morganthau et al., "Losing Ground," 20–21.

16. William Faulkner, *Absalom, Absalom* (New York: Random House, 1936), 100.

17. Alice Miller, *For Your Own Good: Hidden Cruelty in Child-Rearing and the Roots of Violence*, trans. Hildegarde and Hunter Hannum (New York: Farrar, Straus & Giroux, 1983), 250.

18. Malcolm X with Alex Haley, *The Autobiography of Malcolm X* (New York: Grove Press, Inc., 1966), 370.

19. Elisabeth Schüssler Fiorenza, *Bread Not Stone: The Challenge of Feminist Biblical Hermeneutics* (Boston: Beacon Press, 1984), 62–63.

20. Howard Thurman, *The Luminous Darkness: A Personal Interpretation of the Anatomy of Segregation and the Ground of Hope* (New York: Harper & Row, 1965), 44.

21. Howard Thurman, "Mysticism and Social Change," *Eden Theological Seminary Bulletin* 4 (Spring 1939): 27. See also Thurman, *The Search for Common Ground. An Inquiry into the Basis of Man's Experience of Community* (New York: Harper & Row, 1971).

22. Langdon Gilkey, "Events, Meanings and the Current Tasks of Theology," *Journal of the American Academy of Religion* 53, no. 3 (Dec. 1985): 728.

23. In a review of Rebecca Chopp's excellent work, *The Power to Speak: Feminism, Language, God* (New York: Crossroad, 1989), Martha Reineke criticizes Chopp for using ideology critique as "a filter to modify . . . [her] post-structuralist gaze. . . ." Reineke claims that the operations of the social world cannot be identified, opposed, or interrupted, because contradictory subject positions are "created by the order as its border, their words remain effects of the social-symbolic order which do not shatter the borders, but buttress them" (*Journal of the American Academy of Religion* 60, no. 1 [Spring 1992]: 150–53). Without access to an ideology critique, the power of the present order is colossal.

24. Ibid.

25. While addressing the mythic significance of ritual within culture, these words of Karl Kerényi sought to capture this same nuance, "Vom Weisen des Festes," *Pardeuma* 1, no. 2 (1938): 71.

26. Malcolm X, *Autobiography*, 375.

27. "Friends of Mind: A Conversation between bell hooks and Cornel West," *The Other Side* (March-April 1992): 16.

28. Ibid., 21.

29. An insightful evaluation of the King nostalgia in popular culture made by the Rev. Joseph Lowry, then president of the Southern Christian Leadership Conference, "Blacks Remember King and His Dream," *San Francisco Chronicle*, 21 January, 1992, 1.

30. Stephanie Smith, "Why Madonna & All White People with Dread Locks Should Burn in Hell," *San Francisco Bay Guardian*, October 19, 1991, 12.

31. Niki Amarantides, "Education with Savage Intent: An Interview with Jonathan Kozol," *The Other Side* (May-June 1992): 26.

32. Gilkey, "Events," 730. See also the helpful epistemological discussion of praxis within dialogical communities in Richard J. Bernstein, *Beyond Objectivism and Relativism: Science, Hermeneutics, and Praxis* (Philadelphia: University of Pennsylvania Press, 1983).

33. Malcolm X, *Autobiography*, 377.